The Gun Dilemma

The Gun Dilemma

How History Is Against Expanded Gun Rights

ROBERT J. SPITZER

OXFORD
UNIVERSITY PRESS

OXFORD
UNIVERSITY PRESS

Oxford University Press is a department of the University of Oxford. It furthers
the University's objective of excellence in research, scholarship, and education
by publishing worldwide. Oxford is a registered trade mark of Oxford University
Press in the UK and certain other countries.

Published in the United States of America by Oxford University Press
198 Madison Avenue, New York, NY 10016, United States of America.

© Oxford University Press 2023

Library of Congress Control Number: 2022936391

ISBN 978-0-19-764374-7

DOI: 10.1093/oso/9780197643747.001.0001

1 3 5 7 9 8 6 4 2

Printed by Integrated Books International, United States of America

To Tess,

The way you changed my life . . .

Contents

Acknowledgments   ix

1. The Gun Policy Fork in the Road   1

2. Assault Weapons and Ammunition Magazines   25

3. The Sound of Silencers   52

4. Weapons Brandishing and Display   72

5. Second Amendment Sanctuaries: Coloring Outside
   the Lines of Federalism   92

6. Conclusion: Navigating the Gun Fork in the Road   116

About the Author   127

Notes   129

Index   177

Acknowledgments

I WOULD LIKE to thank Joseph Blocher, Jacob Charles, Saul Cornell, David Hemenway, Darrell Miller, and the participants in the Duke University Law School Conference on Historical Gun Laws held on June 19, 2020, for their thoughtful and helpful comments and suggestions pertaining to parts of this project. I also thank Jackie Schildkraut, SUNY Oswego.

In addition, I also extend heartfelt thanks to a number of people at my long-time home institution of SUNY Cortland, including Cortland University Police Chief Mark Depaull, Investigator Amanda Wasson and Officer Dave Coakley, History Professor Kevin Sheets, Center for Civic Engagement Director John Suarez, President Erik Bitterbaum, Provost Mark Prus, and Dean Bruce Mattingly. I've worked with many outstanding people at Cortland over the years, but none was harder working, smarter, more dedicated, or funnier than the Political Science Department's administrator, Debby Dintino. Deb, thank you for everything.

I also extend my thanks, and respect, to Solon Town Supervisor Stephen A. Furlin, Truxton Town Councilperson Gun Wehbe, Cortland County legislator and Minority Leader Beau Harbin, Cortland County legislator Ann Homer, Cortland County Clerk Elizabeth Larkin, and Cortland City Police Chief Paul Sandy. And I am again indebted to Oxford University Press social sciences editor David McBride, the nearest modern equivalent to the great Max Perkins of years gone by, to project editor Emily Mackenzie Benitez, and to editorial Project Manager Jubilee James.

For Teresa, to whom I dedicate this book with all the love and humility I can muster (though more the former than the latter), I conclude with the wisdom of Teresa's Rules: 1. Act faster; 2. Pick up your cues; 3. Don't look at your feet; 4. Enunciate; 5. Think about what you're saying; 6. Project; 7. Play to the balcony (keeps face up and out and eyes shine); 8. Early is on time; on time is late.

I

The Gun Policy Fork in the Road

"When you come to a fork in the road, take it."

YOGI BERRA

THE DECADE OF the twenties would prove to be one of national soul-searching on the issue of guns. The nation had drawn away from the international military entanglements of the previous decade and, in the aftermath of internal national crises, was seeking a return to relative normalcy. Yet guns and gun violence made headlines, especially when large numbers of people were killed with exceptionally destructive firearms. Calls for national and state gun legislation came from many quarters, but gun rights forces argued on behalf of ready gun access for civilians, while groups favoring stricter gun laws conducted studies, issued reports, and tried to transform what appeared to be national consensus on behalf of stronger laws into legislation. These efforts fell short at the national level. The states, however, witnessed a flurry of new gun laws.

The decade in question was the 1920s, not the 2020s. Yet the similarities are many, despite the distance of a century. This suggests a considerable degree of constancy—or paralysis, depending on one's perspective—in the modern gun policy debate in America. The country elected a presidential candidate in 1920 who embraced a call for national normalcy, Warren G. Harding, not so much different from the country's turn to Joe Biden in 2020 after four years of the tumultuous and strident presidency of Donald Trump. America had had enough with military conflict in World War I as it entered the 1920s, and similarly supported the end of American military commitments in Afghanistan, Iraq, and elsewhere in the 2020s. The rise of Prohibition-fueled organized crime in the 1920s was punctuated by criminal use of weapons built for war, including the Tommy gun, the Browning Automatic Rifle or BAR (also called the Browning Machine Rifle), and the sawed-off shotgun.[1] In the modern era, much attention has been focused on assault weapons, also designed for battlefield use but increasingly popular among some gun owners, although also used disproportionately by mass shooters as they have found their way into the civilian gun market. Just as gun silencers came in for special scorn in the 1920s, so too did "bump stocks" in recent years, devices attachable to semi-automatic rifles that allow the operator to fire the weapons in near-fully-automatic fashion. Large capacity ammunition magazines (LCMs), defined as those capable of hold more than ten rounds, have also come under contemporary scrutiny, as they did in the 1920s. (Both silencers and bump stocks were subject to successful regulatory action; LCMs were widely regulated in the 1920s and 1930s; in recent years they have been restricted in some states.)

In the 1920s many good government groups, including the American Bar Association, the National Conference of Commissioners on Uniform State Laws, business groups, and newspaper editorial pages called for gun law reform. Gun groups like the U.S. Revolver Association (USRA) and the still-fledgling National Rifle Association (NRA) opposed some stricter new gun laws but also proposed their own model laws. The USRA drafted a model Uniform Firearms Act, which among other things called for a forty-eight-hour waiting period for purchase of a handgun and gun licensing.[2] In the 1920s, Congress managed to pass only one limited new gun law, the Mailing of Firearms Act of 1927, which prohibited the sale of handguns to private individuals through the U.S. mail.[3] The states, however, enacted a flurry of gun regulations. Most notably, from the 1920s through the early 1930s, more than one-half of the states enacted bills generally termed anti-machine gun laws that barred the sale and possession of fully automatic weapons. During the same period, at least eight states (and perhaps as many as eleven) enacted laws to restrict semi-automatic firearms as well.[4] Also during the same time period, at least sixteen states enacted firearms or ammunition registration laws; another dozen enacted some form of gun permitting.[5] As for the decade of the 2020s, it is not possible to know as of this writing how it will conclude, but early in the decade states continued to enact stricter laws, such as "red flag" laws, also referred to as "extreme risk protection orders." These measures allow authorities to temporarily remove guns from those considered to pose an imminent and dire threat to themselves or others, and to keep the guns away if the threat is found to be justifiable. On the other hand, more conservative states continued a contrary trend of loosening existing gun laws, a phenomenon that does not find parallel with the 1920s. If the recent past (that is, the late 2010s and early 2020s) is any indication, state gun policy action will continue to be prolific, and will far exceed the scope or frequency of national gun policy change.

The Fork in the Road on Guns

Despite the many parallels between the 1920s and the 2020s, the third decade of the twenty-first century is ushering in something new: a sharp, and perhaps even widening, divergence between a political consensus that supports existing public policy on guns as well as new proposed measures, on the one hand, versus an emergent sharp conservative counter-reaction from ultra-conservatives[6] in some courts, including a majority of the Supreme Court. Prevailing public support for stronger gun laws is one of the most durable and consistent public opinion trends measured since the advent of modern polling in the 1930s. A 1938 Gallup poll reported that seventy-nine percent favored "firearms control." Since 1975 Gallup has asked whether Americans favor making firearms laws more strict, less strict, or kept the same. From 1975 to 2020, an average of over fifty-eight percent favored more strict laws. An average of thirty-two percent of respondents during this period have favored keeping gun laws the same. Less strict responses ranged from three to thirteen percent.[7] Thus, clear majorities favor stronger laws; overwhelming majorities oppose rolling back existing gun laws. Gallup polling concluded in 2021 that: "The data show strong public support for proposed legislative changes that would do such things as require background checks for all gun purchases, ban high-capacity ammunition magazines, require all privately owned guns to be registered with the police, and require a 30-day waiting period for all gun sales." It also noted majority support for an assault weapons ban.[8] Other recent polls show overwhelming public support for red flag laws (also called extreme risk protection orders; seventy to seventy-seven percent support in a National Public Radio poll, eighty-six percent support in a Washington Post–ABC poll).[9]

The gap between public support for gun laws and the general failure of the national government to act in line with that consensus is well understood.[10] The new force opposing gun laws this study identifies, however, is not simply resistance to new gun policy proposals (although of course that is part of the movement), but the prospect that existing gun laws will be dismantled by a new generation of very conservative judges and local activists bent on expanding the definition of gun rights.

In the years since the Supreme Court's historic and controversial gun rights decision of *D.C. v. Heller* (2008), when it carved out a new, Second Amendment-based individual right of citizens to own handguns for personal self-protection in the home—let's call it Gun Rights 1.0—the legal system has found a rough equilibrium that balances gun laws with this new gun right.

It has done so as the Supreme Court had consistently refused to weigh in on Second Amendment cases up to the start of the 2020s. Yet the federal judiciary may well now be poised to not only upset, but perhaps throw into gear-grinding reverse, that equilibrium by significantly expanding the definition of gun rights beyond that set out in *Heller*—let's call it Gun Rights 2.0. The animating force behind this possible judicial reversal is a federal bench populated by large numbers of relatively young, very conservative jurists who maintain in particular an unwavering fealty to a singularly expansive definition of gun rights.

Judicial conservatism is nothing new, nor are evolving legal theories. And it is not only customary but expected that presidential administrations appoint to federal judicial positions jurists who share the ideological leanings of the administration and president making the appointments. But here the liberal–conservative parallelism ends. Since the early 1980s, a concerted legal movement has been constructed and mobilized to change what was seen as a too-liberal legal establishment by cultivating a generation of very conservative legal thinkers and practitioners who possess three key traits: a high degree of extremely conservative ideological coherence, including (although hardly limited to[11]) an unwavering fealty to a singularly expansive definition of gun rights; allegiance to a constitutional theory generally identified as constitutional Originalism (see subsequent discussion); and with respect to judicial appointments, relative youth.[12]

This conservative legal movement coalesced in the form of the Federalist Society. The organization first appeared as a chapter at Yale Law School in 1980, and a year later at the University of Chicago Law School. In 1982 it established itself as a nationwide non-profit corporation dedicated to providing a conservative counterweight to what was seen as the prevailing liberalism of the legal profession. The organization's establishment was fortuitously timed in that it coincided with the election of conservative Republican President Ronald Reagan (1981–1989). Reagan's counselor to the president and then attorney general, Edwin Meese, urged Justice Department lawyers to join the society. In turn, it brought into government service Federalist Society lawyers/members. As a result, "[b]y 1986, all twelve of the Assistant Attorneys General in the Justice Department were tied to the Federalist Society."[13] Federalist Society membership and values rapidly came to dominate the legal philosophy and personnel connected to Republican administrations, both with respect to Executive branch law-related positions and judicial selection. This continued through the Reagan and George H.W. Bush (1989–1993) presidencies.

This new conservative legal movement's impact on legal thinking, and especially on the composition of the federal judiciary, picked up momentum and success during the eight years of the second Bush presidency (2001–2009) and flowered fully during the four years of the Trump administration (2017–2021). As a candidate and then as president, Donald Trump essentially threw the judicial selection process entirely to the Federalist Society, proclaiming, "We're going to have great judges, conservative, all picked by the Federalist Society."[14]

During George H.W. Bush's four-year presidency, nine of the forty-two federal appeals court judges he appointed were members of the Federalist Society. For the eight years of the second Bush presidency, a majority of his federal courts of appeal appointees were members, as were his two Supreme Court nominees. In George W. Bush's first term, more than two-thirds of his appeals court nominees were connected to the Federalist Society.[15] With the direct pipeline from the Federalist Society to the Trump administration, in his four years Trump appointed fifty-four judges to the thirteen federal appeals courts (and three Supreme Court justices). Nearly all of them are Federalist Society affiliated.[16] In total, Trump appointed 234 federal judges.[17]

Even though Trump only served four years, he was able to have a disproportionately large impact on the composition of the federal judiciary, compared to his predecessors. Republican leaders in the U.S. Senate, headed by the exceptionally skillful (his critics would say unscrupulous) majority leader Mitch McConnell (KY), swept aside many of the customary barriers in the Senate that traditionally allowed opposition party members to slow and even stymie the judicial confirmation process. For example, only 28.6 percent of President Barack Obama's (2009–2017) judicial nominees won confirmation in the last two years of his presidency in the face of a Senate controlled by the opposition party. McConnell, on the other hand, succeeded in achieving his slogan for the Trump presidency to "leave no [judicial] vacancy behind," meaning that Trump's administration would be the first in decades to leave no unfilled seats at the end of the administration.[18] During his term Trump appointed thirty percent of all active federal appeals court judicial positions and twenty-seven percent of active district court judges.[19]

It should be noted that the process of sweeping aside Senate procedures that allowed the minority party to delay or even stop court nominations dated to 2013 when then-Senate majority leader Harry Reid (D-NV) eliminated the filibuster for lower federal court nominations in response to Senate minority leader McConnell's announcement that his party would block through filibuster any Democratic nominations offered to fill three vacancies on the U.S.

Court of Appeals for the District of Columbia Circuit, regardless of their merit, because, McConnell said, "no more judges are needed." President Obama had nominated three judges to fill the positions. Even though majority leader Reid had historically supported the filibuster, the Republicans' refusal to allow any Democratic nominations to fill vacancies was the last straw. Even in this moment, it was McConnell's tactics that precipitated the change.[20]

Up until the Trump presidency, the Senate witnessed the escalation of the use of the filibuster and other dilatory tactics by opposition party senators. This was a relatively recent phenomenon that led to a swelling chorus of critics, although those criticisms often followed partisan tides. A good argument can be made that presidents, regardless of party, should not encounter roadblocks to judicial nominations of the sort faced by Obama and his immediate predecessors. Given the steps taken by McConnell to sweep aside these impediments, current and future presidential administrations should therefore be able to mimic the Trump–McConnell judicial confirmation success rate when the same political party controls the Senate and the presidency. Indeed, in his first year in office, President Joe Biden was able to successfully appoint more federal judges—forty, including eleven to the appellate courts, out of a total of seventy-three nominees—than any president since Reagan.[21]

Still, this is mostly in the future. The Trump presidency's success in filling judicial ranks with young conservative judges does and will have immediate consequences, in particular for the future of gun laws. On the question of judicial appointee age, one study found that in the last forty years, Republican presidents have indeed appointed younger justices to the Supreme Court than have Democrats, and that this factor by itself has helped push the court in a more conservative direction.[22] For court of appeals judges, Trump appointees have been younger on average than those of any past president going back to the turn of the twentieth century. And Republican presidents from Reagan through Trump appointed the youngest twenty-five federal appellate judges, forty-five of the youngest fifty, and seventy-six of the youngest one hundred.[23]

While the Federalist Society sits at the epicenter of the conservative legal movement, it repeatedly declaims that: "The Federalist Society takes no positions on particular legal and public policy matters."[24] Yet the legal and policy consequences stemming from the appointment of its adherents are unmistakable. Consider a sweeping study of the ideological leanings of Trump-appointed judges (recalling that virtually all of them are or were promoted by and through the Federalist Society), based on a comparative examination of 117,000 opinions issued by over 2400 judges from 1932 to 2020. It concluded that "Trump has appointed judges who exhibit a distinct decision-making pattern that is, on the whole, significantly more conservative than previous presidents . . . . his judges are more to the right than those of any recent Republican president."[25] A different study of 950 en banc federal court decisions (those made by all active members of the respective courts of appeal when they sit together to render decisions for the circuit) spanning fifty-four years through 2020 found "a dramatic and strongly statistically significant spike in both partisan splits and partisan reversals" from 2018 to 2020. No such pattern was observed in any prior period of the study. The authors referred to this "surprising" deviation from the prior relatively non-partisan era as "weaponizing en banc."[26]

The point of this analysis is not that Federalist Society–Trump era judges now possess controlling votes on all or even most of the federal circuits; that is certainly not true. And President Joe Biden will appoint more liberal judges during his time in office. But what is true is that there are now multiple receptive avenues for legal challenges to every sort of gun law that will undoubtedly produce some decisions that have already and will surely widen the definition of gun rights and narrow the range of gun regulations. Such decisions will pave the way for new cases to reach the Supreme Court, and where the current Supreme Court is, I argue, primed to redefine and expand gun rights (Gun Rights 2.0) in a way that will make the 2008 *Heller* decision (Gun Rights 1.0) look like a liberal triumph. Consider the nine justices. Even if this prospect is never realized, it is beyond dispute that the makeup of the federal courts has shifted profoundly to the right.

Among the members of the Supreme Court as of 2021 (years of their birth in parentheses), Samuel Alito (1950), Amy Coney Barrett (1972), Neil Gorsuch (1967), Brett Kavanaugh (1965), John Roberts (1955), and Clarence Thomas (1948) are all Federalist Society affiliated. Lest there be any doubt, during the period of 1937 to 2012, recent Republican appointees to the Supreme Court were far more conservative than earlier Republican appointees, whereas recent Democratic appointees are no more liberal than their Democratic-appointed predecessors. Since 2012, Trump-era appointees, taken together, push the judicial ideological needle even further to the right.[27] Gun rights supporters could hardly ask for a more receptive group. Leading them on matters related to the Second Amendment is Justice Thomas.

Thomas's Steroidal Second Amendment

Among jurists, Clarence Thomas has become a leader of the court's right-ward march on an array of issues. In fact, in 2021 ace journalist Jill Abramson argued that "we may be witnessing the emergence of the Thomas court"[28] as its composition has become ever more conservative.

With respect to the gun issue, Thomas has been a leader on the individualist view of the Second Amendment, codified by the high court in the 2008 *Heller* decision. Yet he has gone beyond that ruling, championing an even more expansive version of that right beyond the parameters of *Heller*. Within the previous decade, Justice Thomas has increasingly chafed at what he has considered the courts' anemic post-*Heller* view.

Justice Thomas's Second Amendment jurisprudential views date at least to 1997, in the case of *Printz v. U.S.*[29] Despite the subject matter of the legal challenge giving rise to this case, this was not a case about the Second Amendment. It challenged provisions of the federal Brady Handgun Violence Prevention Act, enacted in 1993, that required local law enforcement officials to conduct background checks of those seeking to buy a handgun.[30] The constitutional question in the case was based on the argument that Congress had overreached in using its power to regulate interstate commerce to enforce this provision. *Printz* followed an earlier case in which the court, for the first time in decades, struck down a federal law as an overreach of the commerce power and a violation of states' rights under the Tenth Amendment.[31]

The court majority in *Printz* struck down the local law enforcement requirement provision of the act. Thomas voted with the five-member majority, but in his separate concurrence, he wandered off topic, writing:

> This Court has not had recent occasion to consider the nature of the substantive right safeguarded by the Second Amendment. If, however, the Second Amendment is read to confer a *personal* right to "keep and bear arms," a colorable argument exists that the Federal Government's regulatory scheme, at least as it pertains to the purely intrastate sale or possession of firearms, runs afoul of that Amendment's protections.[32]

This was plainly taken for what it was: an invitation to bring to the courts Second Amendment-based challenges to gun laws. That invitation was taken up by a young conservative lawyer, Alan Gura. Indeed, Thomas's comment "was decisive" in persuading Gura to begin litigation that ultimately resulted in the *Heller* decision.[33] Interestingly, the National Rifle Association and its lawyers were unpersuaded by Thomas's invitation and were opposed to Gura's legal initiative, fearing that it could not prevail, and might even produce an outcome inimical to its gun interests. Gura was not deterred, and his efforts were assisted instead by the libertarian Cato Institute. Only later did the NRA weigh in as a party to the case.[34] In any event, the litigation resulted in the reinterpretation of the Second Amendment in 2008 to create, for the first time in history, a personal or individual right to gun ownership, aside and apart from the Second Amendment's traditional militia-based understanding.

Two years later, the Supreme Court applied this new interpretation of Second Amendment rights to the states in *McDonald v. Chicago*.[35] Thomas voted as a member of the five-member majority—the same five who composed the *Heller* majority—but unlike in *Heller*, he wrote his own lengthy concurrence, arguing that the incorporation of the Second Amendment (that is, applying it to the states through the Fourteenth Amendment) should be justified based on the largely abandoned justification of the "privileges or immunities" clause rather than the due process clause of the Fourteenth embraced by the other justices writing in the majority. In his lengthy concurrence, Thomas referred to the Second Amendment as "an inalienable right that pre-existed the Constitution's adoption" that was "essential to the preservation of liberty."[36] This was the first of several expressions on his part of a broader and more encompassing Second Amendment right than that expressed by his brethren on the court.

In the 2017 case of *Peruta v. California*,[37] the Supreme Court refused to hear an appeal to a lower court ruling upholding California's concealed carry law that required permit applicants to show "good cause" for the granting of a carry license. A three-judge panel of the U.S. Court of Appeals for the Ninth Circuit struck down the challenged provisions of the law, but a full, en banc panel reversed and upheld the law. Thomas dissented from the Supreme Court's refusal to hear the appeal, along with Justice Gorsuch. Thomas argued that the court should have taken the case, and in the process expressed displeasure with the California law and the court's treatment of it. Thomas wrote: "The Court's decision to deny certiorari in this case reflects a distressing trend: the treatment of the Second Amendment as a disfavored right." This "disfavored" treatment, by Thomas's account, is reflected in what he sees as the denigration of the Second Amendment compared to rights found in the other amendments: "The Constitution does not rank certain rights above others, and I do not think this Court should impose such a hierarchy by selectively enforcing its preferred rights."[38]

The following year, Thomas again dissented from the court's refusal to hear an appeal to a state gun law upheld by a lower court. In *Silvester v. Becerra*,[39] the federal court of appeals, again from the Ninth Circuit, upheld California's ten-day waiting period. In a solo dissent, Thomas bemoaned the "lower courts' general failure to afford the Second Amendment the respect due an enumerated constitutional right."[40] He continued: "If a lower court treated another right so cavalierly, I have little doubt that this Court would intervene. But as evidenced by our continued inaction in this area, the Second Amendment is a disfavored right in this Court . . . . I do not believe we should be in the business of choosing which constitutional rights are "*really worth* insisting upon . . . ."[41] In order to demonstrate his belief that the Second Amendment is a mistreated, neglected constitutional right, Thomas engaged in a lengthy comparison with three other rights that, in his mind, hold a far more exalted, privileged position: "The Court would take these cases because abortion, speech, and the Fourth Amendment are three of its favored rights. The right to keep and bear arms is apparently this Court's constitutional orphan."[42]

In 2020, Thomas issued yet another dissent from a denial of certiorari in *Rogers v. Grewal*.[43] This time, his dissent was joined by Justice Kavanaugh, in part. This case arose from a challenge to New Jersey's "justifiable need" standard for granting concealed carry permits (what is generally referred to as a "may issue" gun carry law; nine states plus D.C. have such laws as of this writing). In the dissent, Thomas made no effort to conceal his dismay, saying that by refusing to hear the case, "the Court simply looks the other way." Thomas proceeds to state his clear view that "the Second Amendment protects a right to public carry."[44] Most of the rest of his opinion lays out his support for this proposition, including Thomas's repetition of the theme that the historical denial of guns to Blacks in the post-Civil War South was the linchpin of their oppression. He concludes by bemoaning what he believes to be the court's "decade-long failure to protect the Second Amendment"[45] (a reference to the court's refusal to hear new gun law challenges in the aftermath of the *Heller* and *McDonald* decisions). One can almost see the good Justice Thomas's blood pressure rising across these dissents.

A recent, well-regarded book on Thomas that combines biography with an analysis of his jurisprudence by political scientist Corey Robin argues that Thomas's constitutional philosophy identifies two constitutions: a "White Constitution" and a "Black Constitution." The latter Constitution for Blacks in America "features a society that is violent, racist, and regressive, a mix of *Mad Max* and *Do the Right Thing*. The centerpiece of that Constitution is the

Second Amendment." Thomas's expansive individualist view of the amendment, according to Robin, holds that guns and gun rights are "the black man's main protection against a rampaging white supremacy .... a racialized society armed to the teeth."[46] As Robin further explains regarding Thomas's view of Blacks in America: "there is no polity to protect him .... the political element of this vision has been eliminated. We are simply left with arms and the black man."[47]

What is initially most striking about Thomas's view is both its apocalyptic and ultimately anti-law grounding where the final remedy to racial inequity and mistreatment is not the law, or even the Constitution, despite Thomas's proclaimed devotion to the Second Amendment, but the authority that comes from the barrel of a gun. This variant of "insurrectionist" theorizing can be found in elements of Black liberation philosophy. The Black Panthers of the 1960s and 1970s, who armed themselves for personal protection and as an act of defiance against the white establishment, is perhaps the clearest recent example.[48] But Thomas's argument fails for the reason that insurrectionism itself fails: it makes war on civil society, rule of law, and peaceful change. When insurrectionists claim that the Second Amendment somehow protects or carves out a right of citizens to use extra-legal force, they make war on the document itself—something that cannot be allowed in a constitutional system where its defining trait is political expression through peaceful means.[49] And while it is true that this nation was founded on violent revolution against Britain, it was a two-part revolution: against the colonial power but for its own indigenous government that was predicated on a system of representation and republican values missing from British rule. Stupidly, Britain never gave American representatives a seat at the table, so America had no voice in its own rule. It fought to create its own system precisely so that political rule could exist by the people through peaceful mechanisms. More specifically, Thomas's argument calls on a group historically subject to subordination, discrimination, and racism to turn to interpersonal violence in a society where they are outnumbered and outarmed. That suggests these three more specific problems.

First, African Americans in the post-Civil War South were in fact armed by states and the federal government under Reconstruction-era regimes. Blacks formed "Black Militias" for protection and Union Leagues to promote civic responsibility and political participation. The armed freedmen drilled, marched, and paraded with rifles and sabers, staging one of the first such marches in Richmond, Virginia in 1866. "New black volunteer militias were training in every town and county" in Virginia and similar activities occurred in other Southern states.[50] The white reaction, predictably, was to respond with a variety of their own organizations, including armed organizations, the most notorious of which was the Ku Klux Klan. Groups like these disarmed, intimidated, and sometimes killed the Black Militia forces, among others.[51] The lesson of this experience was as predictable as it was depressing. The fundamental problem in the post-Civil War South was not that Blacks were deprived of arms (or didn't have enough arms), but that they were deprived of all rights, especially as Reconstruction came to an end and Jim Crow took hold. All rights for Blacks were under attack: free speech, lawful assembly, access to fair hearings before local magistrates, protection by local governments (as opposed to the intimidation and harassment by local governments that they faced), the right to vote (despite the Fifteenth Amendment), and more. Historian Saul Cornell addresses this issue in a slightly different, although insightful, way. In his extensive analysis of post-Civil War gun laws, he refers to the "false historical narrative" that "Reconstruction-era Republicans opposed gun regulation because it was inherently racist and aimed at disarming Blacks." Racist supporters of the notorious "Black Codes" in the South did promote gun laws to keep guns from Blacks among many other such racially targeted laws, but Republicans promoted "racially neutral gun control measures" aimed at improving public safety in an effort to "demilitarize the public sphere, to restore order and empower freed people to participate in civic life, most importantly elections."[52] Gun laws enacted by Republican-dominated state legislatures during this period were not racist. Their overarching goal was to improve public safety and protect the rights of Blacks and Republicans, including the right to vote, without fear of violence. When Reconstruction ended and white segregationists reasserted control over state and local governments, ushering in the era of Jim Crow, laws of every sort were administered in a way to insure white racist hegemony.[53]

Second, for American Blacks, the prospect that ultimate or final self-defense and safety in society could or can be effectuated outside of peaceful legal remedies in a race-based armed conflict is one that finds no historical or logical support. From the Colfax, Lousiana massacre of 1873 to the Tulsa, Oklahoma race massacre of 1921—instances where Blacks were armed and tried to protect themselves from attack by whites—the result was Black annihilation. In the case of Tulsa, for example, the appearance of Black armed defenders, including World War I veterans, provided the excuse for an escalating white armed response.[54] As one analysis notes about the post-Civil War period: "Extralegal violence and repression were pervasive responses to Black freedom and citizenship."[55] Had Blacks during this period been able to mount a stronger armed response, the ultimate result would have been more killing, more death, but with the same eventual outcome: white dominance and rule. One can find instances where armed Blacks did successfully protect themselves from violent whites, but such instances provide no comfort to any notion that widespread arming of Blacks was somehow a solution to the overarching denial of the right of personal self-defense or equal citizenship in the post-Civil War segregationist South.[56]

Third, the right of personal self-defense is deeply embedded in American law. It long predates the Second Amendment and was never dependent upon it. It is found in the criminal laws of every state and the common law tradition, has existed in America for hundreds of years, and is traceable back to the British legal tradition from the Middle Ages.[57] This common law right can be added to the list of those made mostly unavailable to American Blacks in our history.

Justices Joining with Thomas

Even as Thomas has led the charge for expanding Second Amendment rights, he has not marched alone, as witnessed by Gorsuch and Kavanaugh's agreement in two of the prior cases. In fact, political scientist Matthew J. Lacombe says that President Trump's nomination of "pro-gun" judges Kavanaugh and Gorsuch, "whom the NRA publicly supported—were seen by many as rewards for the organization's efforts."[58] Amy Coney Barrett was also endorsed by the NRA. In his 2010 majority opinion in *McDonald v. Chicago*, Justice Samuel Alito accused the defendants of asking the court "to treat the right recognized in *Heller* as a second-class right,"[59] even though the right had been established two years earlier and was now being applied to the states in *McDonald*. This theme of the Second Amendment as abused orphan would appear often in the years after this case.

Another case prompted Alito to express his displeasure with existing Second Amendment application. It came in a dissent he authored, joined by Gorsuch and Thomas (with the exception of one portion). This 2020 case, *N.Y. State Rifle & Pistol Association v. City of New York*,[60] involved a challenge to an arcane New York City gun law that barred the transport of firearms whose owners possessed premises licenses (i.e., a permit to have a gun at home, not a carry license) to a second home or shooting range outside of the city. The Supreme Court granted certiorari, a fact that was widely and immediately recognized as "the biggest guns case in over a decade,"[61] meaning one that might be used by the now more conservative majority to repeal gun laws and expand gun rights. But the city changed the law to accede to the complaints against it. This prompted the court to render the case moot (that is, there was no longer a live controversy justifying judicial action).

Kavanaugh voted with the court majority to dismiss on the grounds of mootness, but he separately opined: "I share Justice Alito's concern that some federal and state courts may not be properly applying Heller and McDonald. The Court should address that issue soon."[62] Alito's lengthy and testy dissent objected that New York's repeal of the law in order to head off the legal challenge (which conforms to the very definition of mootness[63]) "permits our docket to be manipulated in a way that should not be countenanced."[64] Alito's conclusion was unequivocal: "The City violated petitioners' Second Amendment right, and we should so hold."[65] Had New York not repealed the law, anticipation was widespread that the court's acceptance of the case was the moment gun rights activists were waiting for: a new, even more strongly gun rights-leaning court majority jumping at a chance to further expand gun rights. As was widely noted at the time: "There is little doubt that a majority of the Court believes that the Second Amendment should be read aggressively to strike down a wide range of gun laws."[66]

Both Justices Kavanaugh and Amy Coney Barrett, President Trump's late day appointment to the high court coming a month before the 2020 election, came to the bench with a clear gun rights views consonant with Thomas, Alito, and Gorsuch. In 2011, Kavanaugh served as a judge on the District of Columbia Circuit which heard a follow-up to the 2008 *Heller* case. After losing the case, the District of Columbia wrote a new gun law that barred assault weapons and required gun registration, which resulted in a new challenge in *Heller v. D.C.*[67] (also known as *Heller II*). The D.C. Circuit upheld the new gun law provisions. Judge Kavanaugh issued a dissent in which he argued that even these laws ran afoul of *Heller*: "Our sole job is to faithfully apply Heller and the approach it set forth for analyzing gun bans and regulations. In my judgment, both D.C.'s ban on semi-automatic rifles and its gun registration requirement are unconstitutional under Heller."[68] Despite numerous legal challenges, assault weapons bans, limits on ammunition magazines, and gun registration schemes have been consistently upheld both before and after the *Heller* decision.

Kavanaugh's analysis leaves no doubt that he favors significantly expanding gun rights at the expense of existing gun laws. Seven states plus D.C. have assault weapons bans on the books as of 2021 (the first state to enact a ban, California, passed the law in 1989). But consider existing laws that could be swept aside if Kavanaugh's view prevailed. Ten states plus D.C. restrict large capacity ammo magazines.[69] The federal government has maintained a system of gun registration for fully automatic weapons since 1934.[70] Over two-thirds of the states at one point or another enacted either gun registration or gun licensing or both, with some having such laws in place today.[71] Whether one agrees or disagrees with these laws, there is no doubt that Kavanaugh's view would have a momentous, disruptive effect on existing and otherwise well-established law.

As for Justice Amy Coney Barrett, she served as a federal judge for the Seventh Circuit U.S. Court of Appeals before joining the Supreme Court in 2020. She also clerked for Justice Scalia. In 2019, she dissented in the case of *Kanter v. Barr*,[72] where the majority upheld the denial of gun rights to the plaintiff Kanter, a man who had been convicted of a non-violent felony. Barrett objected, arguing that the historical record supported her contention that "legislatures did not strip felons of the right to bear arms simply because of their status as felons."[73] Rather, this was done "only to people who are dangerous."[74] Barrett's assertion that non-violent felons are entitled to gun rights is consonant with the conclusion of her dissent that, quoting from *McDonald*, the court majority "treats the Second Amendment as a 'second-class right'"[75] compared to other Bill of Rights protections. In her view, "dangerousness is the Second Amendment's exclusive limiting principle."[76] Barrett "appears to have an even broader view of gun rights than Justice Antonin Scalia."[77]

This leads to two questions. Does post-*Heller* Second Amendment treatment by the courts amount to some kind of mistreatment or denigration of gun rights? And what about the single-minded obsession with Originalism as the prism for ruling on the constitutionality of gun laws as reconciled with gun rights?

The Second Amendment as Little Nell

It is clear that Justice Thomas and some of his colleagues are unhappy with the way in which Second Amendment rights have been defined since the *Heller* decision. As the previous sections make clear, a voting majority of the current court, as well as some judges in the rest of the federal court system, believe that gun rights have been defined too narrowly. They are entitled to that belief, of course, but their dismay provides no basis for concluding that the amendment has been treated "cavalierly," as "a disfavored right," a "second class right," or as a "constitutional orphan," especially as compared with other Bill of Rights protections. Nothing in post-2008 Second Amendment caselaw warrants these cartoonish labels (thus the reference to "Little Nell"[78] in the heading), which seem designed mostly to provide a rallying cry for Second Amendment absolutists.[79]

If anything is true about the Bill of Rights, it is that they were not produced in some cookie-cutter-like fashion designed to treat each of them identically. They were, after all, the product of many state recommendations and much bargaining and haggling among the members of the First Congress of 1789. The list of what was to become the Bill of Rights began with around two hundred separate proposals that were finally whittled down to twelve amendments sent to the states for ratification; only ten of them were approved at the time. Bill of Rights supporters had many goals, including the protection of personal liberties, alterations in the balance between national and state government powers, and the structure of the federal government itself.[80] If all the amendments warranted the same dignity and treatment, where is Justice Thomas's umbrage, and that of his like-minded colleagues, at the sad and ignored Third Amendment, protecting citizens against the quartering of troops in people's homes in times of peace? Or the Seventh Amendment's ignored protection of the right of jury trial for suits at common law where the value exceeds twenty dollars? Or the Ninth Amendment's largely slighted enumeration clause (a cause taken up by some liberals)?

Judging the history of constitutional interpretation, it is clear that some rights really are more important than others, a principle reflected in the longstanding "preferred freedoms" doctrine, a principle dating back at least to the 1930s.[81] More generally, the courts undoubtedly "watch some freedoms more carefully than others," that one can observe "gradations *among* the guarantees" and even "gradations *within* the individual guarantees in the Bill of Rights."[82] Surely the First Amendment's protections of free speech and press, for example, are indeed more important than other (or every?) Bill of Rights protections. As one constitutional scholar has noted, the preferred freedoms doctrine "has been absorbed in the concepts of strict scrutiny, fundamental rights, and selective incorporation."[83]

In the minds of some, Second Amendment rights would exist whenever a human hand comes in contact with a firearm, or even a firearm accessory (subsequent chapters will examine this very idea). If that seems extreme, it also comes uncomfortably close to the doctrine of Justice Thomas and company. Yet what kind of case can be made that their view of gun rights maltreatment is justifiable? The short answer is, not much, either as law or policy.

First, the mere existence of *D.C. v. Heller* is a testament to a remarkable success in the effort to carve out a brand-new individualist gun right. In most of our history, a constitutionally based individual right to guns under the Second Amendment as a matter of law did not exist. The direct evidence pertaining to the meaning of the Second Amendment, most especially the debates over the amendment during the First Congress of 1789, as well as its subsequent interpretation over roughly two centuries, explains it as a militia-based right, not a personal one.[84] The court's reinterpretation of the Second Amendment in *Heller* was deeply problematic, both as history and law.[85] My purpose here, however, is not to rehash those arguments, as many others have done that elsewhere. Problematic or not, *Heller* is the law, and courts have made a good faith effort to follow it, given the general roadmap it set out.

My second point is that the courts have carefully and logically implemented the *Heller* principle. The court's roadmap consisted of three parts: that *Heller* established a personal right to own a handgun for self-protection in the home; that laws and restrictions on guns and gun habits were allowable, including, but not limited to, conventional restrictions that the majority opinion listed; and that gun laws' historical provenance—whether they are "longstanding"— would be an important consideration in determining a contemporary law's constitutionality. As the court said:

> Although we do not undertake an exhaustive historical analysis today of the full scope of the Second Amendment, nothing in our opinion should be taken to cast doubt on longstanding prohibitions on the possession of firearms by felons and the mentally ill, or laws forbidding the carrying of firearms in sensitive places such as schools and government buildings, or laws imposing conditions and qualifications on the commercial sale of arms.[86]

The court also said that the list does not purport to be exhaustive. Further, the court said that this right:

> does not protect those weapons not typically possessed by law-abiding citizens for lawful purposes, such as short-barreled shotguns. That accords with the historical understanding of the scope of the right.[87]

In addition, the court said that there was "not a right to keep and carry any weapon whatsoever in any manner and for whatever purpose" adding "[f]or example, the majority of the 19th-century courts to consider the question held that prohibitions on carrying concealed weapons were lawful under the Second Amendment or state analogues"; that "prohibitions on carrying concealed weapons were lawful," as were restrictions on "dangerous and unusual weapons," "laws regulating storage of firearms to prevent accidents," and that "weapons that are most useful in military service—M-16 rifles and the like—may be banned."[88]

This general framework has left unanswered questions. Such unfinished business is hardly unusual when the court issues an important ruling. In areas as diverse as abortion rights and rights of criminal defendants, for example, accumulated lower court rulings (and also Supreme Court follow-up rulings) addressed unanticipated questions and ambiguities. That, after all, is the essence of caselaw.

The federal courts have generally adopted a two-step approach to judging the constitutionality of gun laws. The first step is whether the law in question burdens the Second Amendment right. If not, then no further inquiry is needed, and the law is upheld. If the answer is yes, then the second step involves answering the question of whether the law can sustain examination under "intermediate scrutiny" (the standard of review adopted in most of the circuits), drawing from a longstanding framework pertaining to evaluating constitutional claims that evaluates them based on one of three successively more strict categories: rational basis, intermediate scrutiny, or strict scrutiny. The first of these is a relatively low bar to accept the constitutionality of the law in question; the last is the highest or strictest bar.[89] This has demonstrated not only the ability of lower federal courts to resolve important subsequent questions, but the ability to do so sensibly.

Other questions remain which have been and will be the subject of increasing judicial scrutiny, including gun restrictions for categories of people, categories of weapons, places they may or may not be carried, gun sales restrictions, and licensing and registration restrictions.[90] For those who consider gun law history relevant, and for those who claim fealty to Originalism, America's gun law history provides a useful and instructive roadmap. That is, in fact, a primary theme of this book, along with the Supreme Court's conservatives' anxiousness to recast that history in a way favorable to their desired outcomes.

As laws pertaining to these questions have been challenged in the decade-plus after *Heller*, the Supreme Court has refused to hear virtually every appeal of a lower court ruling on the Second Amendment until the current decade. From 2008 until 2021, the Supreme Court has declined to hear over 150 appeals of lower federal court rulings on the Second Amendment. Moreover, over 1400 legal challenges to gun laws have resulted in the vast majority of the laws being upheld.[91] This, of course, is what really rankles Thomas and friends. They would like to see many more gun laws brushed aside.

I argue, however, that the rulings of lower courts have, to date, produced a reasonable balance between gun laws and gun rights. Both laws and rights remain intact. The Second Amendment is no "cavalierly disfavored second class orphan." While there continue to be areas where its legal application needs clarification, the *Heller* rubric outlined above has been applied by lower courts in a more or less sensible manner to reconcile its newly established right with the legitimate policy concerns of a nation plagued by persistent gun violence. The chapters to come will provide evidence to support this proposition, a subject we will return to in the Conclusion. And despite the evident unhappiness of the Supreme Court's new conservative majority with the current state of affairs, the idea that gun rules and rights are entirely compatible, is one that is consonant with our nation's history. As I have argued elsewhere, gun possession is as old as the country, but so are gun laws. The idea that gun laws and rights exist in a zero-sum world, where a gain for one is considered a loss for the other, is a new framework emerging in the hyper-politically charged world of gun politics of the last few decades. It was emphatically not the lesson of gun laws and rights in the country's first three hundred years.[92] This returns us to legal conservatives' guiding light—their secular religion—constitutional Originalism.

Originalism as Constitutional Spousal Abuse

The legal and political battle over the meaning of the Second Amendment has been fought in the midst of a larger political and legal clash over competing perspectives regarding how the Constitution is or should be interpreted. One view, "Constitutional Originalism," says that judges should interpret the Constitution based on the document's original intent or "fixed" meaning, filtering out contemporary values and preferences. As Justice Scalia said, judges should "begin with the text, and to give that text the meaning that it bore when it was adopted by the people."[93] Constitutional interpretation should avoid anything like contemporary societal values or other similar considerations.

The "Living Constitution" view does not abandon the constitutional text, but notes that the Constitution was the product of many hands, that it is often vague as to meaning, that it often raises more questions than it answers, that the framers themselves disagreed not only about the meaning of the document but about how strictly to adhere to its provisions, that some of the framers changed their minds about important matters (chief among those was James Madison), and that for the document to survive, it must be adapted to modern society and conditions that could not have been anticipated in the eighteenth century.[94] As one analyst has noted, "scholars disagree on the original meaning of almost every important constitutional provision."[95]

The Originalist movement (the antecedent of which was dubbed constitutional "strict construction") is largely the product of the last few decades, arising in reaction to what was seen as the excesses of liberal judicial activism of the 1950s to the 1970s. This reaction to judicial activism was an integral intellectual component of the New Right political movement that arose in the late 1970s and early 1980s. Leading the legal march to the right was the Federalist Society, discussed earlier.[96] Originalist theory is especially important for the framing of gun rights, as the *Heller* case is considered one of the most history-driven, and history-based (as opposed to law-based) rulings in modern times.[97] By one account, Justice Scalia's majority opinion in *Heller* was "a textbook example of how to decide a constitutional law case using originalism."[98] Scalia himself admitted that this opinion "is my legacy opinion insofar as it is the best example of the technique of constitutional interpretation .... the most complete originalist opinion that I've ever written."[99]

Originalism's adherents, it should be noted, began by extolling their deep dive into history to resolve contemporary constitutional controversies rather than engaging in "legislating from the bench," the charge often leveled against those taking a Living Constitution view. This initial version of Originalism, labeled "Originalism 1.0" by Jonathan Gienapp,[100] soon gave way to a new version of Originalism, what Gienapp dubbed "Originalism 2.0." This second version emerged because of the drubbing Originalists took at the hands of historians who pointedly and effectively noted that Originalists were, frankly, bad historians who seemed more interested in cloaking their ends-oriented jurisprudence in an ill-fitting historical guise than in getting the history right, as best as that could be determined. Originalism 2.0 dodged this criticism by shifting their paradigm to "public meaning," meaning "how the words of the document would have been understood by a competent speaker of the language when the Constitution was enacted."[101] By their account, this meant that historical evidence was now irrelevant to their analysis. They simply needed to study word use in the particular legal context, which was framed as a fairly narrow methodological exercise, not "doing history."[102] Except, of course, that it was and is. Moreover, this all assumes that "the words the framers used had settled meanings," which they did not.[103]

If one accepts Originalism as a viable constitutional construct—and that's a mighty big "if"—a case like *Heller* represents a paradigmatic example of the abuse of history in the name of Originalism. As the Pulitzer Prize winning historian Jack Rakove noted: "the main advocates for originalist theory are lawyers, not historians."[104] If a man professes love for his wife yet abuses her, how do we interpret his professed love? Bruce Allen Murphy concluded that Scalia was "adept at manipulating his originalist theory to reach the result that he sought."[105] In that sense, the current court's conservatives are following in his footsteps.

Yet the idea that lawyers bend history to suit their arguments is not new, even if Originalists have taken it to a new level. The derogatory term "law office history" gained currency as early as 1963 when historian Paul L. Murphy noted with disapproval the practice of the legal researcher working on a case who "knows that his job is to find those materials which will best serve to persuade the judges to rule favorably in the immediate case . . . . 'Law office history,' then, is not only deliberately calculated to win cases, but its inadequacy as academic history is never questioned."[106] In his telling criticism of *Heller*, the noted conservative Judge Richard Posner referred to Scalia's opinion derisively as "law office history," where, Posner added, "the derision is richly deserved."[107]

Be that as it may, one need not be an Originalist adherent to agree that the past matters, not only for the sake of understanding how we arrived at the present, but because it can contribute important perspective to the understanding of contemporary problems and issues. Still, in the real world, we live in the present, not the past. In the year of the Constitution's adoption, the United States consisted of thirteen Atlantic-coast-hugging pre-industrial states where over ninety-five percent of its inhabitants were subsistence farmers. By the start of the twentieth century, the nation was an industrial (later post-industrial) giant that spanned the two great oceans consisting of forty-eight (and later fifty) states. Neither modern governance nor the modern American state could exist had the document not possessed the elasticity to, for example, expand and redefine Congress's power to regulate commerce, providing the basis for the government to intervene in and regulate the economy. Many years ago, political scientist Theodore J. Lowi argued that the American republic had evolved through several republics, each with its own distinctive constitutional configuration, even as we were governed under the same basic document. He subsumed this analysis under the umbrella phrase "The Second Republic."[108] With its many flaws, the modern American republic would not have been possible under any notion of Originalism, which mostly hurtles toward an imaginary past to service a parochial contemporary political agenda. At least Living Constitution adherents are honest about their endeavor. As political scientist Susan P. Liebell has written, "Originalism does not provide neutrality; it conceals interpretation."[109]

Navigating the Fork in the Road on Gun Policy

Despite the terminal flaws of Originalism, extending to both concept and implementation, the purpose of this book is to accept, in part, the Originalist challenge to examine and learn from our constitutional, political, and legal history as relevant to, in this case, modern gun policy. Fortunately, intrepid researchers have culled and digitized a treasure trove of old gun laws that shed important new light on our gun law past, which in turn is useful for framing the contemporary gun debate. This perspective will be used to suggest a way forward in the emergent gun dilemma facing America, the rhetorical fork in the road: a country supportive of, and in need of, effective gun laws to address its burgeoning gun violence crisis, contradicted by a conservative Supreme Court including several members who are anxious to not only block that progress but to throw national and state gun laws into gear-grinding reverse by striking them down.

As historians of the courts well know, this is not the first time that the Supreme Court has been out of sync with the national political and policy consensus. And a perfectly respectable argument can be advanced asserting that the courts ultimately do take account of the public mood and opinions on important questions.[110] Unlike past eras, however, the current looming standoff is not between defense of the status quo versus change, but between turning the clock back to an imaginary past era regarding guns (i.e., a fictional past where gun laws were few and imagined gun rights were held in some kind of exalted position) versus the current effort to defend existing gun laws along with pursuit of incremental gun policy change.

It is therefore essential that we get our gun past right, as best we can. This book is one effort to advance that goal. It does so by examining emergent gun controversies with the help of an exploration of that gun past—the methodology of this book. This does not mean, however, that contemporary policy judgments should be chained to a bygone era, what has been sometimes referred to as rule by "the dead hand of the past."[111] The world, and the United States, are profoundly different in the twenty-first century than in prior centuries, and it is not possible to make responsible policy decisions now without taking account of the profound differences between the present and the past. To do so would be a concise definition of political irresponsibility.

The bulk of this book examines emergent gun policy controversies, most of which have received remarkably little attention. Each chapter will address a different case or example, but all represent instances where Second Amendment rights are defined (or more properly redefined) as existing whenever a human hand comes into contact with a gun—or even a gun accessory. Consider that to be a working definition of the new Gun Rights 2.0. The chapter cases also will provide evidence to address the charge that the Second Amendment has been treated as a "disfavored" or second-class right.

The Plan of the Book

The subjects of the chapters to come have several things in common. Each deals with a very specific contemporary and emergent legal, political, and regulatory matter pertaining to guns. Each also has a gun regulatory past that is little known, or even unknown. Each also represents an outer edge of, or new twist in, the contemporary gun debate via a case study of an effort to expand the definition of gun rights.

Chapter 2 examines the contemporary assault weapons debate and its specific relationship to ammunition magazines, especially large capacity magazines (LCMs), generally defined as those capable of holding more than ten rounds. These military-derived high-capacity semiautomatic weapons have been the focus of intense political debate since they first emerged in appreciable numbers in the civilian gun market in the 1980s. Unlike conventional semi-automatic firearms, these weapons have been defined by their military origin and characteristics, a fact that has been the source of some ridicule by gun people—and in part, with good reason. Many of the features of these weapons, like pistol grips, thumbholes, adjustable stocks, and threaded barrels, have nothing directly to do with the weapons' firing capabilities. But the ability to receive LCMs does, and that is why they receive special attention here. Despite assault weapons' recent vintage, however, state regulation of semi-automatic weapons first appeared nearly a hundred years ago. The same is true of ammo magazine regulations, which, as we will see, were regulated far more extensively in the past.

Chapter 3 will examine the historical and contemporary debate over gun silencers, also called "suppressors." These gun accessories were strictly regulated (but not banned) by a federal law enacted in 1934, but firearms manufacturers and gun rights forces launched an aggressive campaign to deregulate them within the previous decade, and also to extend the definition of gun rights to accessories like silencers. After so many decades, why the sudden interest? And is silencer regulation still appropriate? Here again, history sheds revealing light on this issue.

Recent very public demonstrations, organized in particular to protest COVID-19 pandemic restrictions and new gun law proposals, have included public civilian arms carrying, a phenomenon otherwise rarely seen in recent times. Aside from the stated benign motives of the gun carriers, the prevailing public reaction has ranged from puzzlement to dismay to fear. Carry activists have reframed the movement as a simple, benign expression of Second Amendment rights. This sort of activity has, however, been subject to regulation since the colonial era and before, under the general heading of weapons brandishing, and for the very same reason, whether past or present: public arms carrying, by its very nature, induces fear. Chapter 4 will explore the little-known history and contemporary consequences of this phenomenon, including modern allegations by some gun owners that people who fear guns are guilty of irrational "hoplophobia."

Even as the federal government has taken virtually no action on gun policy, the states have witnessed a relative blizzard of actions, but with states taking divergent directions. Some states have tightened their gun laws while others have loosened them. Stricter state measures have spawned a new movement that has spread rapidly among local governments around the country to enact so-called "Second Amendment sanctuary" resolutions. Chapter 5 will examine this seemingly new gun rights development. Here, too, this movement follows a lineage of rebellion against law that was once called nullification. Chapter 6 will offer a brief conclusion in the light of the earlier analysis.

2

Assault Weapons and Ammunition Magazines

LEGAL CHALLENGES TO gun laws are nothing new, including laws restricting access to assault weapons. Such challenges have also included objections to restrictions regarding ammunition magazine capacity (magazines are the box-like containers that attach to guns that hold and feed new rounds into the guns' firing chambers). In general, ammo magazine restrictions have been consistently upheld, until recently.[1]

In 2000, California enacted a law limiting ammunition magazines to ten rounds. This law kept legal the ownership of larger capacity magazines obtained before the enactment of the restriction. That law was expanded by a state referendum in 2016, which now required owners of magazines holding more than ten rounds to dispose of or destroy them. That new law was also challenged, but unlike past challenges,[2] this one prevailed in its initial adjudication. In the 2019 case of *Duncan v. Becerra*,[3] a federal district court judge struck down the ten-round magazine limit. The decision is notable for three reasons: first, because it struck down both the verdict of the state referendum that eliminated the legality of owning pre-2000 large capacity magazines (LCMs), but also the ten round limit itself; second, it concluded that there is a Second Amendment right to own ammunition magazines holding more than ten rounds, repeatedly calling it a "core" right of the Second Amendment;[4] and third, up until this time federal appeals courts had consistently upheld magazine restrictions.[5]

Federal district court judge Roger Benitez was emphatic in his ruling: "the question is whether a magazine is an arm [i.e., a gun] under the Second Amendment. The answer is yes."[6] He went on to say that "restrictions on the possession of firearm magazines of any size have no historical pedigree," adding that the "oldest statute limiting the permissible size of a detachable firearm magazine" dated to 1990.[7] These conclusions are false, as this chapter will demonstrate.

In 2020, a divided three-judge panel upheld the lower court decision to strike down the magazine limit.[8] Interestingly, however, that ruling sidestepped some of Judge Benitez's tendentious claims. Yet that decision ran afoul of basic facts, too. Notably, it said that only "a handful" of states had formerly enacted ammunition magazine restrictions, proceeding to list only three states that did so in the 1920s and 1930s (Michigan, Ohio, and Rhode Island).[9] That, too, is false, and the proof of that predates the arguments presented in this case.[10] This decision was in turn reheard en banc by the full Ninth Circuit panel. In late 2021, it restored the magazine limit in a 7–4 ruling. That decision was appealed to the U.S. Supreme Court.

Regardless of the final outcome, the district court ruling is significant because it raises some key issues about the regulation of ammunition magazines and its relationship, if any, to the Second Amendment. Similar recent arguments have surfaced claiming that the ownership of gun silencers might or should also be protected under the Second Amendment (see Chapter 3). Even for those fully convinced that the 2008 Supreme Court ruling of *D.C. v. Heller* establishing a personal right to own handguns for personal self-defense is correct both as to law and history, it surely must seem a stretch to argue that LCMs are "a gun." Yet this is one example of the new frontier of Second Amendment law that is the focus of this book.

Contrary to much popular culture and frontier mythology, gun laws and regulations in America are old, not new. That is no less true when it comes to the subject of this chapter (and those to come), ammunition feeding devices. Recent analyses of the history of gun laws in America have excavated a surprisingly extensive, diverse, and prolific number and variety of gun laws, extending back to the country's beginnings. While gun ownership is as old as the country, so are gun laws.[11] That is significant because it is commonplace to think of gun regulation as an artifact of the late twentieth century. Yet nothing could be further from the truth.

This chapter will examine the little-known roots of gun magazine[12] regulation, and its relationship to the regulation of semi- and fully automatic weapons, dating to early in the previous century. For reasons of history, policy, and law, a fuller understanding of this regulatory history is essential to understand our past and inform these modern debates. As I argued in the previous chapter, one need not be a constitutional Originalist—or, for that matter, a lawyer—to take an interest in, or seek edification from, the country's gun law past. Because that history is inextricably tied to the regulation of semi- and fully automatic weapons, both will be examined.

The Story of Assault Weapons

Modern guns available to civilians labeled assault weapons and assault rifles are derived from military weapons designed for use on the battlefield. The firearm known today as the assault weapon arose during World War II when the Germans developed the STG 44 or *Sturmgewehr* (literally translated as "assault rifle"). That soldier-carried weapon was studied by the Soviets, who produced the well-known Soviet AK-47 Kalashnikov in 1947, the most successful and prolific soldier-held battlefield weapon in modern times.[13] The AK-47 gave rise to the American AR-15, which then became the military M16. The AR-15 was eventually sold to the civilian market, and that led in turn to many copycat variations.

The AR-15 was first produced by the ArmaLite Company in the late 1950s (the basis for the "AR" name). According to one of its designers, Jim Sullivan, the weapon was "designed for full automatic military use. It wasn't really designed as a sporting rifle."[14] Sullivan also said of the AR-15 in an interview that "[c]ivilian sales was never the intended purpose."[15] ArmaLite sold the rights to the gun to the Colt Company in 1959. A few years later, the weapon was adopted by the American military and produced as the M16, where it came in to use during the Vietnam War in the 1960s. These military weapons came to have three firing capabilities: fully automatic, semi-automatic, and (sometimes) "selective fire" or three-round bursts.[16] Civilian versions could and can fire only in a semi-automatic fashion.

Colt received permission to market a semi-automatic version of the AR-15 to the civilian market, but these weapons did not catch on in the American market in a significant way until the late 1980s,[17] when the Chinese flooded the market with cheap weapons, including their own semi-automatic version of the AK-47.[18] Today, the AR-15-type weapon is manufactured and sold by over thirty companies, including Smith and Wesson, Bushmaster, and Sig Sauer.[19]

Some have insisted that the terms "assault weapon" and "assault rifle" are a "public relations stunt"[20] or are ginned up labels invented by gun control organizations. According to one law journal article, "[p]rior to 1989, the term 'assault weapon' did not exist in the lexicon of firearms. It is a political term, developed by anti-gun publicists to expand the category of 'assault rifles' so as to allow an attack on as many additional firearms as possible on the basis of undefined 'evil' appearance."[21] Not only did these terms exist long before 1989, these were the very terms used by the companies that first produced, marketed, and sold such weapons to the public. Industry use of the terms "assault weapons" and "assault rifles" appeared in the early 1980s (and even earlier), before political efforts to regulate them emerged in the late 1980s.[22]

Gun industry analyst Tom Diaz has chronicled the marketing strategies employed by gun manufacturers and gun publications from the time that such weapons emerged in the American civilian market in a significant way in the 1980s. He reports on, and quotes directly from gun company advertisements and gun magazines, like Heckler and Koch selling its "HK 91 Semi-Automatic Assault Rifle," the "Bushmaster assault rifle," the AKM "imported assault rifle," the Beretta M-70 that "resembles many other assault rifles," the AR10 (made by Paragon S&S Inc.) advertised as a "famous assault rifle [that] is now available in a semi-auto form!", the "AMT 25/.22 Lightning Carbine" that was advertised as an "assault-type semi-auto," among many other examples. The use of military terminology, and the weapons' military character and appearance, were key to marketing the guns to the public.[23] As early as 1984, *Guns & Ammo* magazine advertised a book called *Assault Firearms* that the magazine extolled as "full of the hottest hardware available today."[24]

As a standard buyer's guide on assault weapons noted, the "popularly-held idea that the term 'assault weapon' originated with anti-gun activists, media or politicians is wrong. The term was first adopted by the manufacturers, wholesalers, importers and dealers in the American firearms industry . . . ."[25] The more expansive phrase "assault weapon" is generally used over "assault rifle" because "weapon" also includes not only rifles but some shotguns and handguns that were also subject to regulation in the federal 1994 assault weapons ban and subsequent laws.

In the 1990s, both the gun industry and the National Rifle Association (NRA) abruptly changed course in their labeling of such weapons as pressure built on Congress and in some states to enact curbs, and that led to the remarketing and rebranding of such weapons as no different from typical, traditional hunting weapons that also fired in semi-automatic fashion. That effort has persisted to the present, with terms like "tactical rifles" and "modern sporting rifles" typically offered by gun organizations including the NRA and the National Shooting Sports Foundation (NSSF) as preferred terms for such weapons.[26]

Persistent efforts at rebranding—and parallel denials of assault weapons' past—accelerated through the 2010s as national concern about assault weapons escalated, as seen, for example, in the NSSF website and literature.

A widely circulated "Modern Sporting Rifle Pocket Fact Card"[27] says that such weapons are "widely misunderstood" because of their cosmetic resemblance to military weapons (even though these are intentional design features). It urges gun owners to use the information on the card and website "to correct misconceptions about these rifles." Among the "corrections" it offers: "AR-15-style rifles are NOT 'assault weapons' or 'assault rifles.' An assault rifle is fully automatic—a machine gun." It adds "Please correct them" if they use the term "assault weapon," claiming further that it "is a political term" created in the 1980s. (As noted above, this assertion is incorrect.)

An article in *Outdoor Life* belied the claim that assault weapons are limited only to those that fire fully automatically. That article, too, urged its readers to share its information with non-shooting friends to dispel "myths" about "assault weapons." In its account, it correctly noted that "the term 'assault weapon' . . . generally referred to a type of light infantry firearm initially developed in World War II; a magazine-fed rifle and carbine suitable for combat, such as the AK-47 and the M16/M4. These are selective-fire weapons that can shoot semi-auto, full-auto, or in three-round bursts."[28]

The effort to rebrand "assault weapons" as something more benign and severed from its military origins was seen in the publication struggles of Phillip Peterson, whose book, titled as recently as 2008, *Gun Digest Buyer's Guide to Assault Weapons*,[29] is a well-known reference work on the subject. As Peterson explained, the gun industry "moved to shame or ridicule" those who used the phrase "assault weapons," insisting that the term should now only apply to fully automatic weapons. Peterson noted that the origin of the term "assault weapon" was the industry itself.[30] He found that the NRA refused to sell his book until he changed the title, which in 2010 he renamed *Gun Digest Buyer's Guide to Tactical Rifles*.[31] The very same pattern played out in Canada, where gun companies also used the term "assault rifle" in the 1970s and 1980s until political pressure began to build to restrict such weapons in the aftermath of the mass shooting in Montreal in 1989. By the 1990s, Canadian companies and their allies also adopted terms like "modern sporting rifles."[32]

The Regulatory History of Semi- and Fully Automatic Firearms

Mass shootings in the late 1980s and early 1990s raised public concerns about whether to regulate assault weapons. Complicating this call was the fact that, like many other common weapons not modeled after military weaponry, the guns marketed to civilians fired semi-automatically—that is, firing one round with each pull of the trigger. Still, California became the first state to enact restrictions on assault weapons in 1989, shortly after a mass shooting at an elementary school earlier that year where the shooter used an AK-47 semi-automatic assault rifle. After several years of pressure, Congress enacted a limited national assault weapons ban in 1994. Written into the bill was a sunset provision that called for the bill to lapse in 2004.[33] Congress did not renew the ban, despite repeated efforts to do so in subsequent years.

Even with the law's limitations, a study reported to the National Institute of Justice found that assault weapons crimes studied in selected cities declined at a minimum of seventeen percent in the city with the smallest decline to seventy-two percent in the city showing the greatest decline during the ban. In addition, three studies concluded that it reduced the rate of mass shootings and fatalities, which then climbed after the law lapsed.[34]

As of 2021, seven states (California, Connecticut, Hawaii, Maryland, Massachusetts, New Jersey, and New York) plus the District of Columbia ban assault weapons. (Hawaii bans assault pistols only.) Two more states, Minnesota and Virginia, regulate but do not ban them.[35] Relevant to this discussion, nine states (California, Colorado, Connecticut, Hawaii, Maryland, Massachusetts, New Jersey, New York, and Vermont) and D.C. ban high-capacity ammunition magazines. In 2022, Washington State also enacted a ban on these magazines. All these states limit capacity to a ten-round maximum except Colorado, which puts the limit at fifteen.[36] Yet the regulation of semi-automatic weapons and ammunition magazines dates not just to the 1980s, but to the 1920s.

Invention versus Regulation

As researchers and experts of gun history have noted, multi-shot guns existed in the eighteenth century (with multi-shot experimental designs dating back as much as two centuries earlier). The example often cited is the Girandoni air rifle, a gun developed for crack shots in the Austrian army that was capable of firing up to twenty rounds. One of these was taken along on the Lewis and Clark expedition of 1804–1806.[37] But such guns were a rarity, as they were extremely expensive, fragile, and complex, and few were made.[38] An early multi-shot gun, the "Puckle Gun," developed in the early 1700s, could fire nine rounds per minute (hardly comparable to the far more rapid firing capabilities of semi- and fully automatic weapons of the modern era). It sat on a tripod, was too large and heavy to be used as a hand-held weapon, and was basically a military weapon.[39] Even this weapon "never advanced beyond the prototype stage."[40] The more well-known "pepperbox," a multi-shot firearm where the number of shots fired coincided with the number of barrels bundled together, found some popularity in the early 1800s, but it was rapidly eclipsed by the superior Colt revolver. The reason: pepperboxes were "heavy, lumpy, and impractical."[41] Indeed, the Colt revolver was "the first widely used multishot weapon."[42]

Colt notwithstanding, single shot guns were the ubiquitous firearm until after the Civil War.[43] The idea of an available, affordable, feasible multi-shot firearm did not arise until the development of Colt's multi-shot revolver in the 1830s. Indeed, Colt biographer Jim Rasenberger says that Colt's pistol was the first practical firearm that could shoot more than one bullet without reloading.[44] Even then, Colt could not make a go of manufacturing multishot weapons for many years because he could find no market for them, either from the government or the public. The government, in fact, dismissed such weapons as mere "novelties."[45] After an 1837 test of Colt's gun and others the government concluded that it was "entirely unsuited to the general purposes of the service."[46] Colt's early failure to cultivate either a military or a civilian market in the U.S. drove him to bankruptcy and then to market his guns to European governments in the 1840s. The gun made appearances in the pre-Civil War West, but it took the Civil War to finally witness the proliferation of the Colt-type revolver and similar firearms.[47]

Nevertheless, in the *Duncan v. Becerra* case mentioned earlier, both the district court and appeals court made much of the fact that multi-shot guns existed in these early times, including a few capable of firing more than ten rounds. In the words of the appeals court: "After the American Revolution, the record shows that new firearm designs proliferated throughout the states and few restrictions were enacted on firing capacities."[48] This reasoning provided important support for striking down California's ten-round magazine limit. But the problem with this logic is not difficult to discern. It would be as logical to reject modern governmental regulation of electric power through such government agencies as state power commissions and the Federal Energy Regulatory Commission because no such regulation was enacted after Benjamin Franklin's experiments with electricity in the mid-eighteenth century. The fact that "firearms designs proliferated"—itself an arguable proposition—tells us nothing about the consequences of such designs for society. And more importantly, the existence of designs does not equal general availability, much less general use of these weapons.

Aside from the six-shot revolver and long guns like the Winchester rifle, very few guns in circulation in the late nineteenth and early twentieth centuries fired anything like ten or more rounds without reloading. Yet the rise in the circulation of multi-shot handguns was accompanied by the rapid spread of anti-concealed carry laws, precisely because of their contribution to escalating interpersonal violence.[49] By the end of the nineteenth century, virtually every state in the country prohibited or severely restricted concealed gun carry.[50] It was only in the post-World War I era when multi-shot long guns came into criminal use that they became a regulatory and public policy concern.

The Roaring Twenties and Gun Violence

As discussed in Chapter 1, the 1920s was a time of considerable gun regulatory activity. At least twenty-eight states enacted laws to bar fully automatic weapons from the 1920s through 1934.[51] In 1934, Congress responded by enacting the first significant national gun law, the National Firearms Act.[52] It imposed restrictions on gangster-type weapons like the Tommy gun and other fully automatic weapons, sawed-off shotguns, and silencers.

Aside from prolific regulation of fully automatic weapons at the state and federal levels, however, at least eight (including D.C.), and as many as eleven states enacted laws to restrict or bar all semi-automatic weapons. These laws were enacted between 1927 and 1934. All eleven states also barred fully automatic weapons, often lumping semi-automatic and fully automatic (often referred to as "machine guns" and "submachine guns") under the same regulatory rubric.

For example, a Massachusetts law enacted in 1927 said this: "Any gun of small arm calibre designed for rapid fire and operated by a mechanism, or any gun which operates automatically after the first shot has been fired, either by gas action or recoil action, shall be deemed to be a machine gun."[53] A 1927 Rhode Island measure defined the prohibited "machine gun" to include "any weapon which shoots automatically and any weapon which shoots more than twelve shots semi-automatically without reloading."[54] Michigan's 1927 law prohibited machine guns or any other firearm if they fired more than sixteen times without reloading.[55] Minnesota's 1933 law outlawed "[a]ny firearm capable of automatically reloading after each shot is fired, whether firing singly by separate trigger pressure or firing continuously by continuous trigger pressure."[56] It went on to penalize the modification of weapons that were altered to accommodate such extra firing capacity.[57]

Ohio restricted to permit holders both fully automatic and semi-automatic weapons in a 1933 law, incorporating any gun that "shoots automatically, or any firearm which shoots more than eighteen shots semi-automatically without reloading."[58] The law defined semi-automatic weapons as those that fired one shot with each pull of the trigger.[59] South Dakota restricted access to machine guns by defining them as weapons "from which more than five shots or bullets may be rapidly, or automatically, or semi-automatically discharged from a magazine, by a single function of the firing device."[60] Virginia restricted weapons "of any description . . . from which more than seven shots or bullets may be rapidly, or automatically, or semi-automatically discharged from a magazine, by a single function of the firing device, and also applies to and includes weapons, loaded or unloaded, from which more than sixteen shots or bullets may be rapidly, automatically, semi-automatically, or otherwise discharged without reloading."[61] A 1932 law applying to the District of Columbia barred fully automatic weapons, described as those operating "Automatically, more than 1 shot by a single function of the trigger," and semi-automatic weapons "designed to shoot or can be readily converted to shoot . . . semiautomatically, more than 12 shots without reloading."[62] Aside from these eight states, another three—Illinois, Louisiana, and South Carolina—included language that may also have extended regulations to semi-automatic weapons as well as to fully automatic weapons.[63]

Regulating Ammunition Feeding Devices

As an examination of these old laws shows, restrictions on fully automatic and semi-automatic firearms were closely tied to the regulation of ammunition magazines or their equivalent, as both types of weapons are predicated on some kind of reloading function or device that automatically feeds new rounds into the firing chamber after the previous round is fired. As is the case with contemporary state regulations restricting ammo magazine capacity, all the state laws previously quoted imposed regulations based on the number of rounds that could be fired without reloading, ranging from more than one (Massachusetts and Minnesota) up to a high of eighteen (Ohio).

Magazine firing limits were imposed in three categories of state laws (see Table 2.1): twelve states regulating semi-automatic and fully automatic weapons (District of Columbia, Louisiana, Massachusetts, Michigan, Minnesota, Ohio, Rhode Island, South Carolina, South Dakota, and Virginia; New Jersey had a 1920 law making it "unlawful to use in hunting fowl or animals of any kind any shotgun or rifle holding more than two cartridges at one

Table 2.1 Ammunition Magazine Firing Limits in 23 State Laws, 1917–1934*

Semi-automatic and Fully Automatic Firearms (barred weapons holding more than the number of rounds stipulated)	Fully Automatic Firearms (barred weapons capable of firing a set number of rounds without reloading or that could receive ammunition feeding devices)	All Firearms (barred any weapon capable of receiving rounds through certain named round-feeding devices)
-District of Columbia (12 round maximum; 1932)	-Illinois (8 round maximum; 1931)	-California (1927)
-Louisiana (8 round maximum; 1932)	-New Jersey (any removable device holding rounds; 1927)	-Hawaii (1933)
-Massachusetts (more than 1 round; 1927)	-North Dakota (loadable bullet reservoir; 1931)	-Missouri (1929)
-Michigan (16 round maximum; 1927)	-Oregon (2 rounds or more; 1933)	-Washington State (1933)
-Minnesota (more than 1 round; 1933)	-Pennsylvania (2 rounds or more; 1929)	
-New Jersey (more than 2 rounds; hunting only; 1920)	-Texas (5 round maximum; 1933)	
-North Carolina (more than 2 rounds; hunting only; 1917)	-Vermont (6 round maximum; 1923)	
-Ohio (18 round maximum; 1933)	-Wisconsin (2 round maximum; 1933)	
-Rhode Island (12 round maximum; 1927)		
-South Carolina (8 round maximum; 1934)		
-South Dakota (5 round maximum; 1933)		
-Virginia (7 round maximum; 1934)		

*Including the District of Columbia. Note that New Jersey appears twice in this table. The dataset from which this information is drawn ended in 1934, so it does not include any states that might have enacted similar restrictions after 1934. See "Repository of Historical Gun Laws," Duke Law Center for Firearms Law, https://law.duke.edu/gunlaws/.

time, or that may be fired more than twice without reloading"[64] and North Carolina made it "unlawful to kill quail with any gun or guns that shoot over two times before reloading" in 1917[65]); eight states regulated fully automatic weapons only, where the regulation was defined by the number of rounds that could be fired without reloading or by the ability to receive ammunition feeding devices (Illinois, New Jersey, North Dakota, Oregon, Pennsylvania, Texas, Vermont, and Wisconsin[66]); and four states restricted all guns that could receive any type of ammo feeding mechanism or round feeding device and fire them continuously in a fully automatic manner (California, Hawaii, Missouri, and Washington State). A 1927 California law, for example, was titled this way:

> An Act to Prohibit the Possession of Machine Rifles, Machine Guns and Submachine guns Capable of Automatically and Continuously Discharging Loaded Ammunition of any Caliber in which Ammunition is Fed to such Guns from or by means of Clips, Disks, Drums, Belts or other Separable Mechanical Device.[67]

The other three states in this category (Hawaii, Missouri, and Washington[68]) used this same description. In all, at least twenty-three states enacted gun restrictions based on the regulation of ammunition magazines or similar feeding devices, and/or round capacity. Note also that the original version of the legislation that became the National Firearms Act of 1934 included this definition of semiautomatic and fully automatic firearms that were to be subject to regulation: "The term 'machine gun' means any weapon designed to shoot automatically or semiautomatically 12 or more shots without reloading."[69] (The final version of the bill was limited to fully automatic firearms.) Without question, one may reasonably conclude that regulations concerning removable magazines and magazine capacity were in fact common as early as the 1920s.

As this discussion demonstrates, the regulation of semi-automatic weapons and magazines predates the modern debate over these questions by seventy years. This fact is notable because it uncovers a hither-to unknown gun regulatory past, and because, as the Supreme Court noted in *D.C. v. Heller*, historical gun law provenance is relevant to determining the constitutionality of modern gun laws.[70]

History is important, but as I argued in Chapter 1, it is not and should not be the sole criterion for judging the utility, necessity, or legality of contemporary gun laws. As was true decades ago, the debate over contemporary gun regulations is directly shaped by changing technology and access to firearms like assault weapons and accessories like LCMs when that access began to have adverse societal consequences. Each will be considered in turn.

Assault Weapons, Magazines, and Crime

The military-style features of assault weapons are important because many bear directly on how the weapons are fired, like these weapons' lighter weight, more compact design, pistol grips, flash suppressors, collapsible or telescoping stocks, threaded barrels for attaching silencers, extensive use of plastic stampings, and the ability to receive large capacity magazines (LCMs). These features make them more maneuverable and concealable, and also facilitate a key trait for battlefield use: their ability to fire large numbers of rounds without reloading to lay down "spray fire," also referred to as "hosing down" an area.[71] Among these features, however, the one feature usually considered of greatest importance, as the discussion here emphasizes, is the ability to receive detachable magazines, which normally would include LCMs (as noted earlier, defined as those capable of holding more than ten rounds). The effort to restrict LCMs, and/or to require in law that such weapons have fixed, non-detachable magazines, is designed "to reduce gunshot victimizations by limiting the stock of semiautomatic firearms with large ammunition capacities and other features conducive to criminal use."[72] Considerable research has been brought to bear on this question.

Contemporary Assault Weapons Concerns

No precise count of the number of assault weapons owned in America is maintained. In 1994, the year Congress enacted the federal assault weapons ban, there were roughly 1.5 million such weapons in the country.[73] Several estimates in 2012 pegged the number at about four million.[74] One 2016 estimate put the number at "upward of 3.5 million,"[75] whereas another estimate that same year said about five million.[76] The National Shooting Sports Foundation, a pro-gun industry group, estimated in 2020 that about fifteen to twenty million were produced and in circulation (although not necessarily sold). But that estimate is considered unreliably high because it included weapons produced for law enforcement, because the NSSF did not offer any explanation or methodology as to how it produced that number, and because of the NSSF's pro-industry orientation.[77] In 2019, CBS News pegged the number of assault weapons at "over 11 million."[78]

If, for the sake of argument, we take a high number of fifteen million assault weapons in the country and divide by roughly 300 million guns in civilian hands today, it equals about five percent of all guns in America. While there is general agreement that assault weapons, led by the AR-15, are the biggest selling type of gun in recent years, they still represent a very small percent of all guns in America. The sale of handguns far outstrips that of assault weapons. And assault weapons sales only began to rise dramatically in the U.S. after the expiration of the federal assault weapons ban in 2004.[79] This date also coincided with an increase in the use of assault weapons and LCMs in crime. (The 1994 law also limited LCMs to ten rounds, a limit that disappeared when the law lapsed in 2004).[80]

Assault weapons' use in crime continues to be relatively small in relation to all gun crime in America. Most gun crime is committed with handguns. For example, roughly 80 percent of all gun murders and gun robberies are committed with handguns.[81] Yet, as noted, assault weapons' use in crime has increased since 2004, as has the use of LCMs. According to a recent study, firearms capable of receiving LCMs (including but not limited to assault weapons, which account for an estimated two to twelve percent of guns used in crimes) account for twenty-two to thirty-six percent of guns used in crime, and over forty percent of guns used in cases of "serious violence."[82] Beyond overall gun crime, assault weapons play a disproportionately large role in three types of criminal activity: mass shootings, police killings, and organized criminality.

Mass Shootings

Mass shootings are defined by the FBI as those where four or more people are killed, excluding the perpetrator.[83] Among mass shootings that have garnered significant national attention, such as the Stockton, California elementary school shooting in 1989; the Columbine High School shooting in 1999; the Aurora, Colorado movie theater shooting and the Sandy Hook elementary school shooting, both in 2012; the Orlando night club shooting in 2016; the Las Vegas shooting in 2017; and the Parkland shooting in 2018, all involved the use of assault weapons. From 2009 to 2019, the five deadliest mass shootings in the U.S. involved assault weapons with LCMs.[84] LCMs were used in the ten deadliest mass shootings in the decade of the 2010s.[85] From 2017 to mid-2021, assault weapons were used in at least thirteen mass-casualty shootings.[86] Aside from these specific horrific events, the mass shooting phenomenon possesses three traits: they have increased over time, both in terms of the number of incidents and number of people killed and injured; the number of incidents involving or including assault weapons also continues to increase; and assault weapons are more lethal than other firearms.[87]

A study of sixty-two public mass shootings from 1982 to 2012 found that of the 143 firearms used in these events, thirty-four percent of them were assault weapons, using as a metric the definition of assault weapons that would have been restricted under the 2013 federal assault weapons bill proposed by Sen. Dianne Feinstein (D-CA; the Senate voted the measure down). Handguns continue to be the firearm most likely to be used, as fifty percent involved semiautomatic handguns, and another fourteen percent were revolvers.[88]

In terms of the number of shooting incidents rather than number of guns, seventy-five percent of the sixty-two mass shootings involved semi-automatic handguns, eighty-seven percent had handguns of some type, and over one-third of mass shootings had assault weapons (note that attackers often had more than one firearm).[89] A Congressional Research Service study of mass shootings from 1999 to 2013 concluded that assault rifles were used in twenty-seven percent of public mass shootings; taking the data back to 1982, they were used in twenty-four percent of mass shootings.[90] A more recent study notes that from 2000 to 2017, semi-automatic assault rifles were used in twenty-five percent of active shooter events. Handguns continued to be used in over one-half of such incidents, more frequently than any other type of firearm,[91] but the twenty-five percent assault rifle number overrepresents their use in these incidents compared both with all gun crime and the percentage of assault weapons in society.[92] Further, mass shootings have become more lethal, a fact attributed in substantial measure to the wider availability and use of assault weapons and LCMs.[93] And as noted, the number of such incidents, both public and non-public, has been increasing.[94]

Killings of Police

Using FBI data, the Violence Policy Center reported that from 1998 to 2001, forty-one of 211 police officers (twenty percent) killed in the line of duty with firearms were shot with assault weapons (in all, 224 police officers during this period were killed in the line of duty from all causes).[95] An updated VPC study also found that twenty percent of police officers killed in the line of duty in 2016 and 2017 died from assault weapons fire.[96] Data from 2009 found that of forty-five officers killed by firearms nationwide, eight (eighteen percent) were shot with assault weapons.[97] While this represents a minority of all police gun deaths, it is a far higher proportion than that of assault weapons in society.

A 2018 study reported that assault weapons and LCMs were disproportionately more likely to be used in murders of police from 2003 to 2014: thirteen to sixteen percent of police murders used assault weapons, and over forty percent involved LCMs.[98] Law professor and economist John J. Donohue argues that "one of the most dangerous acts that any police officer can take" is approaching a mass shooting. That danger is magnified when the shooter has an assault weapon. Donohue added that "an officer with a handgun is outgunned against someone with an AR-15."[99] Police organizations like the International Association of Chiefs of Police and other police force leaders have long supported restrictions on assault weapons.[100]

Gang, Criminal, and Extremist Activity

Assault weapons are also preferred weapons for gang activity. A report by the International Association of Chiefs of Police recommended "Enacting an effective ban on military-style assault weapons . . . and other weapons that enable criminals to outgun law enforcement."[101] A report by the Police Executive Research Forum (PERF) noted "significant support for the proposition that the expiration of the law [the 1994 assault weapons ban] has caused problems for local police. Thirty-seven percent of the police agencies responding to PERF's survey reported that they had seen noticeable increases in criminals' use of assault weapons."[102] When New York State's tough new gun law, the New York SAFE Act of 2013, was challenged in court, the counsel for the New York State Police filed a brief on behalf of the law, defending in particular the strengthened assault weapons ban and magazine limit provisions. The 2013 law included a provision (upheld by the courts) that pre-ban magazines capable of holding more than ten rounds be destroyed, turned in to police, or sold out of state where their possession is legal.[103]

Widely noted prolific gun trafficking between the U.S. and Mexico has been motivated in large part by the appeal of assault weapons to Mexican drug gangs.[104] A study of gang members in the American Midwest by a team of researchers from the National Gang Crime Research Center of 1206 respondents, including 505 gang members, found that over forty-three percent reported owning an assault rifle, as compared with fifteen percent of non-gang member criminals. Gang members were also much more likely to report having used an assault rifle in a crime (twenty-eight percent) than non-gang members (four percent).[105] Other analyses note the appeal of assault weapons to American crime gangs and extremist paramilitary militias.[106] A spokesperson for the Drug Enforcement Agency said of the appeal of assault weapons to those involved in the drug trade: "There's a machismo to carrying the biggest, ugliest, and most powerful weapon available."[107]

Assault weapons have long found special allure to extremist groups. For example, an account of the activities of "paramilitary groups and cults" in California in 1980 identified what state authorities then described as the "phenomenal" growth of such groups there. The groups themselves were wide-ranging but had in common the amassing of weaponry (including but not limited to assault weapons, which were then relatively uncommon), systematic arms and military-style training, and various predictions of a coming apocalypse or collapse of societal order that, they claimed, necessitated "self-defense" steps. Some of the listed groups, like the Jewish Defense League, organized and trained openly, while others, like the Legion of Zion Army (an extremist Christian group), the Healthy Happy Holy Organization (radical American Sikhs), a Hare Krishna breakaway group, a Synanon splinter group, and the Brotherhood of the Sun operated covertly. Even in 1980, these groups were drawn to assault weapons like the Ingram Mac 10 submachine gun and the German-made HK-91semiautomatic military assault rifle.[108]

In more recent times, self-styled militia and similar extremist groups routinely armed themselves with assault-type weapons, as well as other arms and explosives. An FBI report of such groups spanning the two decades of the 1990s to the 2000s reported assault weapons to be typically included in their arsenals.[109] When one adds the dark, apocalyptic views of extremist groups about the government representing impending tyranny, it suggests a powder keg. As political scientist Melissa K. Merry notes, "futility arguments are pervasive in the rhetoric of gun rights organizations."[110]

A 2020 report by the gun safety group Everytown for Gun Safety explored the connections between what it labeled the gun lobby, exotic weapons, and the far right. They argue that gun rights forces "enshrine guns as tools of the Extreme Right" through aggressive marketing of guns, ongoing efforts to weaken gun laws and apocalyptic appeals to stoke the far right to both buy guns and mobilize, with arms, for action.[111] A recent book by former gun industry insider Ryan Busse deeply implicates the gun industry in its relentless effort to not only market more exotic and destructive weaponry to fringe groups, but to play to and stoke fear, anger, and resentment among those vulnerable to its messaging as a way to boost sales. Busse's account—that political paranoia and radicalism are good for the gun business—is a stinging indictment of the industry in which he worked for over two decades. Among other things, he noted that "military guns were the symbols of an entire political movement," and the AR-15 in particular, "had become the most important political symbol for President Trump's base."[112] The Trump phenomenon reached its apex in the January 6, 2021 storming of the U.S. Capitol by Trump supporters after an incendiary speech by the outgoing president in front of the White House urging them to do the very thing they did. Strict D.C. gun laws discouraged the vast majority of protestors from carrying guns at the event; still, at least a dozen people were charged with weapons possession crimes, some of those involved in the attack had stashed guns outside of D.C. for possible deployment, and AR weapons imagery was prominently displayed as a rally symbol.[113]

Commenting on the presence of heavily armed protestors at public demonstrations in 2017, a former FBI swat team leader observed that they "appeared to be better equipped than he was as an FBI tactical agent deployed to Afghanistan after the 9/11 attacks." In that year alone, protestors showed up in the hundreds, heavily armed, typically including assault weapons, at demonstrations in Charlottesville, Virginia, Austin, Texas, and Pikeville, Kentucky, among other places. "Why," asked the former FBI official, "would you let someone bring an AR-15 to a hate rally? . . . It's absolute insanity."[114]

The start of the 2020s witnessed the rise of more radical, aggressive, and heavily armed extremist groups for whom assault weapons became a de facto symbol of their armed defiance.[115] The prominent public display of assault weapons was prolific in numerous demonstrations held around the country in 2020 and 2021, organized to protest COVID-19 anti-pandemic measures and as counter-protests to the Black Lives Matter movement (see Chapter 4). Scores of cities witnessed armed protests by various groups and individuals including the Boogaloo Bois, Oath Keepers, and Three Percenters.[116] Data gathered by the Armed Conflict Location and Event Data Project and the Bridging Divides Initiative at Princeton University tabulated at least one hundred incidents of gun carrying in state capitals during a nine-month period from 2020 to 2021.[117] During the two-year period of 2020 to 2021, it tabulated a total of 610 armed demonstrations around the country (including 114 of these on legislative grounds). The rate of such demonstrations actually increased in 2021, compared to 2020.[118]

Assault Weapons' Firing Traits and Injury

Some think that, with respect to the damage done to the human body, a gun is a gun (i.e., that the type of firearm is incidental or relatively unimportant in relation to the damage it can inflict), or that larger caliber rounds necessarily equal more damage. But these assumptions conceal important distinctions.

Semi-automatic rifles are more likely to produce injuries and deaths than other types of firearms. For example, a study of FBI data on 248 active shooter incidents from 2000 to 2017 concluded that "more people were wounded and killed in incidents in which semiautomatic rifles were used compared with incidents involving other firearms."[119] The reasons for this greater lethality are straightforward.

The ammunition fired by assault rifles is smaller caliber and exits the barrel at a very high velocity (often between 3000 to 3500 feet per second)—higher than do rounds fired by typical small-game hunting rifles or handguns.[120] They "deliver a more devastating blow to bones and organs" and are "more likely to break apart as they pass through the body, inflicting more damage." According to one trauma surgeon, such rounds are more likely to produce "severe injury and bleeding and dying than with lower muzzle-velocity munitions."[121] A study by physicians who performed autopsies on soldiers killed by gunfire in Iraq reported that rounds fired at a speed greater than 2500 feet per second resulted in "a shock wave of compression" passing through the victim that caused catastrophic injuries even in locations distant from the direct bullet path.[122] In the case of assault weapons' higher muzzle velocity combined with expanding bullets, the damage to the human body is magnified because once they enter the body, "they fragment and explode, pulverizing bones, tearing blood vessels and liquefying organs."[123]

To cite a different analysis: "Compare the damage an AR-15 and a 9mm handgun can do to the human body: 'One looks like a grenade went off in there,' says Peter Rhee, a trauma surgeon at the University of Arizona. 'The other looks like a bad knife cut.'" Even though an assault rifle round is small, its greater speed increases its kinetic energy, which is "equal to one-half the mass of the bullet times its velocity squared." Even if the bullet does not fragment, its velocity causes "cavitation"—the shock wave previously described— that causes devastating injury away from the bullet's direct path.[124] The ability of assault weapons, especially with high-capacity magazines, to deliver numerous rounds rapidly multiplies the prospect of even greater injury. Trauma surgeons and those who treat battlefield wounds are well aware of the greater destructive features of AR-15-type inflicted wounds.[125] These studies are endorsed by researchers at Brigham and Women's Hospital, who analyzed 248 active shooter incidents from 2000 to 2017. Their study concluded that the use of semi-automatic rifles doubles the chance of injury or death compared to other firearms.[126] The destructive consequences of rounds fired by assault-style rifles can surely also be attributed to some weapons that are not so classified, especially given the thousands of types of firearms available for civilian purchase. Yet the traits described here are characteristic of the assault-style rifle.

Large Capacity Magazines (LCMs)

LCMs are not a gun. They are a gun accessory. To be sure, many firearms can only operate with a magazine inserted into the weapon, but magazines can be easily manufactured or altered to conform to a set capacity, or to permanently attach them to a weapon. As noted earlier, LCMs are defined as those holding more than ten rounds. Magazines holding thirty, fifty, or one hundred rounds are legal in most states. Unsurprisingly, they often appear at mass shootings. Still, critics of restrictions on magazine limits argue that such rules would have no appreciable effect because a shooter can simply interchange smaller-capacity magazines rapidly and easily if larger-capacity magazines are unavailable.

Yet there are three problems with this objection. The first is that, in real shooting instances, shooters have been stopped when they tried to reload. It happened to the Long Island railroad shooter in 1993,[127] the Gabby Giffords shooter in 2011 (the shooter dropped the full magazine he was trying to insert after emptying the initial one, and a woman there picked it up), and the Parkland shooter in 2018 (in his case, his weapon jammed when he was trying to switch out an empty magazine for a full one). These incidents, admittedly, are anecdotal, but they illustrate that in a live fire instance, opportunities for action can be exploited.

Second and more importantly, numerous studies support the efficacy of LCM restrictions in reducing shooting casualties. Some of those studies are discussed next.

Third, an alternative and quite simple strategy can be even more effective in reducing shooting deaths and injuries: either manufacturing or altering weapons so that magazines are permanently fixed in place. In the case of assault rifles, for example, the firearms can be either manufactured or altered so that the magazine is a permanent part of the weapon, such that reloading occurs through a process other than removing and replacing it with a new full magazine.[128] Were fixed magazines of limited capacity the norm for assault weapons, the consequences for mass shootings would be obvious—no more discharging of dozens of rounds without reloading, or rapid substitution of an empty magazine for a full one.

A study of sixty-two mass shootings up until 2012 found that LCMs were used in at least thirty-one of these instances. A later study covering the period from 2009 to 2017 found that fifty-eight percent of mass shootings involved LCMs. The preference for magazines holding more rather than fewer rounds underscores the utility and appeal of less reloading for those seeking to kill multiple people.[129] A study of mass shootings from 2009 to 2018 found that shooting incidents involving high-capacity magazines resulted in twice as many deaths and fourteen times as many injuries, than in those instances where the perpetrators did not use such magazines.[130]

A study conducted in 2017 by CNN covering the period from 2012 to 2016 found that states with LCM bans in place had a sixty-three percent lower rate of mass shootings, controlling for other factors; in fact, "Whether a state has a large capacity ammunition magazine ban is the single best predictor of the mass shooting rate in that state."[131] A 2019 study in the *American Journal of Public Health* examined high-fatality mass shootings from 1990 to 2017, and concluded that attacks with LCMs resulted in a sixty-two percent higher death toll than when LCMs were not used. It also found that states without LCM bans had more than twice as many mass shootings and three times as many gun deaths as states with such bans in place.[132]

A study published in *Criminology & Public Policy* in 2020 punctuated the particularly adverse consequences of LCMs. It concluded: "Restrictions on large-capacity magazines are the most important provisions of assault weapons laws in part because they can produce broader reductions in the overall use of high-capacity semiautomatics that facilitate high-volume gunfire attacks." It further concluded that magazine restrictions could result in a reduction in mass shooting deaths by from eleven to fifteen percent and reduce the overall number of persons shot by one-quarter. The study cautioned, however, that a lag effect would result in these reductions not appearing for several years.[133] A different study concluded that, along with handgun licensing, "laws banning LCMs are the most effective gun policies for reducing fatal mass shootings."[134] Finally, a 2021 study by the Regional Gun Violence Research Consortium of the Rockefeller Institute of Government found that bans on LCMs were associated with a thirty-eight percent reduction in public mass shooting fatalities and a seventy-seven percent reduction in non-fatal injuries.[135]

Some high-profile mass shootings illustrate LCMs' appeal. For example, the 2012 Colorado movie shooter had a one hundred-round drum magazine (he killed twelve and wounded fifty-eight). The 2012 Sandy Hook elementary school shooter used thirty-round magazines (twenty-six killed). The perpetrator of the 2016 Pulse Nightclub shooting in Florida used thirty-round magazines (forty-nine killed). The attacker in a 2019 mass shooting in

Dayton, Ohio also used a one hundred-round magazine (he fired forty-one shots in about thirty seconds, killing nine and injuring twenty-seven). Such LCMs are not new. The notorious Tommy gun of the 1920s could receive one hundred-round magazines (see earlier discussion).[136]

The consequences of LCMs were vividly illustrated by one particular mass shooting. In 2011, then-Arizona Congresswoman Gabrielle Giffords was shot in the head by a deranged man at a public event. Giffords survived the attack. In 2013, Giffords' husband, Mark Kelly (a former Navy captain and astronaut, now a U.S. senator from Arizona, elected in 2020) offered this account of his wife's shooting in congressional testimony, indicating how the shooter's larger capacity magazines resulted in more deaths and injuries:

> The shooter in Tucson showed up with two 33-round magazines, one of which was in his 9 millimeter. He unloaded the contents of that magazine in 15 seconds. Very quickly. It all happened very, very fast. The first bullet went into Gabby's head. Bullet number 13 went into a nine-year old girl named Christina Taylor Green . . . . When he tried to reload one 33-round magazine with another 33-round magazine, he dropped it. And a woman named Patricia Maisch grabbed it, and it gave bystanders a time to tackle him. I contend if that same thing happened when he was trying to reload one 10-round magazine with another 10-round magazine, meaning he did not have access to a high-capacity magazine, and the same thing happened, Christina Taylor Green would be alive today.[137]

As noted earlier, opponents of LCM limits often argue that a minimally skilled person can rapidly interchange an empty magazine for a full one, suggesting the futility of any magazine limits as an impediment to lethal criminality.[138] In a live shooting situation, however, shooters often succumb to the tension and confusion of the moment and take extra time, fumble or drop a magazine (as did the man who shot Giffords), or commit other errors that open the door to intervention. Even if they interchange magazines successfully, the few seconds that elapse do provide a window of opportunity for others to fight or flee. Even some gun enthusiasts draw the line at LCMs. According to one gun rights supporter, otherwise critical of the assault weapons ban: "Can anyone think of a really good reason to have a magazine that holds more than 10 rounds?"[139]

Without seeking to in any way minimize the awful consequences of mass shootings, it is important to remember that they account for about one percent of annual gun homicides.[140] Yet this does not mean that LCMs' deadly consequences occur only in mass shootings—far from it. LCMs account for between twenty-two and thirty-six percent of crime guns.[141] A 2018 study found that over forty percent of guns used in murders of police had LCMs.[142]

Finally, companies producing gun accessories have developed a new generation of magazines that are "compact, lightweight, and strong" and that are increasingly dominating the ammo magazine market. This newer generation of magazines functions more reliably with better antifriction "self-lubricating" technology. They can hold from forty to one hundred rounds. Beyond this, these manufacturers have found that gun accessories are highly profitable, including magazines.[143] The same is true of assault weapons' profitability, compared to other firearms.[144]

Assault Weapons, LCMs, and Self-Defense

In theory, any firearm can be used for self-defense, including assault weapons. As part of the effort to justify their ownership and resist efforts to restrict access to them, arguments have been mounted to extol their use for personal self-defense, such as by former NRA president David Keene.[145]

In a 2021 federal district court case, Judge Roger Benitez issued a ruling, immediately appealed, that struck down California's three-decades-old assault weapons ban. (This is the same judge who struck down the state's restriction on LCMs discussed earlier. Within a month of his ruling, a three-judge panel imposed a stay without time limit on his ruling.) In that decision, *Miller v. Bonta*,[146] Judge Benitez devoted considerable attention to the use of assault weapons for self-defense, arguing that they are uniquely well suited for that purpose. "The evidence shows that one reason for the popularity of the modern rifle is that it makes a good weapon for self-defense at home. The AR-15, in particular, is an easy firearm to shoot accurately and is generally easier to fire accurately than a handgun. The AR-15 rifle is light in weight, and has good ergonomics, and is suitable for people of all statures and varying levels of strength."[147] He even went so far as to claim of assault weapons: "They could just as well be called 'home defense rifles' or 'anti-crime guns.'"[148] These assertions all play fast and loose with the truth. More specifically, his evidence and arguments do not support his conclusion.

For example, he emphasizes the dire threat facing civilians by noting: "The defense of home and family by using a gun is not a hypothetical event. While there are not hard numbers, it surely happens a lot. Approximately 1,000,000 burglaries of a home while occupied take place each year, according to Department of Justice statistics."[149] According to the FBI, there were a total of roughly 1.1 million burglaries in 2019, but most burglaries occur when no one is home, not, as Benitez says, one million "while occupied."[150] During the period from 2003 to 2007, according to the National Crime Victimization Survey, burglaries occurred with someone home about twenty-seven percent of the time.[151] Aside from failing to note that the vast majority of home burglaries occur when no one is home, this information has nothing to do with assault weapons. In fact, guns are often stolen in burglaries where guns are found. Judge Benitez's only actual, direct evidence of assault weapon use for self-defense consists of six news accounts of individuals who apparently used them for that purpose.[152] Yet none of these incidents provides any evidence or reason to believe that a different type of firearm would not have worked at least as well. (In his decision Judge Benitez decides, without explanation, to refer to assault weapons as "modern rifles," as though he is substituting rebranding for legal analysis.)

Despite claims of this sort, even some gun enthusiasts reject the utility of assault weapons for personal defense. A co-founder of *Rambler Magazine* labeled the arguments on behalf of assault weapons for personal defense and hunting as "insufficient" and went on to explain that: "AR-15's are one of the most difficult guns to fire accurately in self-defense scenarios; mobility is extremely difficult and accuracy is successful only when sitting and scoping. Gun sites themselves, report that both pistols and shotguns both act as a better tool in self-defense situations."[153]

Even if all assault weapons disappeared, Americans would still have thousands of models and hundreds of millions of guns to choose from for self-defense purposes. Handguns are, however, the clear choice for those citizens seeking a gun for self-protection, and they were identified specifically by the Supreme Court as the self-defense firearm of choice for use in the home.[154]

For self-defense purposes, an assault weapon has obvious limitations. Its length and weight, compared with a handgun, make it more unwieldy to deploy in the often-tight confines of a home. It requires two hands to handle and operate. The higher velocity of the smaller caliber bullets assault weapons fire means that it is more likely that rounds fired may "overpenetrate," entering nearby buildings, automobiles, and other surroundings, resulting in unintended damage, injury, and even death.[155] And within the confines of a person's home, long guns contribute nothing to accuracy of fire, which is largely determined by the ability of the shooter to deal successfully with the stress and surprise of an actual confrontation with an intruder at close quarters.

Further, actual civilian gun self-defense situations do not involve anything resembling a protracted firefight necessitating the ability to fire many rounds without reloading. A study of self-defense shootings based on data cumulated by the National Rifle Association's Institute for Legislative Action conducted by Lucy P. Allen of National Economic Research Associates (NERA) examined data from the NRA's "armed citizen" stories—accounts compiled in a database of private citizens who self-report instances when they claim using guns for self-defense. These stories are often reprinted in NRA publications. Data compiled from 1997 to 2001, and from 2011 to 2013, found that during the earlier time period defenders fired an average of 2.2 shots, and in twenty-eight percent of these instances, defenders fired no shots (i.e., mere display of a weapon stopped or thwarted the incident). For the later time period, the average number of shots was 2.1, and no shots were fired in sixteen percent of the instances. For this later time period, there were no instances in which the defender fired as many as ten shots or more.[156] Allen later expanded her study to the period of 2011 to 2017, again finding that defenders fired an average of 2.2 shots. Out of a total of 736 incidents of firing, in only two did the defender fire more than ten rounds. Given the NRA's well known positions favoring gun ownership and use for self-defense and the non-random, self-selecting, unverifiable nature of the NRA data, one may assume that it likely represents the most positive face of gun self-defense uses. Allen also conducted an analysis based on news media stories of home defense incidents when firearms were deployed for the same seven-year period and found that the average number of shots fired per incident was 2.34; in no incident were more than ten rounds fired by the defenders.[157]

One notable instance of an effort to defend the use of LCMs for personal self-defense came in the 2019 federal district court case, *Duncan v. Becerra,*[158] discussed earlier. In a challenge to California's ten-round limit on magazines, the same Judge Benitez issued a decision striking down the law (the decision was appealed). Judge Benitez began his decision with the breathless retelling of three cases of self-defense which purport to show that actual instances of self-defense with a gun were or could have been effective only with the defenders' possession of a large capacity magazine. These three stories were the only actual evidence offered to support the self-defense utility of LCMs in his decision.

The first case cited by Judge Benitez involved two armed intruders who entered the home of Susan and Mike Gonzalez of Jacksonville, Florida, in

August 1997. Both were armed; nevertheless, Susan and her husband resisted. Both were shot. Susan called 911, retrieved her husband's handgun and emptied it, shooting one of the intruders, who died after exiting the house. One of the intruders then confronted her and, holding his gun to her, told her to give him her car keys to make his escape, which she did; he then fled. Susan and Mike were each shot twice, but both survived. Susan expressed deep sorrow for killing one of the intruders, believes in gun locks, but also carries a sidearm. She reported that neither she nor her husband were members of the NRA. In March 2000, their house was burgled while they were away. Among the items taken were at least two handguns.[159]

Like every real-life case, this one raises a host of questions: would all have survived unharmed if they had not tried to resist, especially because the one intruder didn't kill her after she emptied her husband's handgun? What of the bad consequences of having their guns stolen? One need not question the right of the couple to defend their home with guns to imagine that their decision to deploy their own guns might have worsened the situation, although there is no way to know. What is certain is that this amounts to a unicorn event: an incident of such rarity that it provides no rational justification for concluding that the civilian possession of LCMs somehow is necessary, desirable, or should come under the umbrella of Second Amendment rights.

The other two cases cited by Judge Benitez simply do not support his argument. One involved a woman who emptied her handgun during a 2013 home intrusion, successfully driving the wounded man away in the process.[160] The other involved a woman whose home was entered by three men in 2016 with whom she exchanged gunfire, driving them away.[161] As one gun safety organization observed about these latter two cases after the *Duncan* case was announced, "high capacity magazines were not an issue."[162] In fact, the one trait all three instances have in common is one that police forces have long known: that in a high stress situation, a shooter is prone to firing all of the rounds in the weapon at hand, regardless of necessity. Police standards are designed to train the police to shoot to stop a person, not to empty the magazine, although police are often accused of firing too many rounds in such situations.[163]

In his 2021 assault weapons ruling, Judge Benitez insisted that LCMs are uniquely valuable to home defenders because "one may need many rounds to overcome the difficulty of aiming in the dark at multiple attackers making furtive movements."[164] His advice: if a person is literally shooting in the dark and cannot see what one is shooting at, the best course of action is to fire lots of rounds. This is advice that no sane gun instructor would ever offer.

The particular fixation on the use of firearms by civilians as a preferrable alternative for personal self-defense too often leaves aside numerous other non-firearm self-defense alternatives for individuals, whether at home or in public. That by itself is a problem. As for guns, however, Judge Benitez declared in his 2019 ruling that "[t]he size limit [of LCMs] directly impairs one's ability to defend one's self."[165] Yet his own best evidence fails to support that conclusion. As a matter of public safety and personal protection, it is difficult to muster a coherent argument on behalf of civilian LCM acquisition for self-defense.

Finally, one might well be tempted, and with ample justification, to decry the "judicial activism" of a judge who seems to simply disregard evidence that is both readily available and that so thoroughly contradicts the judge's conclusion. I leave that line of argument, however, to others.

Conclusion: Regulatory Regimes Followed Gun Proliferation

The lesson of our gun history is clear: when firearms became a threat to the public, regulations followed. Laws against the concealed carrying of dangerous weapons, including multi-shot handguns, proliferated as interpersonal violence rose, most notably in the nineteenth century. By the end of the 1800s, virtually every state in the country had laws restricting or barring concealed gun carrying. As historian Saul Cornell noted: "By the era of Reconstruction, gun violence had emerged as a serious problem in American life and legislators responded to this development by enacting scores of new laws."[166] When a new generation of weapons found favor with criminals in the 1920s, the states acted to impose restrictions. That included restrictions on fully automatic firearms, semi-automatic firearms, and ammunition feeding devices in many states. History repeated itself in the 1990s when some states and, for a time the federal government, restricted assault weapons.

The new gun era in which we find ourselves raises the specter of jurists and legislators who, despite claiming fealty to history, either do not know or do not appreciate the lessons of that history. Our forebears demonstrated more wisdom when it came to gun laws. As discussed in this chapter, the best arguments offered to justify rolling back or blocking contemporary gun measures are based on what could charitably be called flimsy evidence. The continuing debate over the regulation of assault weapons is at least a debate. The debate over the regulation of LCMs is hardly even that. An examination of the extant arguments yields no coherent public policy case against their regulation. LCMs are not "a gun"; they are a gun accessory, and a frivolous one at that. Their use in crime without question rachets up the scale of mayhem and destruction no less today than was true in the 1920s.

We turn in the next chapter to a very similar debate over what is also a gun accessory: gun silencers.

3

The Sound of Silencers

ON A HUMID, overcast morning in June 2021, I took the opportunity to fire, and witness the firing of an AR-15 with attached silencer[1] at a local gun range. The weapon was the property of the SUNY Cortland University Police Department, so it had three features available to the police but not available to New York civilians: an adjustable stock, a thirty-round magazine, and the silencer. Contrary to some writing about silencers discussed in this chapter, my personal (and purely anecdotal) experience contradicted standard claims about silencers in certain respects. First, the silencer weighed in at a little over one pound, so it added a fair amount of weight to the barrel end of the weapon, thus adding to the semi-automatic's cumbersomeness. Second, the silencer didn't seem to have any appreciable dampening effect on barrel rise when fired. (When I asked the four gun experts present at the range about whether silencers reduced rise, they all said that it did not in their experience. Silencer advocates claim that it reduces barrel rise.) Third, my hearing protection equipment consisted of the inexpensive ear muffs I use when I mow the lawn, but they were effective in dampening the firing noise of both the AR and of nearby handgun firing where silencers were not being used at the range. Fourth, after firing fewer than ten rounds, the silencer heated up considerably, making it initially too hot to touch. Fifth, the silencer tended to send discharging gases back toward to operator instead of forward, as would otherwise occur. Shooters then tend to get black dust on their face if firing multiple rounds. Sixth, like a James Bond movie, the discharge noise made an unobtrusive "poof" sound, although louder than that replicated in the movies.

In recent years gun advocates have argued that gunfire noise poses a distinct hazard: namely, the loss of hearing by gun owners. In 2017,[2] a bill was introduced in Congress as part of a larger piece of legislation called the

Sportsmen's Heritage and Recreational Enhancement Act or SHARE Act. A subset of that bill, called the Hearing Protection Act, aimed to deregulate the process for obtaining a gun silencer (also referred to as "suppressors"[3]). Under the terms of the National Firearms Act (NFA) of 1934,[4] the process for obtaining a gun silencer was (and is to date) the same as for acquiring an automatic weapon: the applicant needs to pay a $200 fee, submit fingerprints and a photograph, and undergo a detailed background check by the FBI in a process that normally takes at least several months. As with the firearms regulated under the NFA, the government also keeps track of silencer ownership.

The 2017 bill would have eliminated these regulations, making silencer purchase legal as long at the prospective purchaser passed an instant background check—the same check applied to gun purchasers. Hearings on the bill were scheduled for 2017 but were postponed, as was a subsequent floor vote, in the face of public dismay over contemporaneous mass shootings. Thus, the bill died at the end of 2018. A similar bill was introduced in the U.S. Senate at the start of the new Congress in 2019. That bill, according to its sponsors, would not have affected nine state laws that bar silencer purchase (California, Delaware, Hawaii, Illinois, Massachusetts, New Jersey, New York, Rhode Island, and the District of Columbia).[5] In 2021, a new silencers bill was introduced in the Senate and House, called the Silencers Helping Us Save Hearing or SHUSH Act by its primary Senate sponsor, Mike Lee (R-UT). This bill would eliminate any background check for the acquisition of silencers and was touted as one that would work in tandem with the reintroduced Hearing Protection Act,[6] designed to "remove silencers from the federal definition of 'firearm,' allowing for interstate transfers and sales, and the purge of the existing registry."[7]

The effort to reduce or eliminate barriers for citizens to obtain silencers also proceeded on a Second Amendment-based track. In 2014, two Kansas men were charged with violating federal law when one of the two sold the other several weapons without following federal sales and registration requirements. Included among the items was a silencer. The men argued in part that they were exempted from the terms of the NFA of 1934 because Kansas had enacted a state law, the Second Amendment Protection Act, which stated that any firearms and firearms accessories manufactured in the state and remaining in the state were not covered by the federal law. (The idea that purely intrastate commerce is exempted from the federal government's power to regulate interstate commerce has been rejected for decades.) A federal district court rejected the motion of the two men to dismiss the indictment against them in 2016.[8] The following year, the district court specifically rejected the claim that silencers were protected under the Second Amendment.[9] In 2018, the U.S. Court of Appeals for the Tenth Circuit upheld the lower courts' rulings in *U.S. v. Cox*, rejecting the argument that there was a right to own silencers under the Second Amendment.[10] In 2019, the Supreme Court turned aside without comment a request from Cox to consider whether firearms accessories including silencers are protected by the Second Amendment as part of a challenge, also refused, to federal firearms registration.[11]

The unsuccessful effort in this case was no anomaly. Groups like Gun Owners of America argue that the right to own "bearable arms" under the Second Amendment includes the right to own gun accessories like silencers.[12] Eight state attorneys general from conservative states agreed and argued as much in a 2019 brief before the Supreme Court appealing the Tenth Circuit ruling.[13]

This little-noticed effort to peel back regulations pertaining to silencers is another instance of a firearm accessory, like ammunition magazines discussed in the previous chapter, that has become part of the new campaign to expand gun rights chronicled in this text. It also poses another instance where gun law history casts a useful and important light on contemporary regulatory concerns. This chapter will begin by examining that history—seemingly lost, forgotten, ignored, or perhaps unknown—and then turn to the contemporary debate.

Silencer Definition

Most Americans' impressions of gun silencers probably begin and end with popular culture imagery, connected especially to crime and spy movies where villains, and sometimes heroes, screw onto the barrel end of a gun a threaded cylindrical-shaped attachment designed to deaden the sound of a gun discharge. While James Bond's silencer all but eliminated gunfire noise, yielding nothing more than a quiet pop, in real life silencers are not quite so effective in reducing noise. Silencers have indeed been tied to criminality since their invention. But there is also an argument for legitimate silencer use by law-abiding gun owners. But more about that later.

According to the Bureau of Alcohol, Tobacco, Firearms, and Explosives (ATF):

The term "Firearm Silencer" or "Firearm Muffler" means any device for silencing, muffling, or diminishing the report of a portable firearm, including any combination of parts, designed or redesigned, and intended for the use in assembling or fabricating a firearm silencer or firearm muffler, any part intended only for use in such assembly or fabrication.[14]

An estimate from the mid-1990s said that Americans owned over sixty thousand silencers.[15] By 2010, Americans owned 285,000 silencers.[16] By 2016, the number was reportedly about 900,000.[17] As of early 2021, the ATF reported civilian ownership of over 2.6 million silencers registered with the agency, a clear indication of escalating civilian interest.[18]

This returns us to a central question: why the recent effort to roll back a federal regulation that has been in effect for over eighty years, and that has, with the rarest exceptions, successfully kept silencers out of the hands of criminals while still making them available to civilians who go through the background check process? Before addressing this contemporary question, we first turn to the methodology that organizes this text: the gun law history of silencers and early efforts at regulation.

Silencer History

The gun silencer, also referred to as a muffler, was invented by engineer Hiram Maxim in the early 1900s and patented by him in 1908.[19] Maxim sought immediately to sell his invention to the American military, as well as to those of European nations.[20] According to Maxim's biographer, "The primary purpose of the gun silencer was its use by the United States Army."[21] Extensive news coverage hailed the new invention, but objections to civilian use of silencers appeared almost immediately. The prestigious publication *Scientific American* reported in 1909 on a direct demonstration of the device, discussing in detail its technological traits and value for military use: "If it were possible to confine the possession of the new weapon [i.e. silencers] to the military, for whose use, and for whose use alone, it was designed, we would have nothing to say against the device." But, the article continued, it warned of "the menace" of silencers that "greatly enlarged the opportunities for the commission of undetected crime .... It is well understood," the editorial continued, "that fear of detection is one of the most powerful deterrents to the commission of crime." Therefore, it concluded, silencers "should be made the subject of immediate and very stringent legislation."[22] A 1909 newspaper article asked: "Who shall be authorized to carry and use firearms" equipped with silencers? "No private person, surely. A true sportsman," opined the author, "would not use it .... The burglar, the highway robber, and the Black Hand assassin are the only other persons to whom it could be of advantage."[23]

The first state law outlawing silencers' sale or possession came within a year of its patent, when Maine enacted a ban in 1909.[24] Pittsburgh moved against silencers that same year. As the city's superintendent of police warned, "the use of the 'silencer' will prove disastrous to the peace of every city where precautions against its use are not taken . . . . The risk of shooting is too great; the discharge of the weapon makes too much noise and attracts too many people. But with a silencer in use this would be different."[25] Two years later, New Jersey outlawed the use of "any silencer, when hunting for game or fowl, on any gun, rifle or firearm."[26]

These early restrictions underscored the two primary concerns about un-regulated possession of silencers: that they would be used by criminals seeking to avoid detection, and that they would be used by hunters with a similar moti-vation. As a news article from 1916 noted regarding both criminal and hunting concerns, that "[t]he Silencer is an incentive to crime" and "in the shooting of game it is forbidden in some states . . . because it is believed that it gives too great an advantage to poachers and to those who are shooting out of season."[27] In 1913, the director of the New York Zoological Park, William T. Hornaday, published a book decrying the imminent extinction of many animal species throughout the country. One of the chief causes, he argued, was the enhanced firepower of ever-more people engaged in indiscriminate hunting. Included in his list of weaponry technology that allowed for mass slaughter of animals was "silencers," which he dubbed "grossly unfair," arguing that they "should immediately be prohibited."[28] The fear of the spread of silencers was not merely hypothetical. A 1916 news article reported that, in New York City, "silencers for .22 calibre rifles were sold in considerable quantities."[29] Chicago police discovered as early as 1922 that "the city's lawbreakers were ordering sales catalogs from the Maxim Silencer Company," and New York authorities reported similar criminal interest in silencers around the same time.[30]

From 1909 to 1936, as listed in Table 3.1, at least fifteen states enacted silencer restrictions,[31] with seven of them specifically barring their use in hunting.[32] Unlike other categories of early gun laws, the statutory wording pertaining to silencer restrictions varied from state to state, but the purpose and goal of these laws is perfectly clear. Notably, these enactments did not cluster around a particular date (as was true, for example, for many states enacting anti-machine gun laws starting in 1927; see Chapter 2) but began only a year after silencer patenting and continued progressively across the suc-ceeding three decades.

Table 3.1 Laws Restricting Silencers in Fifteen States, 1909–1936*

STATE	YEAR	PROVISIONS
Maine	1909	"It shall be unlawful . . . to sell, offer for sale, use or have in his possession any . . . firearm, fitted with any device for deadening the sound of explosion."
New Jersey	1911, 1920 (hunting)	"It shall be unlawful to use any silencer, when hunting for game or fowl, on any gun, rifle or firearm."
Vermont	1912	"A person who manufactures, sells, or uses, or possesses with intent to sell or use, an appliance known as or used for a gun silencer shall be fined."
Michigan	1913, 1927, 1929	"Every person, firm or corporation . . . in the business of selling . . . silencers for fire-arms shall keep a register . . . of each and every purchaser" (1913); "It shall be unlawful . . . to manufacture, sell, offer for sale, or possess any . . . muffler, silencer or device for deadening or muffling the sound of a discharging firearm" (1927).
Minnesota	1913	"Use of silencers prohibited. No person shall . . . sell or offer or expose for sale . . . any silencer."
New York	1916	"A person who sells or keeps for sale, or offers, or gives or disposes of, or who shall have or carry . . . any gun . . . to be silent or intended to lessen or muffle the noise of the firing of any gun . . . shall be guilty of a felony."
Louisiana	1918 (hunting)	"It shall be unlawful for any person to hunt, or kill wild deer with any gun . . . with any device for deadening the sound of the explosion attached or fitted thereto . . . called a silencer."
Wyoming	1921 (hunting)	"It shall be unlawful . . . to take into . . . or have in possession while in the game fields or forests . . . for the purpose of hunting the game animals or game birds of this State any device or mechanism designed to silence or muffle or minimize the report of any firearm, whether such device or mechanism be separated or attached to any firearm or not."

(continued)

Table 3.1   (Continued)

STATE	YEAR	PROVISIONS
Pennsylvania	1923 (hunting)	"It is unlawful to hunt for, or catch or take or kill or wound, or attempt to catch or take or kill or wound, game of any kind, excepting raccoons, through the use of . . . an automatic gun or an automatic firearm of any kind . . . or the apparatus known as a silencer, or from an automobile or vehicle or boat or craft of any kind propelled by any mechanical power."
North Carolina	1925 (hunting and general)	"It shall be unlawful . . . to use while hunting any gun having a 'Maxim silencer' or any other device thereon that will muffle the report of such gun, nor shall any gun be used that does not produce when discharged the usual and ordinary report."
Massachusetts	1926	"Whoever sells or keeps for sale, or offers, or gives or disposes of, or uses, any instrument, attachment, weapon or appliance for causing the firing of any gun . . . to be silent or intended to lessen or muffle the noise or the firing of any gun . . . shall be punished by imprisonment."
Delaware	1927 (hunting)	"It shall be unlawful to use any silencer or noise-reducing contrivance on any gun, rifle or firearm when hunting."
Rhode Island	1927	"It shall be unlawful within this state to manufacture, sell, purchase or possess . . . any muffler, silencer or device for deadening or muffling the sound of a firearm when discharged."
Hawaii	1933	"The manufacture, possession, sale, barter, trade, gift, transfer, or acquisition of any . . . silencers or devices for deadening or muffling the sound of discharged firearms . . . is prohibited."
Arizona	1936 (hunting)	"It shall be unlawful for any person to take into the field or forest, or to have in his possession, while hunting wild animals or birds, any device designed to silence, muffle or minimize the report of any firearm, whether separated from or attached to such firearm."

Source: Duke Center for Firearms Law, https://firearmslaw.duke.edu/repository/search-the-repository/. Note that this dataset ends in 1936, so other states may have adopted similar laws after that date.

No statistics are available on early silencer ownership and use, but an examination of newspaper archives during this period, including the *New York Times*, revealed a prodigious number of news stories where silencers were used in gun crimes. The nation's largest city, New York, is an unfortunate exemplar. One early case in 1915 involved a triple murder and suicide in New York City. Herman Auerbach, who had recently purchased a Winchester repeating rifle equipped with a silencer, killed his wife and two daughters before turning the gun on himself. (Auerbach was reportedly despondent over financial troubles.) The family lived in several adjacent rooms in a nine-story apartment building bordering Central Park. The dead family members were discovered the morning after the shootings by the family's fourteen-year-old son, who found the bodies when he went to check on his family members. The boy slept through the shootings, according to the account, because "the Maxim silencer had prevented even the boy from hearing the shots that killed his sisters in the next room."[33] Within days of this killing, members of the State Legislature introduced a bill, enacted the following year, to bar the manufacture or sale of silencers in the state.[34]

Among other reports of New York-area silencer crimes were that of the suicide of a New Jersey man in 1917,[35] the murder-robbery of a city jewelry store in 1920,[36] a drive-by shooter who fired shots randomly as he sped up Broadway in 1920,[37] a 1921 city jewelry store robbery, a bootlegger murder in a tenement house in 1921, and a gangster murder in 1930 in Hoboken, New Jersey where the victim, known to carry a gun with a silencer, was killed with his own weapon.[38] The *Times* also reported the 1926 arrest of a man in Omaha charged with committing random killings in a dozen cities in the Midwest who also used a silencer.[39]

A similar examination of newspapers nationwide[40] revealed prolific accounts of guns equipped with silencers being used in crimes. (What follows is the proverbial tip of the iceberg of silencer accounts and reporting. I have deliberately included a wide range of cases, from the seemingly innocuous to the most lethal, to provide a flavor of what Americans were reading during this period.) These accounts began to appear shortly after silencers became available. For example, a protracted taxi drivers' strike in 1911 in St. Louis was marred by repeated silencer gunfire over the space of several weeks. News accounts referred to "silent-gun men" who fired on strike-breakers and others. During this crisis, Hiram Maxim authored a front page article for the city's most prominent newspaper defending his invention.[41] A plot to kill the mayor of San Diego and other top city officials in 1912 noted that the alleged perpetrator was armed with a rifle fitted with a silencer.[42] Also in 1912, members of the Texas militia were fired on in El Paso by multiple individuals reportedly using guns with silencers.[43] A sailor walking through a dock yard in San Diego in 1921 was shot and killed by a silencer-equipped gun.[44]

As soon as the devices began to appear, calls for their restriction or banishment also appeared. For example, the *Brooklyn (N.Y.) Times* editorialized in 1912 that the silencer was a "useless and dangerous invention." It argued that the federal government "can forbid its transportation in inter-State commerce, and the various States can forbid its manufacture and sale.... Do away with this instrument," it concluded.[45] In 1921 the *Yonkers (N.Y.) Statesman* opined that "bandits have adopted the Maxim silencer for their revolvers as another strictly up-to-date device."[46]

Returning to other contemporaneous stories, two boys were shot and killed by a "crank" with a silencer-attached gun in the Detroit area in 1921.[47] The *Daily Telegram* of Long Beach, California reported on an apologetic armed robber who held up a man under a street light using a gun with silencer in 1921.[48] An arsonist in Lagrange, Maine, identified as "an ill-tempered giant" who had terrorized the local community for months, was arrested in 1921 for possession of a silencer along with a cache of weapons.[49]

A crime more typically identified with silencers during the Roaring Twenties was that of three Brownsville gangsters who entered a stag party at a local New York City social club and murdered, execution-style, "Doggy" Henry Ginsberg plus another man who were waiting for the festivities to begin. The shooter used a gun with a silencer.[50] An account of a police raid in Cicero (a Chicago suburb dominated by gangsters in the 1920s) in 1926, spurred by the machine gunning of a prosecuting attorney driving through the town, discovered a vast cache of sawed-off shotguns, machine guns, bombs, pistols, and rifles fitted with silencers.[51]

In 1928, a St. Louis man returning home with his family saw a light on in his house. Suspecting trouble, he entered from the back to retrieve his pistol to confront what turned out to be two burglars. The burglars had found his pistol with attached silencer, however, and shot him several times with it.[52] A Camden, New Jersey "phantom sniper" using a silencer was responsible for at least twenty random shootings in the city in 1928.[53] That same year, two young men in Dover, Ohio were shooting sparrows with a rifle with silencer, when one of their shots ricocheted, went through the window of a nearby home and narrowly missed a child inside. They were fined.[54] Also the same year, an unfortunate man in Paterson, New Jersey was held up twice by two different highwaymen armed with silencer-fitted revolvers.[55]

Al Capone was both the most notorious gangster of the 1920s, and also the regular target of opposing gangs. In 1929, however, the targeting of Capone reached the boiling point in the aftermath of the St. Valentine's Day massacre, when some of "Scarface" Al's men, dressed as Chicago police officers, gunned down seven members of George Clarence "Bugs" Moran's gang in their garage headquarters. Friends of the deceased sought revenge. Tracking Capone relentlessly, they followed him around the country. Sensing that danger was closing in, Capone and his bodyguard decided to turn themselves in to local authorities in Philadelphia on the prearranged charge of carrying concealed deadly weapons. The trio of assassins, all carrying guns with silencers, narrowly missed their target.[56] Capone served nine months of a one-year sentence. The year after his release, he was convicted of income tax evasion.

Stories like these lace newspapers during this nearly three-decade period. Several conclusions arise from this brief newspaper archive excursion. First, from the beginning, these local stories often became national news, as indicated by the fact that accounts of a shooting in one city would subsequently and typically appear in many dozens of local newspapers around the country. Second, incidents of criminal silencer use occurred in cities big and small, and from one end of the country to the other. And the incidents themselves run the gamut from the minor to the catastrophic. Third, judging by the reports of these events, the silencers did their job—that is, victims, witnesses, and bystanders reported consistently that they heard no gunshot sounds when shots were fired from guns with silencers. Fourth, silencers had their defenders as reflected in articles, interviews, and advertisements. And they were often advertised for sale in newspapers or otherwise extolled. These ads and articles emphasized their value for hunting or shooting in places where the noise of gunfire might be particularly troublesome.

Fifth, references to Maxim silencers rapidly entered and thoroughly suffused the popular culture, as seen in prolific and often comical newspaper references where "Maxim silencer" became a term or euphemism to identify a silencer-type device that could or should be fitted to anyone or anything needing quieting, from crying babies to over-zealous sports fans, from soup slurpers to any kind of loud machinery or activity, and to loud-mouthed politicians. For example, this sarcastic jibe appeared in dozens of newspapers around the country in 1911, in the midst of the campaign to win the right to vote for women: " 'What shall we wear?' the suffragists are asking, and a wag suggests a Maxim silencer, a muzzle, or a gag."[57]

Political applications of the term proliferated, especially in election years, as during the 1912 presidential election. For example, this jibe appeared in many newspapers: "Champ Clark continues to rant about the United States annexing Canada. He needs a Maxim silencer for his tongue."[58] Clark was a Democratic member of the U.S. House of Representatives from Missouri who was speaker of the House at the time. That same year, former president Theodore Roosevelt's unsuccessful campaign to recapture the White House prompted this oft-reprinted quip: "Nobody has been able to slip a Maxim silencer over Roosevelt's head."[59]

It is impossible to gauge how often silencers were used in crimes in the 1910s, 1920s, and early 1930s, or what percentage of gun crimes included silencers. But it is equally clear that they appeared frequently enough to be considered a nationwide menace that was both well-known and well understood by civic and political leaders, and the public.

Maxim repeatedly defended his invention throughout this time in articles, lectures, and advertising. But in 1930, he "discontinued manufacturing silencers because of the popular impression that this invention was an aid to crime" and turned his attention to the development of automobile mufflers and other sound-deadening technologies.[60]

Given the close association between the use of silencers and criminal acts, Congress moved to subject their purchase to the same requirements attached to citizens who sought to own the weapons targeted to be regulated under new law, like submachine guns and other fully automatic firearms: a substantial fee, an extensive background check, and registration. Congress did so when it enacted the National Firearms Act of 1934. In the bill's 166 pages of committee hearings and testimony in the House of Representatives, silencers received very little mention. But this was clearly not an oversight or mistake.

In an exchange during the hearings between Rep. Claude Fuller (D-AR) and Milton Reckord, Adjutant General of the State of Maryland and NRA chief executive, Rep. Fuller said to Reckord: "If a man is carrying that type of weapon . . . he ought to be taken into custody . . . because we know that he is carrying it for an unlawful purpose; I am referring to such a weapon as a sawed-off shotgun or machine gun, or a silencer." Record replied: "We agree with that."[61]

Gun rights lawyer Stephen Halbrook has argued on behalf of repealing NFA silencer regulations by noting of the 1934 congressional hearings on the bill this: "Astonishingly, no facts or data were ever set forth in the legislative record suggesting that suppressors were a crime problem."[62] Like Halbrook, gun specialist Adam Paulson also seemed puzzled by the 1934 regulation of silencers, speculating that it might have been because of game poaching during the Depression.[63] That explanation was repeated without comment or evidence by lawyer Paul Clark.[64] David Kopel of the libertarian Independence Institute opined: "We simply have no idea what (if anything) Congress thought it was doing about them [silencers]."[65] A 2012 article otherwise critical of the effort to deregulate silencers noted that a "quarter-century" after the 1908 patenting of the devices, "silencers still hadn't acquired the bad rep they have today."[66]

Most astonishing in these observations is not only their inaccuracy but their degree of historical amnesia. The full account of numerous old silencer laws discussed in this chapter is new information, but the use of silencers by criminals early in the last century certainly is not. The foregoing account demonstrates that the absence of any more detailed discussion of silencers at the 1934 hearings was not "astonishing" at all. Debate is rarely necessary in the presence of ample supporting evidence, history, and political consensus. By the early 1930s, the nation well understood that (a) silencers had been and continued to be prominently used in crimes for over two decades, (b) silencers therefore warranted the strict regulatory standards applied to the other weapons named in the 1934 law, and (c) possible legitimate uses of silencers, also prolifically repeated in the public press by Hiram Maxim and others (including the National Rifle Association), posed no basis for rejecting federal regulation (remembering that the federal law did not bar silencers, but rather provided for regulated access to them). Members of Congress promoting this silencer provision knew exactly what they were doing. President Franklin D. Roosevelt's first Attorney General, Homer S. Cummings, reported that in the first three years of the law's enactment, it had resulted in the registration of 9316 submachine guns, 11,520 machine guns and machine rifles, 16,456 miscellaneous weapons, and 769 silencers.[67]

The Contemporary Debate: Hearing Protection

The debate over the then-new silencer gun technology that played out across the first few decades of the last century came to a clear conclusion: meaningful silencer regulation was amply justified. That debate has now been restarted within the last few years—as though the earlier debate never happened or occurred in an information vacuum. Contemporary silencer regulatory questions are mostly framed around an issue that received relatively little attention a century ago: hearing protection.

Modern advocates of silencer use cite several benefits, including reducing muzzle flash, gun recoil, and improved firearm stability when firing. Silencers trap the explosive gas that exits the barrel after the bullet, reducing recoil.[68]

With less recoil, the shooter experiences less "muzzle rise"[69] and therefore more control (contrary to my anecdotal experience cited at the beginning of this chapter). The National Shooting Sports Foundation also argued that silencers "help make shooting ranges more neighborly."[70]

The political push has been promoted in part by a little-known organization, the American Suppressor Association (ASA). The organization was founded in 2011 by an employee of a firearms and firearm accessory company, Knox Williams. Williams left his job to form a non-profit trade association that received initial start-up funding from gun and silencer manufacturers. From then until 2017, it claimed credit for getting three states to legalize silencer ownership and eighteen to allow their use in hunting, leaving only nine states (including the District of Columbia) that bar silencers.[71]

As noted earlier, those who seek to repeal the 1934 standards for silencer purchase have hung their hats primarily on the health benefits associated with the suppression of the noise that accompanies gunfire—ergo, the name of legislation advanced in Congress in recent years, the Hearing Protection Act. Clearly, the sound generated when a weapon like an assault-style AR-15 is fired generates enough noise to harm hearing, especially when that firing is repetitive, as at a firing range. As has been frequently reported, many guns produce noise levels of between 140–160 decibels (including the AR-15), at which level hearing can be permanently impaired.[72] A study of the National Institute for Occupational Safety and Health (NIOSH) studied firearms instructors' exposure to firearms noise and found that they were subject to noise levels exceeding 150 decibels, whereas the NIOSH recommends exposure to no more than 140 decibels.[73] These and similar reports typically focus on the noise of a small number of weapons, especially assault weapons.[74] Yet it is important to remember that firearms come in thousands of models, sizes, and styles, from derringers to elephant guns, which in turn generate a wider range of noise than that in the 140–160 decibel range. Thus, many firearms do not pose the degree of threat to hearing that others do. For example, among long guns, an AR-15 was tested as producing 167 decibels of noise, whereas a Ruger 10/22 .22 LR Rifle produced 140 decibels of noise.[75]

In this connection, as silencer advocates point out, silencers do not eliminate all or even most of the noise caused by gun firing, but do reduce the noise of louder firearms by about twenty to thirty decibels, to roughly 135 decibels, below the 140 decibel threshold.[76] According to a noise-reduction rating (NRR) scale developed by the Environmental Protection Agency, both silencers and ear-protective equipment (depending on the particular product) can each reduce noise by around thirty decibels.[77] As hearing experts and many gun enthusiasts advise, even in the case of less noisy weapons, and those with attached silencers, they still generate enough noise that shooters should wear proper hearing protection—even when firing a weapon with an attached silencer. The chief reason, according to the National Hearing Conservation Association (NHCA), is that "[s]uppressors cannot reduce the noise caused by the supersonic flight of the projectile breaking the sound barrier once it leaves the barrel of the firearm." Operators can use subsonic ammunition (which travels below the speed of sound to avoid the sharp "crack" noise) to address this problem produced by a supersonic bullet. Subsonic ammunition is becoming increasingly available, and marketed to gun enthusiasts by companies such as Hornady.[78] In the words of one silencer maker, even with that, the NHCA recommends that shooters "wear hearing protection whenever shooting firearms, including when employing a noise suppressor device."[79] The American Speech-Language-Hearing Association (ASHA) also recommends that gun users "[a]lways use some type of hearing protection any time you fire a gun."[80]

Both the NHCA and the ASHA note that, for hunters or others disturbed by the prospect of wearing ear plugs or earmuffs while in the field, some hearing protection devices are available that allow for the audibility of soft sounds while still blocking out the loud, sharp crack of firearm discharge. Such hearing protection devices are inexpensive, effective, and readily available.[81] Some hunters avoid hearing protection, saying that they could prevent the hunter from "hearing their prey," a claim that one expert in silencers calls "laughably ridiculous." "The animals you are hunting have better hearing than you do . . . . They'll hear you before you hear them."[82] The combination of hearing protection plus a gun silencer would of course reduce the noise even further, and that option is readily available for those willing to go through the paperwork to make a silencer purchase according to current federal law. On the other hand, hearing protective technologies continue to improve, some better-quality devices obviously reduce harmful noise more than others, and they may well provide the best long-term remedy to hearing damage caused by firearm discharge.

Under virtually all actual firing circumstances, those firing guns have no time problem in taking the few seconds needed to put hearing protection into place. The only instance where time constraints would not allow a gun user to employ hearing protection is in an emergency firing situation, such as a home intrusion, when an individual would not only deploy but actually wind up discharging a weapon in defense of person or property. Yet such events are extremely rare, and involve few shots fired. One study based on data from the FBI and the National Crime Victimization Survey (NCVS) noted that from 2008 to 2012, there were a total of 1018 justifiable homicides by civilians (about 204 per year). According to NCVS data, from 2007 to 2011, there were a total of 235,700 self-protection actions involving firearms. This number (yielding a yearly average of 47,140) does not distinguish the type of firearm involved and does not indicate whether it was actually fired or not.[83] It is clear that the number of self-defense firing events is tiny relative to the gun-owning population, that the number of rounds fired is few, and that such events rarely if ever repeat themselves among those who do fire in self-defense. Even among police officers, most never fire their service weapons in the line of duty. According to a nationwide survey of nearly eight thousand police officers, for example, only about twenty-seven percent reported having ever fired their service firearm while on the job, and multiple firing instances among officers are extremely rare.[84]

In short, hearing experts always recommend the use of properly fitted ear protection devices, whether the shooter is using a silencer or not. What, then, would be the consequence of silencer use for those around a shooter? Might it not be beneficial if bystanders were exposed to less noise?

The Safety Value of Noise

Former President George W. Bush press secretary Ari Fleischer chanced to be passing through the Ft. Lauderdale airport on January 6, 2017, when he heard what he described as "multiple gunshots ringing out" coming from just below where he and others were standing. "We all realized it was gunfire and it was coming from the level below us at the escalator." Those shots resulted in five deaths and six injuries. By Fleischer's own account, that sound may have saved his life, and those of others, who otherwise might have walked straight into the line of fire.[85]

The sound of gunfire—loud, sharp, rude, abrupt—is one of a firearm's most important de facto safety features (this of course does not mean that noise is somehow engineered into firearms; noise is simply a byproduct of firing small projectiles at a high speed). From potential mass shooting victims who seek to escape a deadly encounter to someone walking in the woods suddenly alerted to a hunter firing a projectile that travels hundreds of yards in the blink of an eye, the sound warns bystanders of potentially lethal danger.

Proponents of silencers argue that because silencers do not eliminate noise but merely reduce it, the residual noise can provide any warning to others that might be required. But this downplays the importance of gunshot noise as a critical safety component. In fact, the noise caused by gunfire is a key, even vital, de facto safety feature of firearms—not for the operator, but for those nearby.[86] The Ari Fleischer story illustrates the important and underappreciated yet obvious value of firearm noise (again, this is not to suggest that noise is somehow manufactured into firearms). Anything that reduces the alert value of gunfire sound is an impediment to bystanders taking effective defensive action. Almost without exception, bystanders who find themselves near a shooting—whether a mass shooting, a robbery, a gang shootout, a disgruntled neighbor, or any other instance of pernicious gunfire—know instinctively that people's best warning of danger is the sound of shots being fired.

Such critical noise warning is not limited to the commission of a gun crime. The same applies in a lawful (and certainly unlawful) hunting situation, especially when it occurs in places where line of sight is limited. Other hunters, sportspeople, recreationists, and residents are best warned of gunfire when it is loud. Given that rounds travel hundreds of yards in the blink of an eye, anything that inhibits gunshot sound decreases awareness and therefore increases the danger to bystanders. This by itself is a powerful argument on behalf of the protective value of gunshot noise.

The idea of sound as a protective warning is not limited to firearms. For example, in 2016, the federal government issued a new rule requiring hybrid and electric cars to "make noise when traveling at low speeds" of up to 18.6 mph so that pedestrians or those with poor eyesight can hear them coming. The rule was put into place in 2021.[87]

Silencers and Crime

Advocates have pointed out that silencers are rarely used in crimes in the contemporary era, and thus suggest or imply that criminals are little interested in using silencers, whether easy to obtain or not. A 2017 internal draft report by the ATF that was leaked to the public noted that "expanding demand and acceptance of silencers" by the public might warrant elimination of the current background check process for silencer applicants as an increase in applications has produced a backlog, even though the ATF and the Department of Justice have historically opposed altering federal requirements. The report also noted the relative rarity of silencer crime, saying that, in recent years, the ATF has averaged only about forty-four prosecutions per year for silencer violations.[88] In 2015, the ATF traced 125 registered silencers connected with crimes.[89] In 2017, it traced 1004 silencers, indicating a possible upswing in criminal

silencer use.[90] A 2007 study produced an estimate of about thirty annual federal prosecutions for illegal silencer ownership or use, with a combined total
of perhaps 200 federal and state prosecutions yearly.[91] It is highly likely that
the number of silencer crimes exceeds the number of prosecutions.

But there are several problems with the ATF's argument (which it never
formally adopted, and which may not represent ATF thinking since the end
of the Trump presidency). The first is that the ATF backlog problem is a thin
reed upon which to base changing silencer law. The devotion of more staff to
background investigations would resolve that problem.

Second and more importantly, the history of silencers, as recounted in
this chapter, tells us that they were used by criminals almost from the very
time that they were available, dating to the start of the second decade of the
twentieth century. As noted earlier, the inclusion of silencers in the National
Firearms Act of 1934, along with other gangster weapons, demonstrated the
consensus that criminal silencer use was a significant and remediable threat.
Given that criminals do pretty much the same things in the modern era as
they did a century ago, why should there be less criminal interest now if they
became more easily available? As if to punctuate that point, the man who
shot up a Virginia Beach municipal building in May 2019 used a silencer attached to one of the two handguns he used to kill twelve people and injure
four others. According to one expert, a silencer "will distort the sound in such
a way that it would not immediately be recognizable as gunfire." Survivors
reported that "they were caught off guard and initially puzzled by what was
happening."[92] One survivor said the gunfire sounded at first like a nail gun: "If
it was a regular gunshot we would've definitely known a lot sooner, even if we
would've had 30 or 60 seconds more . . . . I think we could've all secured ourselves. All of us could've barricaded ourselves in."[93]

More to the point, numerous studies conclude that gun licensing and registration systems are strongly correlated with reductions in gun crime.[94] Thus,
the registration system currently in place for the purchase of silencers may
well be a primary reason for their rare use in crime.

Third, silencers have indeed been used in a small number of crimes in
recent years. The Violence Policy Center chronicled eighteen serious criminal cases between 2011 and 2019 involving the use of silencers.[95] Does this
small number mean that criminals would have no interest in silencers if they
were more easily available and not subject to background checks and careful
record-keeping? Or does it mean that the 1934 federal law has been successful
in mostly keeping them out of the hands of criminals? The criminal record before 1934 alone suggests it is the latter, especially because the federal database

of silencer owners provides a valuable source to trace and track silencer ownership and use.

Fourth, the use of silencers in crime would surely escalate for one reason alone: more and more cities are installing ShotSpotter technology, designed to pinpoint the location of gunfire. Anything that modifies or muffles that sound could impede or even defeat that technology, a concern expressed by the Minnesota Chiefs of Police Association when its State Legislature was considering a bill to make them available to state residents.[96] By one account: "if the sound of a gunshot is suppressed, it may not trigger gunshot alert systems."[97] And a rogue hunter who is hunting out of season, or on posted or private land, would have an obvious and powerful incentive to use a silencer in hopes of avoiding detection, as was true a century ago. As the earlier examination of silencer history noted, silencer hunting was one of the very earliest concerns about the devices.

Commercial Considerations

One additional reason explains the push to make silencer purchase easier and quicker, and it has nothing to do with safety or hearing. Like accessories for any commercial product, an explosion of silencer sales offers the prospect of enhanced revenues for manufacturers. According to Josh Waldron, founder and CEO of SilencerCo, a Utah-based company, the silencer industry is "the highest-growth niche of the firearms industry right now."[98] Since 2013, when Waldron was quoted, silencer sales increased significantly, even with current restrictions (sales increased by 400,000 from 2015 to 2016).[99] From 2014 to 2017, SilencerCo's business increased six hundred percent, according to the company's chief revenue officer. The company anticipates that with deregulation, the silencer market could expand ten-fold.[100] Further, silencer deregulation would allow the gun industry to manufacture guns with "integral silencers" as a separately manufactured item that would surely boost sales.[101] According to *Forbes Magazine*, "[s]oftening suppressor regulations would be a boon to domestic business."[102] In 2020 the Trump administration reversed State Department policy dating to 2002 that barred the sale of silencers to private foreign sources, opening the gates for non-government international sales. The decision meant roughly $250 million in annual silencer sales, but the reversal received critical scrutiny from Congress and others because the policy change involved a top White House aide, Michael B. Williams, who "played a leading role" in the decision and had personal and professional ties to the American Suppressor Association, the chief lobbying group for silencer manufacturers.[103] Aside from Williams, President Trump's son, Donald Jr., became an outspoken proponent of loosening silencer regulations, although Trump senior had voiced opposition to them.[104]

Gun accessory manufacturers are perfectly entitled to engage in legal and profitable commercial activity. Profit considerations, however, do not out-weigh concerns for safety or sound public policy, especially for those who might find themselves in the line of gun fire, whether produced by a hunter, a criminal, or an international assassin.

Conclusion: Safety First

Consider these observations. First, silencers are today perfectly legal to purchase, except for the nine states that otherwise prohibit them. Second, silencers are an accessory, not a gun. No firearm requires a silencer for its op-eration. The federal government determined decades ago that a system of thorough background checks and registration was an appropriate step to dis-courage their use for criminal purposes. Judging by contemporary writing, si-lencer proponents are at best unaware of, or at worst willfully ignorant about, the notorious history of silencers that led to numerous state laws and the 1934 NFA. Third, the 1934 NFA is an exemplar of an effective gun law, in that the items it regulates—including automatic weapons and silencers—have rarely appeared in crime. Most notably, the law's effectiveness derives not from an outright ban of the items, but rather a careful regulatory mechanism of reg-istration, meaningful background checks, and a tax. As noted earlier, studies have found that gun licensing and registration systems are strongly correlated with reductions in gun crime. One may reasonably infer that the same lesson applies to silencers in explaining their relative rarity of criminal use. Fourth, the chief stated purpose behind the drive to make silencers easier to acquire— the protection of shooters' hearing—is achievable by using proper hearing protection gear.

The legislation to deregulate silencers discussed at the start of this chapter would be truer to its stated purpose of protecting shooters' hearing if it subsidized the purchase and dissemination of good quality hearing protec-tive devices (in cooperation with gun manufacturers), promoted a public ser-vice campaign to remind shooters to wear proper protective hearing gear, and subsidized further research into improving hearing protection technologies, which would benefit not only gun owners but others regularly exposed to other kinds of harmfully loud noise. The protection of hearing is a worthy goal, but the deregulation of silencers is hardly the best or most sensible route to that goal.

In the light of silencer history and contemporary politics, the press to push aside existing silencer regulation is more well understood as one front of the broader effort to expand the definition of gun rights, notch a political win for gun rights forces, and increase profitability for the gun industry. These themes pervade the subjects covered in this text. Gun noise provides a real, life-saving benefit. Just ask anyone caught in the vicinity of a mass, or simply misdirected, shooting.

4

Weapons Brandishing and Display

IN MAY 2020, 46-year-old George Floyd, an African American, was arrested by police in Minneapolis for allegedly passing a phony $20 bill. After initially resisting, Floyd was handcuffed and pushed to the ground. One of the four officers on the scene kneeled on the back of Floyd's neck for roughly nine minutes. Despite his pleas and those of bystanders, the man suffocated and died on the scene. The event was recorded and seen by millions. The reaction was spontaneous nationwide outrage, and under the banner of the Black Lives Matter (BLM) movement, organized several years earlier, protests spread like wildfire across the country. In fact, this sequence of events sparked an uncharacteristically rapid and decisive (if short-term) shift in public attitudes about policing and racism. Within weeks of the killing, a *Washington Post* poll reported that sixty-nine percent of Americans agreed that Floyd's death reflected a larger problem of police treatment of African Americans. This sixty-nine percent support represented a tripling in that number compared with poll results from nine years earlier.[1] Six years earlier, after other police killings of unarmed Black men, forty-three percent of the public agreed.[2] Other polls found similarly seismic shifts in opinion.[3]

One such post-Floyd killing protest was held in St. Louis on June 28, when a group of protestors marched on a private street called Portland Place to stage a protest at the home of the St. Louis mayor, who lived on the street. Entering through an unlocked gate, the protestors walked past other homes, including that of Mark T. and Patricia N. McCloskey. Both are personal injury lawyers. As protestors passed, the McCloskeys came outside of their palatial historic home—both carrying firearms—and stood on their property. Mr. McCloskey carried an AR-15 assault-style rifle; Mrs. McCloskey held a silver handgun with her finger on the trigger, which she pointed at the marchers. The McCloskeys claimed that the marchers had broken through the gate to the street, were trespassing on the private road, and had shouted threats and obscenities at them. Mr. McCloskey labeled the marchers "terrorists" and said: "I really thought it was storming the Bastille." Without the display of firepower, he insisted, "we'd be dead and the house would be burned."[4] For their part, the marchers said that they neither made nor posed any threat to the McCloskeys, that none of them stepped onto the McCloskeys' property, that they were simply passing his house on the way to their destination, and that the gate they entered was unlocked and open—all of which was confirmed by video footage and other accounts taken at the time. The protestors considered the private road trespass an act of civil disobedience, although locals report that such trespass on private roads by pedestrians is not uncommon.[5]

Shortly after the encounter, the McCloskeys were each charged with a felony count of unlawful use of a weapon by St. Louis Circuit Attorney Kim Gardner, who said that "it is illegal to wave weapons in a threatening manner at those participating in nonviolent protest." Ms. Gardner proposed as a penalty that the couple complete a diversion program rather than face jail time. Gardner's allegation of wrongdoing against the McCloskeys was that they engaged in firearms "brandishing," succinctly defined by her statement. (Local police also seized the two guns in question.)[6] In an ironic twist, the McCloskeys were invited to speak before the August 2020 Republican National Convention. In October, a grand jury indicted them on felony charges of unlawful use of a weapon and evidence tampering.[7] In 2021, both pleaded guilty: Patricia to misdemeanor harassment with a $2,000 fine, and Mark to fourth-degree assault with a $750 fine. They also agreed to give up the weapons they deployed in the encounter, although they did not lose their right to own firearms. When asked by the judge if he admitted to putting people at risk, Mark replied, "I sure did your honor." Outside of the courthouse, however, he said, "I'd do it again." A month before the plea, Mark announced that he was running for the U.S. Senate. In August of 2021, Missouri's governor pardoned the couple.[8]

Several interrelated legal principles were immediately raised by those on both sides of the dispute, including so-called "stand your ground" laws that allow individuals to employ force, to the point of lethality, if confronted with a perceived threat in public places if they have a right to be where they are; the Castle doctrine, a related idea that people have no duty to retreat to protect their homes and property from intruders; open carry laws that make it legal to openly carry and display firearms in public; the Second Amendment, which by the reckoning of some protects a wide range of gun-related activities;

and brandishing laws that criminalize the threatening display of weapons. In the case of Missouri, state gun laws are relatively lax. It has expansive stand your ground and Castle doctrine laws, open carry is allowed, and the state has a long gun owning tradition. The state also has a brandishing law that defines as a criminal offense whenever anyone "[e]xhibits, in the presence of one or more persons, any weapon readily capable of lethal use in an angry or threatening manner."[9] In the modern era, nearly all states have some kind of brandishing law on the books. States without specific brandishing laws can still prosecute threatening behavior with a firearm under the categories of assault or menacing.[10]

The St. Louis case poses a contemporary exemplar of the complexities of gun brandishing behavior. Yet the case is hardly unique. Since the start of 2020, when states and localities began to impose restrictive measures to combat the spreading COVID-19 coronavirus, protests sprang up in many states, often including armed protestors, who rankled against measures they considered excessive, draconian, and even a violation of fundamental freedoms. Armed protests and protesters, composed mostly of right-wing private militia groups and sympathizers, spread even more rapidly as Black Lives Matter protests continued into the summer of 2020. By one account, armed counter-protesters during this time appeared at anti-racism rallies in at least thirty-three states. Predictably, "the presence of weapons at protests is ratcheting up tensions at a time when stress is high for protesters, counterprotesters and law enforcement alike." As this account observed: "Carrying a loaded firearm at a protest is an inherently dangerous situation."[11]

If asked why they carried guns, the armed protesters would surely respond that it is their right to do so. Strictly speaking, that is usually correct, as open gun carrying, including at public events, is legal in most states.[12] In addition, gun activists view gun carrying as a positive action or symbol, based on motivations to "desensitize" or "normalize" the idea of gun carrying,[13] and also as an effort on their part to somehow keep the peace.[14] A Utah state legislator who introduced a bill in that state to expand public gun carrying justified the effort by saying, "Carrying openly causes lots of consternation for anti-gunners . . . . They see the weapon, wet their pants, and call the police. We're trying to eliminate the public consternation."[15]

To take a different example, a member of the extremist so-called "Boogaloo" movement gave a radio interview in 2020 when he discussed his motivations for carrying a gun. He and others showed up at an otherwise peaceful rally in Las Vegas "armed to the teeth," calling for the reopening of businesses and other services during the pandemic. The armed protestor explained his actions by saying, "We're aware there's those that might be a little terrified of it. The point isn't to make people afraid, it's to show people and to bring up a dialogue."[16]

To cite another example, during a May 2020 armed protest in Michigan against strict state quarantining guidelines, one of the armed protestors, identified in a news report only as Mike S. of Detroit, said regarding the guns he and others were carrying that there was "obviously no intention to use it." Rather, he viewed gun carrying at the public rally to draw attention to the "[c]onstitutional rights protesters are defending." Others at the rally strongly objected to the presence of guns at the event.[17] Another armed protestor in Michigan who identified himself as part of a private militia group was described by a reporter as someone who "presents himself as an impartial guardian of the Bill of Rights."[18]

The fears of those who object to the presence of guns at public demonstrations were realized during a demonstration in Kenosha, Wisconsin in August 2020 that was sparked by the August 23 police killing of a Black man, who was shot by police seven times in the back. Film of the shooting enraged many who then took to Kenosha streets in unplanned protests that began peacefully but degenerated into mayhem. The moment attracted both protestors and armed counter-protestors. One of the latter, a seventeen-year old from Illinois carrying an assault-style rifle named Kyle Rittenhouse, was interviewed on the street during the evening of August 25. When asked what he was doing in the midst of the disorder, he replied: "People are getting injured and our job [he and other armed individuals] is to protect this business [referring to a business that had been recently vandalized] and part of my job is to help people. If there's somebody hurt, I'm running into harm's way. That's why I have my rifle—because I can protect myself obviously, but I also have my med[ical] kit."[19] News accounts described him as a "police admirer." Shortly after the interview, the teenager shot three people, killing two of them. He was charged with murder. Open gun carrying without a license is legal in Wisconsin, but carriers must be at least eighteen.[20] This event was obviously not like the orderly protests previously described, but the intentions of the Kenosha shooter, as he described them, could be taken as honorable, even noble. Yet the end result was anything but that. We cannot know the shooter's true motivations, but the shooting could only have occurred by virtue of the fact that he was armed. Despite the circumstances of this incident, Rittenhouse was found not guilty in a jury trial in late 2021. Decisive in that verdict was a provision in state law that placed the burden on the prosecution to demonstrate that the defendant did not feel in fear of his life, a difficult prosecutorial burden.[21]

Regardless of the political or other motives of public gun carrying, such carrying is an act freighted with meaning and consequences. This simple fact is a central concern in the contemporary gun debate in America, but it is not a new concern, a fact reflected in early American law, and earlier British law.

Myth and Reality in America's Gun Past

Thanks in large part to popular culture and American myth, a prevailing view of our gun past holds that gun laws and regulations are a product of modern American society, and that in the nineteenth century and before, guns were widely owned and little regulated, if at all. Yet the opposite is true. Gun possession is as old as the country (although far less widespread than popular culture suggests), but so are gun laws. Indeed, from the earliest British settlements in America up to the start of the twentieth century, Americans enacted literally thousands of gun laws of every imaginable variety.[22] Among those many laws were measures pertaining to the brandishing, and in some cases the mere display, of firearms in public. These restrictions found roots in early British law. As gun law expert Adam Winkler noted: "As long as people have been able to carry guns in public, there have been concerns about them terrorizing people."[23] Historian Saul Cornell concludes similarly that "[t]he liberty interest associated with the right to arms was always balanced against the concept of the peace."[24] In fact, Cornell notes, under early British law the very act of riding armed "terrorized the King's subjects and therefore violated the peace." To do so "did not require any intentional act [i.e., no *mens rea* standard], or menacing behavior, to run afoul of the law; the mere act of arming itself was sufficient to trigger criminal prosecution."[25] This principle, found in law from Britain in the Middle Ages to the present in the U.S., has long been summarized as, "going armed to the terror of the public."[26] Even gun rights lawyer Stephen Halbrook concluded that "the right to bear arms does not include the carrying of dangerous and unusual weapons to the terror of one's fellow citizens."[27]

For example, in one of the most influential English legal handbooks dating to the early colonial period that also served as a model for the development of American law, Dalton's *Country Justice*, justices of the peace were granted broad powers to bind over individuals for a variety of violations of the King's Peace. Infractions included any who "go or ride armed offensively . . . . For these are accounted to be an Affray and Fear of the People, and a Means of the Breach of the Peace."[28] Blackstone defines "affray" this way: "Affrays (from *affraier*, to terrify) are the fighting of two or more persons in some public place, to the terror of his majesty's subjects."[29] (A private fight, Blackstone added, is an assault.) Another section of *Country Justice* expressly said that the mere carrying of guns and certain other weapons was an offense: "All such as shall go or ride armed (offensively) in Fairs, Markets or elsewhere; or shall wear or carry any Guns, Dag[ger]s or Pistols charged; any Constable, seeing this, may arrest them." The section ends with this: "And besides, it striketh a Fear and Terror into the King's Subjects."[30]

Saul Cornell traces these restrictions back to the British Statute of Northampton of 1328. It said in part that all subjects were bound to "bring no force in affray of the peace, nor to go nor ride armed by night nor by day." The law was enforced by the monarch's agents, who could arrest violators and cause them "to forfeit their armour to the King, and their bodies to prison at the King's pleasure."[31]

In American law, several prominent legal treatises adopted the British model. For example, the American edition of William Russell's *A Treatise on Crimes and Misdemeanors* from 1824 said: "if a number of men assemble with arms, in terrorem populi [to the terror of the people], though no act is done, it is a riot."[32] The same standard was found in J.A.G. Davis's *On Criminal Law* (1838), James Stewart's version of *Blackstone's Commentaries* (1849), Francis Wharton's treatise, *Precedents of Indictments and Pleas* (1849), and Oliver Barber's *Treatise on the Criminal Law of the State of New York* (1852).[33]

Statutory Law

In statutory law, two types of provisions penalized the mere public appearance of weapons (short of their actual use), including but not limited to firearms, in two circumstances: the brandishing of weapons—that is, to display them in a menacing or threatening manner, and the mere display of weapons. A 1642 provision in the colony of New Netherland (soon to be New York) stated: "No one shall presume to draw a knife much less to wound any person, under . . . penalty."[34] This reference did not mention firearms but allowed for penalties for merely drawing or displaying a weapon, even if no wounding occurred. Similarly, a 1786 Massachusetts law criminalized the mere assemblage of "any persons to the number of twelve, or more, being armed with clubs or other weapons." If they did not disperse within an hour of being warned, they could be subject to arrest.[35] That is, the mere appearance of such an armed assemblage was sufficient to justify legal action against them, although other provisions of the act penalized such groups who also behaved in a threatening manner.

Some of these American laws mirrored the British Statute of Northampton, where "[t]he very fact of carrying a firearm was considered to be in terror of the people and was therefore prohibited by that statute."[36] For example, in 1686 New Jersey adopted "An Act against wearing Swords, &c" as a reaction to "great complaints by the inhabitants of [the] Province, that several persons [were] wearing swords, daggers, pistols, dirks, stilladoes, skeines [small Irish-derived swords], or any other unusual or unlawful weapons."[37] New Hampshire enacted a law in 1699 that punished anyone who "went armed offensively" or "put his Majesty's subjects in fear."[38] Virginia enacted a measure in 1786 saying that no man was to "go nor ride armed by night nor by day, in fair or markets, or in other places, in terror of the Country, upon pain of being arrested and committed to prison."[39] North Carolina enacted a very similar measure in 1792, saying that no man shall "go nor ride armed by night nor by day, in fairs, markets nor in the presence of the King's Justices, or other ministers, nor in no part elsewhere."[40] Massachusetts added to its existing firearms regulations in 1795 that authorized justices of the peace to arrest those who "ride or go armed offensively, to the fear or terror of the good citizens."[41] In 1801, Tennessee enacted a law saying that no one was to "go armed to the terror of the people, or privately carry any dirk, large knife, pistol, or any other dangerous weapon, to the fear or terror of any person."[42] Maine's 1821 law outlawed "affrayers, rioters, disturbers or breakers of the peace, and such as shall ride or go armed offensively, to the fear or terror of the good citizens."[43]

Note that Virginia, Massachusetts, Tennessee, and Maine all invoked some version of the old British phrase "to the terror of the people" with New Hampshire's law referencing the similar "fear" of the public. And in the Tennessee law, concealed weapons carrying was also identified as a source of "terror."

These laws, it turns out, were ubiquitous. Between the late 1600s and the early 1930s, a total of at least thirty-six states and territories enacted laws that penalized weapons brandishing or display (see Table 4.1). Of these, twenty-one states criminalized weapons brandishing[44] by combining two elements: the display of the weapon plus the manner of the display. For example, an 1840 Mississippi law said that "any person having or carrying any . . . deadly weapon" who "shall, in the presence of three or more persons, exhibit the same in a rude, angry and threatening manner, not in self-defense" shall be subject to prosecution.[45] Note the two key elements: the "exhibit" or

Table 4.1 COLONIAL, STATE, AND TERRITORIAL WEAPONS BRANDISHING AND DISPLAY LAWS IN 36 STATES, 1642–1931*

BRANDISHING LAWS IN 21 STATES	DISPLAY LAWS IN 18 STATES
-The Statutes of the State of Mississippi, 1840, § 55	-1642 N.Y. Laws 33
-1854 Wash. Sess. Law 80, ch. 2, §30	-1686 N.J. Laws 289, ch. IX
-Digest of the Laws of California, 1858, Page 34, Image 340 (1861)	-1692 Mass. Acts 10, 11-12; 1786 Mass. Sess. Laws (included Maine); 1795 Mass. Acts 436, ch. 2; 1836 Mass. Acts 748, 750, ch. 134
-A Digest of the Laws of Pennsylvania, 1860, page 250	-1699 N.H. Laws 1, 1–2;
-1867 Ariz. Sess. Laws 21-22, § 1	-1786 Va. Acts 33, ch. 21
-1868 Ark. Acts 218, § 12-13	-Francois Xavier Martin, *A Collection of Statutes of the Parliament of England in Force in the State of North Carolina*, 60–61 (Newbern 1792)
-1870 Id. Sess. Laws 21	
-1873 Nev. Stat. 118, ch. 62, § 1	
-A Digest of the Laws of Texas, 1873, Annotated Page 1321, Image 291 (Vol. 2, 1873)	-1801 Tenn. Pub. Acts 260, ch. 22 § 6
-1875 Ind. Acts 62, § 1	-1821 Me. Laws 285, ch. 73 § 1
-The Revised Charter and Ordinances of the City of Boonville, MO., 1881, § 6	-Revised Statutes of the State of Delaware, 1852, § 3
-The General Laws of New Mexico, 1882 Page 313	-1880 Ga. Laws 151
	-1883 Ind. Acts 1712, chap. 87, § 6678
	-1886 N.M. Laws 56, ch. 30, § 4
-The Revised Statutes of the State of Illinois, 1883, Page 453, Image 512 (1884)	-1889 N.C. Sess. Laws 502, ch. 527, § 1
	-1893 Or. Laws 29–30, § 1
-1884 Wyo. Sess. Laws 114, ch. 67, § 1	-The Code of Alabama, 1897, § 4342
-1885 Mont. Laws 74	-Book of Ordinances of the City of Wichita, Kansas, 1899, § 1
-1897 Fla. Laws 59, chap. 4532, § 1	
-Annotated Code of the State of Iowa, 1897, Page 1898, § 4775	-Revised Statutes of Wyoming, 1899, Pages 1252–1253, Images 1252–1253
-The Session Laws (Washington) of 1897, Page 1956	-1910 S.C. Acts 694
-Annotated Statutes of the Indian Territory (Oklahoma), 1899, Second Session of the Fifty-fifth Congress, Page 228, Image 312	
-1925 W.Va. Acts 25–30, ch. 3, § 7, pt. a	
-1931 Mich. Pub. Acts 670, ch. 37, § 233	

Sources: Duke Center for Firearms Law digital archive of gun laws, https://firearmslaw.duke.edu/repository/search-the-repository/; *Young v. Hawaii*, 992 F.3d 765, 794–95 (9th Cir. 2021); Jonathan E. Taylor, "The Surprisingly Strong Originalist Case for Public Carry Laws," *Harvard Journal of Law & Public Policy* 43 (Spring 2020): 347–356. Note that three states—Indiana, New Mexico, and Wyoming—appear in both lists totaling thirty-nine laws in thirty-six states.

display of the weapon combined with doing so "in a rude, angry and threatening manner." The latter element brings to mind the perpetrator's *mens rea* or "guilty mind,"[46] revealing a criminal intent as invoked by the terms "rude, angry, and threatening." Of the twenty-one states with these laws, eleven used the identical "in a rude, angry and threatening manner" phrase; five used the word "threaten," and the others used wording including "for the purpose of frightening or intimidating," "in a manner likely to cause terror," or simply "point."

A total of eighteen states enacted laws that penalized the mere display or wearing of firearms and other "deadly weapons."[47] (While thirty-six states enacted one of these types of laws, three states—Indiana, New Mexico, and Wyoming—enacted both display and brandishing laws, for a total of thirty-nine laws in thirty-six states.) Several state laws in this category used the phrase "to point," as was true for a couple of laws in the brandish category, but the laws here had additional language that made clear that the intent of the person was irrelevant. An 1880 Georgia law, for example, made it a crime to "point or aim" a gun but added "loaded or unloaded,"[48] a distinction not made in the brandishing laws. Another criminalized gun pointing "in jest or otherwise";[49] another added "with or without malice";[50] a fourth said "in fun or otherwise."[51] The thrust of these laws is that intent does not matter. The mere act of display is sufficient to warrant prosecution. Invariably, these laws made exceptions for justifiable arms carrying including weapons transport, travelers carrying weapons, law enforcement, the military, militias, and cases of self-defense.

To raise a final point about these laws, the weapons to which they referred included (with one exception) firearms, but also included certain named types of knives. While this may seem odd to contemporary readers, certain types of knives were widely used for interpersonal fighting. These named types of knives, including Bowie knives, Arkansas toothpicks, Spanish stilettos, sword canes, swords, dirks, or other bladed "deadly weapons," shared the trait of having long, thin blades that were favorites for fighting and were widely reviled for that reason. The very same list of firearms and knives was invariably included among those weapons barred from concealed carry in the colonies and states from the seventeenth through the start of the twentieth centuries. Indeed, by early in the twentieth century, forty-seven states had enacted laws severely restricting or barring the concealed carrying of such weapons.[52] These state laws mostly remained on the books until the National Rifle Association launched its effort in state legislatures to liberalize and repeal these strict anti-gun-carry laws starting in the 1980s.[53]

In addition to laws restricting concealed carry and brandishing, states commonly enacted gun carrying time and place restrictions. These also stretched back to the seventeenth century, and restricted gun carrying in any number of public places, at communal gatherings, schools, churches, circuses or shows, parades (if the weapons were loaded), certain meeting places including legislative houses, entertainments, on Sundays, or election day, among others. Separate measures commonly and strictly regulated firearm discharges.[54]

Guns and Elections

In the seventeenth, eighteenth, and nineteenth centuries, America was a developing, but still immature nation-state. It was founded on democratic principles, but tightly bounded principles, excluding women, African Americans, Native Americans, and non-property owners from full (or any) citizenship rights and voting. As the nation matured, its definition of democracy expanded—one sign of a maturing nation-state. At the core of this developmental process was the conduct of its electoral process. Mature democratic nations conduct elections within a framework of peace, order, and fair procedures governed by law. Yet "the United States was not a particularly stable political system in the middle of the nineteenth century."[55] The drive to modernity in the U.S. witnessed electoral violence and intimidation. Political scientist Richard Franklin Bensel characterized the American electoral regime during this time as "a basically democratic model against which fraud, intimidation, and corruption could have been identified as pathologies."[56]

These pathologies were eventually met by the enactment and implementation of more orderly, fair, peaceful, and consistent elections administration. Yet violence and intimidation, including intimidation by men with arms, left a deep scar on those compelled to confront it at election time. As historians Glenn C. Altschuler and Stuart M. Blumin chronicled in their deep dive into nineteenth century American political practices, aptly titled *Rude Republic*, an armed presence at the polls was a "menace" that "was an experience that voters remembered for the rest of their lives."[57] The Progressive movement around the turn of the twentieth century was mobilized in part to address electoral corruption and malfeasance, and produced an array of reforms, including the secret ballot and governmental administration of elections, a task formerly controlled by the political parties.[58] Table 4.2 lists at least eleven states that specifically barred weapons from its elections, polling places, or related electioneering.[59] In addition to the laws in Table 4.2, Maryland enacted a measure in 1637 that said: "No one shall come into the house of Assembly

Table 4.2 State Laws Barring Weapons at Polling Places, on Election Days, Governmental Buildings*

STATE	PROVISION
Maryland	Proceedings of The Conventions of the Province of Maryland, Held at the City of Annapolis in 1774, 1775, & 1776 185 (1836)
Delaware	Del. Const. art. 28 (1776)
New York	Act of Jan. 26, 1787, ch. 1, 1787 N.Y. Laws 345
Tennessee	Act of Dec. 1, 1869, ch. 22, sec. 2, 1869 Tenn. Pub. Acts 108
Louisiana	Act of Mar. 16, 1870, sec. 73, 1870 La. Acts 159
Georgia	Ga. Code § 4528 (1873)
New Mexico	The General Laws of New Mexico: Promulgation of the "Kearney Code" in 1846, to the End of the Legislative Session of 1880, with Supplement, Including the Session of 1882 Page 313, Image 313 (1882)
Texas	1879 Tex. Crim. Stat. tit. IX, Ch. 4 (Penal Code); 1895 Tex. Crim. Stat. 93
Missouri	1883 Mo. Laws 76, An Act To Amend Section 1274, Article 2, Chapter 24 Of The Revised Statutes Of Missouri, Entitled "Of Crimes And Criminal Procedure," § 1.
Oklahoma	Terr. Okla. Stat. ch. 25, art. 47, § 7 (1890)
Arizona	1901 Ariz. Acts 1252, Crimes and Punishments, §§ 387 and 391

* *Sources:* Darrell A.H. Miller, "Constitutional Conflict and Sensitive Places," *William & Mary Bill of Rights Journal* 28 (December 2019): 472–475; Duke Center for Firearms Law, https:// firearmslaw.duke.edu/repository/search-the-repository/. Note that this dataset ends in 1936, so other states may have adopted similar laws after that date.

whilst the house is set with any weapon upon peril of such fine or censure as the house shall think fit."[60]

The Delaware Constitution of 1776 stated the matter plainly: "To prevent any violence or force being used at the said elections, no person shall come armed to any of them, and no muster of the militia shall be made on that day." It also barred "any battalion or company" from congregating within a mile of the places where elections were to be held, and for a day before and after elections.[61] New York's 1787 law required that "all elections shall be free and that no person by force of arms nor by malice or menacing or otherwise presume to disturb or hinder any citizen of this State to make free election upon pain of fine and imprisonment."[62]

In 1869 Tennessee made it unlawful "for any qualified voter or other person attending any election in this State" to carry any weapon whether concealed or visible.[63] The other states in the accompanying table enacted similar measures.

The ubiquity and generality of laws penalizing weapons brandishing and display would have undoubtedly extended them to such threatening behavior in the specific context of elections, which probably suggests why laws barring weapons at elections were not more common. Yet the very fact of these laws in some states speaks to the importance of a simple message that, sadly, bears repeating for contemporary elections: that weapons have no place during the conduct of a democratic society's elections.[64]

The Modern Debate About Firearms Brandishing and Intimidation

This brings us to an important question: what happens when gun carrying intersects with public demonstrations? Considerable contemporary legal analysis has examined the relationship between free speech and arms carrying, generally framed as the intersection or collision of First and Second Amendment rights.[65] My purpose in this chapter is not to wade into that constitutional law question. The issue of weapons brandishing is a matter of criminal law,[66] and as the prior discussion illustrates, brandishing restrictions are deeply and firmly embedded in American law dating back hundreds of years. This legal tradition alone recognizes that weapons brandishing and even simple public weapons display when others are present is intimidating *per se*—by its very nature. First Amendment free speech considerations are about words (and occasionally expressive conduct). Gun carrying is about the human carrying of dangerous devices. By one account, "open [gun] carry is action, not speech."[67] Still, some of this writing addresses the focus of this chapter.

For example, Darrell A.H. Miller argues that "the presence of a gun in public has the effect of chilling or distorting the essential channels of a democracy—public deliberation and interchange . . . . A right to freely brandish firearms frustrates one of the very purposes of a constitution, which is 'to make politics possible.' "[68] Eugene Volokh takes issue with Miller's claim, calling it "speculation." His counterargument is that states with liberalized concealed carry firearms laws have shown no evidence of less free speech than those with strict carry laws, and thus gun carrying evinces no intimidation.[69]

That argument, however, is not based on any actual data or measurement of comparative degrees of speech freedom. Further, it fails to address the fact, consequences, and real-life instances of actual public gun carrying. Only a small percent of people with gun carry licenses actually carry guns at any given time (and therefore a tiny percent of all adult Americans),[70] and the presence of guns must be visible and made known to others in a public setting in order for the public consequences of gun display or brandishing to be felt. The question pertaining to brandishing is not whether the law allows gun carrying, but what people actually do, and under what circumstances. When visibly armed citizens appear in public, especially at a public demonstration or other event, it invariably makes news and raises alarm. The earlier examination of historical gun brandishing laws alone provides abundant evidence that public gun carrying engenders fear sufficient to warrant public sanction, and that this, contrary to Volokh's unfounded assertion, has been universally understood for hundreds of years.

In modern times, the Black Panthers armed protests in Sacramento, California in 1967, armed protestors in Virginia while that state was considering new gun control laws in 2019 and early 2020, or armed demonstrators in numerous state capitals protesting strict quarantine measures in response to the COVID-19 pandemic in 2020 are but a few examples of the dismay and alarm that accompanied those actions, and the public attention these and other incidents received.[71] These incidents are not mere artifacts of subjective "perceptions" or "feelings," but predictable, even inevitable consequences arising from the visible presence of dangerous weapons in public places where others are gathered. Joseph Blocher and Bardia Vaseghi, for example, describe the vanishingly thin line between certain core Second Amendment conduct and torts and crimes like brandishing and assault.[72] Garrett Epps has argued similarly that gun carrying in a public context "is not like words or ideas. It [a gun] is an instrument of violence and death, and its display amid a crowd is a threat."[73] Beyond that, dozens of studies dating to the 1960s, including in the field of psychology, have identified a "weapons effect," meaning that people "act more aggressively" when carrying a weapon.[74] According to one researcher, "it really doesn't matter if a good guy or a bad guy is carrying the gun—it creates the bias to *interpret* things in a hostile way."[75] For example, a study of those driving cars with firearms were more likely to exhibit road rage.[76]

As noted, our forebears well understood the inherently intimidating nature of weapons display. Two disparate but analogous examples will help illustrate how this is more than a matter of mere perception.

Police Interrogation and the Security Dilemma

In 1966, the Supreme Court ruled in *Miranda v. Arizona* that suspects being questioned while in police custody had to be informed of their constitutional rights, including the right to remain silent and to have the assistance of an attorney. The reason police were required to provide these "Miranda rights" to those being interrogated was because, as the court said, "the very fact of custodial interrogation exacts a heavy toll on individual liberty," and "in-custody interrogation is inherently coercive."[77] Coerced confessions are, by definition, unreliable and a violation of the protection against self-incrimination. In other words, custodial interrogation, *by its very nature*, is inherently coercive, regardless of the good intentions or friendly demeanor of the police. The same can be said of the presence of guns in a political or public setting. The fact of gun carrying outweighs the stated intention of the carrier, no matter how benign or well intentioned.

Another analogy is found in international relations theory's "security dilemma." This bedrock principle states that the very steps nations take to protect themselves militarily from attack, through arming and fortification, have the perverse effect of ratcheting up the insecurity of other nations. Stated another way, "the means by which a state tries to increase its security decrease the security of others."[78] As international relations expert John J. Mearsheimer observed, "the measures a state takes to increase its own security usually decrease the security of other states."[79] One need not doubt the desire of nations to avoid war and increase their own security to also understand that these good intentions are not sufficient. Intentions and perceptions, relatively speaking, do not matter, because they are eclipsed in the realities of nation-state relations by the factual consequences of military build-ups. The same principle applies, with greater force and clarity, to nations that seek or acquire nuclear weapons. Nations like Iran and North Korea have pursued the possession of nuclear weapons, despite the economic and diplomatic costs of doing so, as a potent power resource—not by their use, but by their mere possession.[80] The same logic applies, on a much smaller scale, with firearms. In fact, a recent study confirms this very trend within the U.S.—escalating violence with a greater likelihood of lethal threats and deaths—in places where few or no restrictions on open gun carrying exist along with expansive stand your ground laws that allow individuals to employ force, including lethal force, if they feel threatened in public places.[81] In these instances, the objective circumstances and consequences of the actions taken outweigh the intentions (no matter how noble or even altruistic) of police interrogation practices and military security policies of nations. The same can be said of the presence of guns in a public or political setting. The fact of gun carrying outweighs the stated intentions of the carrier, no matter how noble or sincere.

Gun Owners Know

Considerable evidence supports the proposition that some gun carriers do so with less than honorable motives. A 2019 nationwide survey of over two thousand gun owners lends inferential support for the proposition that at least some gun owners are drawn to guns precisely because firearms display in a public or political context is intimidating. The survey was designed to assess "the extent to which guns have a symbolic meaning to gun owners." For example, when asked the reason for their gun ownership, most cited personal defense and recreation; 15.8 percent of respondents, however, said that guns gave them a feeling of "empowerment," and 7.9 percent said they owned guns "to exercise their constitutional rights or to give them a feeling of power."[82] A recent study of the meanings given to guns by gun owners identified three distinct assessments of gun meaning: freedom, personal identity, and empowerment. This latter category identifies those who own guns "because they facilitate individual control over one's immediate environment," a sentiment consonant with guns as a source of intimidation, power, and empowerment.[83]

General public opinion data also supports the bifurcation of reactions to gun carrying. On the one hand, those who acquire guns for self-defense— mostly handguns—say that the guns give them a feeling of security or make them feel safer (even among gun owners, however, many oppose or are skeptical of public carrying).[84] Yet when others are asked their reactions to gun possession or gun carrying, the sentiments are invariably negative. For example, in a 2004 Gallup survey of Americans asking how safe they would feel in a "public place" that allowed the concealed carry of firearms, sixty-five percent said less safe, twenty-five percent more safe, and eight percent no difference. When asked who they thought should be allowed to carry concealed firearms in a public place, forty-four percent said only "safety officials," twenty-six percent said only those with a "clear need," and twenty-seven percent said private citizens.[85] A 2017 nationwide survey found even less support for public gun carrying, with between seventeen and thirty-three percent of respondents saying that they favored public gun carrying in various listed public places, with clear majorities expressing opposition to gun carrying circumstances.[86] Political scientist Alexandra Filindra conducted a nationwide survey of Americans in 2021 to gauge their reactions to the idea of gun carrying to public gatherings and protests. She found that respondents overwhelmingly disapproved of the idea. Clear majorities also said that they would not attend events if such carrying were allowed—a clear indication that gun carrying defeats the very purpose of holding a lawful demonstration. Among gun owners she surveyed, clear majorities (sixty percent) also said they would not bring guns to such events, although twenty percent said they were very or somewhat likely to bring guns.[87]

Hoplophobia Phobia

Some gun rights supporters have sought to belittle the unease or fear of gun possession and carrying felt by others by invidiously labeling it "hoplophobia"— the supposedly irrational fear of guns (despite the clinical-sounding name, the term is not recognized by the American Psychiatric Association[88]). According to self-described "gun fanatic" and author Dan Baum, the term was coined in the 1960s by a military veteran who wrote on gun topics and taught gun safety, Jeff Cooper. By Baum's account, the supposedly irrational fear of guns by non-gun owners explains why the latter focus on the gun as the culprit to explain terrible shootings. To gun owners, according to Baum, "imbuing an inanimate metal object with that kind of agency seems genuinely crazy," justifying the "phobia" label attributed to those leery of guns, as though such feelings were irrational or unjustifiable. To Baum, hoplophobia "is a pretty good way to delineate differences between what might be called the pro- and anti-gun camps."[89] Baum's comments are typical for those who seek to marginalize, delegitimize, or belittle the fears of non-gun owners.[90]

Baum's (and Cooper's) analysis and explanation fails on four grounds. First, it fails to recognize the fact, established here and as recognized in the law going back hundreds of years, that guns pose an inherent and objective threat as soon as they come into contact with humans. The very rules of gun ownership, handling, and use that Baum touts verify this fact. The original five rules, expanded by others, and apparently developed by Cooper, are (or should be) well known to all gun owners: that all guns should be treated as though they were loaded; never aim a gun at anything you are not willing to shoot; one's finger should be kept off the trigger until the shooter is ready to shoot; confirm the target and what might be behind it; and keep control of the firearm.[91] Why treat these simple, inanimate objects with such extraordinary caution if they are simply innocuous "inanimate metal objects"? Refrigerators, for example, are inanimate metal objects, too, but hardly require similarly hyper-cautious treatment. The answer is obvious: guns are inherently and uniquely dangerous, a danger that is evident and universal when individuals carry them in a public setting. Automobiles, as many point out, historically killed more people than guns in America annually (although the death gap was reversed by 2021 with more gun deaths than auto deaths[92]). Yet automobiles serve a very different manifest function—to carry people and commodities from place to place. Moreover, automobiles and their operators are subject to a blizzard of safety-based rules, regulations, and design features to minimize harm to humans. The startling absence of similar features, rules, and regulations for firearms in modern society—as of today, for example, no training whatsoever is required in a majority of states as a prerequisite for handgun ownership and carrying[93]—has also been widely noted. Many other objects in daily life cause harm and death, but all of them have other, manifest purposes, and are almost certainly subject to more regulation than guns. And guns have one and only one purpose.

The second problem with Baum's analysis is summarized by the "weapons instrumentality effect." This phrase refers to the independent effect of weapon type on crime and the likelihood of injury or death. No interpersonal weapon is more effective in causing injury or death than a gun, and none is easier to use. Numerous studies verify this simple fact, demonstrating, for example, that assaults with guns are five times more likely to result in death than knife assaults (the second most-commonly used weapon). The successful completion of robberies is more likely when guns are used as compared with other weapons. Indeed, the mere presence of guns sometimes precipitates violence that would not otherwise occur. These findings extend to firearm homicide, suicide, and accident.[94] Further, emergency room physicians have long chronicled in great detail the uniquely devastating and destructive consequences of gunshot wounds on patients as compared with wounds from other sources or implements.[95]

The third problem is that the gun community knows perfectly well that public gun carrying is inherently intimidating. No better example is found than in the shifting positions of the nation's preeminent gun group, the National Rifle Association. The NRA has long been leery of open gun carrying in public, yet it had to act cautiously about the question for fear of alienating staunch gun people among its base. In a remarkably frank moment, it explained its reticence about public gun carrying in a post on its website in 2014:

Let's not mince words, not only is it [public open gun carrying] rare, it's downright weird and certainly not a practical way to go normally about your business while being prepared to defend yourself. To those who are not acquainted with the dubious practice of using public displays of firearms as a means to draw attention to oneself or one's cause, it can be downright scary. It makes folks who might normally be perfectly open-minded about firearms feel uncomfortable and question the motives of pro-gun advocates.[96]

The NRA rapidly backed away from this statement after angry reactions from some of its supporters, and it has maintained an official position that it supports open carry. Yet the concern it expresses is that of a political realist: people instinctively recoil from the presence of armed civilians in public, just as they did hundreds of years ago, therefore impeding the gun rights cause. Far from normalizing the presence of guns, public carrying merely stokes fear and anxiety. The reason: such carrying is threatening *per se*, by its very nature.

Government officials have reported feeling the same intimidation when confronted with armed civilians in the seat of state government. At least eight states have laws allowing civilian gun carrying in capitol buildings in state capitals. State legislators in three of those states have moved to restrict such carrying, and for the same reason: they all found such action intimidating. In fact, Republican leaders in Michigan canceled several legislative sessions in 2020 because armed civilian gun carrying in their chambers was expected.[97]

Fourth, gun carrying during public demonstrations is more likely to result in violence, injuries, and deaths than when guns are not present. An ambitious study issued in 2021 by the Armed Conflict Location and Event Data Project (ACLED) and Everytown for Gun Safety examined over thirty thousand demonstrations nationwide held from January 2020 through June 2021. (The types of demonstrations included those protesting COVID19-related restrictions, the Black Lives Matter movement, and demonstrations related to support for or opposition to Donald Trump, policing, and gun rights.) Of those, participants carried or brandished firearms in 560 instances. While these 560 incidents account for only about two percent of the total number, they were much more likely to result in mayhem. The armed demonstrations turned violent or destructive sixteen percent of the time, whereas non-armed demonstrations resulted in violence less than three percent of the time—an increase by a factor of more than six for armed instances. The fatality rate at unarmed demonstrations was one out of every 2963 events (.03 percent), whereas the fatality rate at armed demonstrations was one out of every sixty-two events (1.6 percent). The study also notes that violence in these armed instances often comes from, or is contributed to by, those who are armed.

The groups involved in armed demonstrating were dominated by right-wing organizations. In order of frequency, the most common armed participants were the Boogaloo Boys, followed by Three Percenters, the Proud Boys, Oath Keepers, the New Black Panther Party, Patriot Prayer, and the Michigan Liberty Militia.[98] The organization expanded its study of armed demonstrations to cover all of 2020–2021. It tabulated over 610 incidents of armed demonstrations during this period and concluded that armed demonstrations were 6.5 times more likely to become violent or result in destruction than unarmed demonstrations.[99] This analysis flatly contradicts the old slogan that an armed society is a polite society. Far from it. In addition, it lends further evidence in support of the real-life consequences of arms escalations as predicted by international relations theory.

Conclusion

Whether public gun carriers admit it or not, gun carrying at public events or locations, like those described here, is by its nature intimidating. Indeed, firearms are carried precisely because they possess this trait.[100] This does not mean that guns in these settings will be fired—they rarely are, or that the carriers have nefarious intentions. But sometimes intentions change, or things go wrong.

In the summer of 2020, Portland, Oregon was the scene of some of the most intense public demonstrations and counter-demonstrations of the Black Lives Matter movement. As protests continued, counter-protestors responded with increasing numbers. Some of them came armed with guns. In turn, some of the BLM protestors began to do the same. The arrival of firearms escalated tensions—very much like arming escalations between nations discussed earlier. In short order, at the end of August, a self-identified member of Antifa (short for "anti-fascist"), a left-wing movement, allegedly shot and killed a member of a right-wing group called Patriot Prayer. Both men were armed with handguns. The alleged shooter, in turn, was tracked by the police who then shot and killed him the next day in a nearby city as they attempted to arrest him. Police and witnesses said he displayed and fired his handgun, although that account has been disputed. Before being killed by the police, the man said in an interview that he was armed during the demonstration to provide "security." He explained his shooting of the other man by saying that he was defending himself and another man, and that he "had no choice."[101]

Like the fatal shooting incident described at the start of this chapter, the participants stressed positive, even noble motives. But they represent the unspoken end point of weapons brandishing. Commenting on the escalating violence and presence of guns in Portland, former acting assistant U.S. Attorney General and now law professor Mary McCord said that the right to peaceful protest is trampled when "you have armed factions ideologically opposed to each other." Another observer referred to it as an "escalating arms race."[102]

Recent writing has argued that guns have "agency," suggesting that they are not simply objects indistinguishable from other objects, but that "guns themselves might be active . . . they might have their own 'lives."[103] Whether this argument has merit or not, this chapter establishes that, as a matter of history, law, and behavior, public gun carrying, especially in a social or political context, transmits a universally understood message of intimidation. That message is utterly at odds with any notions of free speech, lawful expression, and democratic governance in a democratic society. New Hampshire's Republican governor, Chris Sununu, would certainly agree. Re-elected to his post in 2020, he canceled the outdoor inauguration ceremony set for January 2021 because of armed protestors who dogged his trail after he ordered mandatory pandemic-related mask-wearing in public places. "For weeks," according to the governor, "armed protesters have increasingly become more aggressive, targeting my family, protesting outside my private residence, and trespassing on my property—an outdoor public ceremony simply brings too much risk."[104] In New Hampshire, as in many other places, weapons brandishing had again reared its ugly, undemocratic head.

5

Second Amendment Sanctuaries

COLORING OUTSIDE THE LINES OF FEDERALISM

"SANCTUARY! SANCTUARY!" THESE words were famously shouted by the deformed bell-ringer Quasimodo as he dramatically rescued the young, beautiful, and innocent Esmeralda from public hanging by scooping her up and retrieving her to Notre Dame cathedral in the 1939 movie *The Hunchback of Notre Dame*. The moment embodies the idea of a religious haven where people might seek immunity from the hand of the state.

While America of today bears no relationship to Victor Hugo's nineteenth-century novel set in fifteenth-century Paris, new cries of "sanctuary" resonate in our politics. In recent years, local governments, especially in Western states, began to enact so-called "Second Amendment sanctuary" resolutions in which they asserted their right to refuse to enforce any federal or state gun laws they believed violated Second Amendment rights. These actions came largely in response to new state and federal gun law proposals and enactments, following a rising tide of public demand for such measures. Sanctuary resolutions enacted range from purely symbolic expressions of gun law disapproval and support for gun rights to specific declarations that localities would ignore or flout laws they would be otherwise bound to follow, or even punish those who tried to abide by gun laws. Such actions have swept across conservative states and localities around the country. The impact and consequences of such measures are, at the least, uncertain. Yet this movement, like the others examined in this book, represents another front in the ongoing effort to expand or redefine gun rights, although it differs from the other efforts examined in this book in some particulars.

The sanctuary movement idea is part of a lengthy lineage in America. Most importantly, it is a descendent of the tendentious notion of nullification, the underlying theory that ultimately helped precipitate the American Civil War. It also occurs in the context of American federalism, the fundamental governing structure that divides governing power between the national government and the states. After summarizing the nature of the contemporary movement, this chapter will examine the relevant legal and political history, and then turn to a microscopic examination of this movement in the author's home state and county.

Sanctuary Movements

Second Amendment sanctuary advocates claim that they have mimicked and followed an earlier sanctuary movement, one on behalf of undocumented immigrants, that sprang up in the 1980s during which American authorities and individuals organized to provide protection to refugees fleeing political persecution and violence. Central American nations including El Salvador and Guatemala witnessed mass killings and human rights abuses that caused thousands to flee through Mexico to seek refuge in the U.S. American churches played a leading role in this effort to help refugees, invoking the 1980 Refugee Act and other relevant laws as justification. In a watershed moment, six congregations in California and Arizona declared that they were sanctuaries for refugees in 1982. These measures allow for the granting of asylum for refugees who demonstrate a "well-founded fear of persecution."[1] Still, these actions violated federal immigration law, opening them to federal prosecution. This movement was in large part inspired by past, similar efforts to aid runaway enslaved persons before the Civil War, in violation of the federal Fugitive Slave Act, and sometimes state laws, and sanctuary efforts on behalf of Vietnam War-era draft resisters in the 1960s and 1970s. In the decade of the 2010s, a renewed immigration sanctuary movement sought to provide protection for Central Americans fleeing violence and persecution. By 2017, at least five states and over six hundred counties had enacted immigration sanctuary declarations.[2]

This more recent effort to help refugees was facilitated by two changes. First, the Supreme Court had ruled in the intervening years that state and local governments could not be required to carry out federal regulatory programs, opening the door to local non-cooperation with federal enforcement efforts.[3] Second, this made it easier for localities to decide not to participate in the administration of federal immigration laws without frontally flouting their legal obligations (the non-cooperation principle generally did not apply to instances of serious criminality).

As noted, the Second Amendment sanctuary movement drew its name, and arguably inspiration, from the immigrant sanctuary movement. Yet the two differ in important respects. First, immigration regulation is a strictly federal function. Gun laws exist at both the federal and state levels, although most gun laws in America are state laws, and localities stand on far less firm ground if they attempt to sidestep or contradict state law, for reasons to be discussed. Second, immigration sanctuary efforts are motivated to a great degree by the concern that local law enforcement and social service activities would be stifled if local officials aggressively targeted undocumented immigrants for purely immigration-related matters (excepting serious immigrant criminality). Local officials must rely on individuals to report crime victimization and to cooperate with police investigations—both activities that would be undercut by local police administration of immigration laws. The Second Amendment sanctuary movement possesses no similar or analogous motivation. Third, the Second Amendment sanctuary movement seeks to undermine or delegitimize the very idea of gun laws and regulations. The immigration sanctuary movement certainly objects to what it views as unduly harsh and unjust treatment of refugees seeking asylum in the U.S., but they do not pretend that they can somehow unilaterally neutralize federal immigration law by declaring it invalid. According to legal analyst Rick Su, "while the two share similarities in rhetorical framing and political strategy, they are divided by substantial differences in their legal framing. As a result, many of the legal vulnerabilities of Second Amendment sanctuaries are not shared by immigration sanctuaries."[4]

This comparison notwithstanding, the Second Amendment sanctuary movement deserves to be examined and evaluated on its own terms. To begin, Second Amendment sanctuary resolutions serve some or all of three broad purposes: to express support for gun rights, to criticize enacted or proposed gun laws, and to reserve to themselves a self-proclaimed right to judge which gun laws or possible laws apply to them through their assertion of self-defined Second Amendment rights.[5] In 2018, for example, a county in Illinois enacted a resolution vowing not to enforce "unconstitutional" gun measures then before the state legislature, including proposals to ban bump stocks, assault weapons, and large-capacity magazines (those holding more than ten rounds; see Chapter 2). A Virginia county enacted a resolution that "would oppose unconstitutional restrictions on the right to keep and bear arms." Over seventy local governments in Illinois enacted similar measures as of the start of 2020; as of the same time in Virginia, where the state legislature enacted several new gun laws, more than 120 municipalities had approved sanctuary provisions, including ninety-one of the state's ninety-five counties.[6] As of 2021, local governments in forty states have done the same. As many as seventeen states have enacted some version of these measures since the advent of the modern movement although most of those state laws did not include frontal challenges to federal law. A recent state enactment in Missouri, however, did (see discussion at the end of this chapter).[7]

These sanctuary enactments roughly conform to a longer, older, and similarly contentious (if not tendentious) anti-law movement in America, identified generally under the umbrella term nullification.

Mangling Federalism: The Doctrine of Nullification

One of the fundamental building blocks of the American political system, and an indispensable part of any Introduction to American Government course curriculum, is the principle of federalism—that governing powers are divided between a national government, on the one hand, and state governments on the other. Each maintains distinctive powers upon which the other may not encroach, and some powers are shared between the two levels of governance.[8] Yet that is not the end of the matter. Having learned the bitter lesson of weak national governance under the nation's first constitution, the Articles of Confederation, the founders inserted the Supremacy Clause in the Constitution's Article VI. It affirmed that "This Constitution, and the Laws of the United States which shall be made in Pursuance thereof . . . shall be the supreme Law of the Land." Further in the article, an additional provision noted that members of Congress, as well as those "of the several State Legislatures, and all executive and judicial Officers . . . shall be bound by Oath or Affirmation, to support this Constitution."[9] Thus, the federal Constitution and its proper laws have the final say.

The Second Amendment sanctuaries movement, in some of its iterations, challenges the tenets of federalism, as well as the supremacy of state governments over local governance units (more on that later). Such challenges are not new.

Roiling disputes early in American history challenged the idea of national supremacy. In 1798, Kentucky and Virginia declared the federal (and infamous) Alien and Sedition Acts, enacted by Congress that same year, to be null and void within their states.[10] Notably, however, neither resolution proposed any specific provisions to block enforcement of the federal law, nor did the two states attempt any such effort, and no other states adopted similar measures.[11] Within the succeeding four years, most of the offending provisions lapsed or were repealed, defusing the crisis.

A far more serious threat to federalism and the constitutional order arose in the 1820s with the nullification crisis, which ultimately helped precipitate the Civil War. At the dawn of the 1820s, the principle of nationalism was well established and widely accepted, including in the American South. But a series of economic shocks, starting with the banking Panic of 1819, hit southern states with particular force. Cotton planters were especially hard hit, nowhere worse than in South Carolina. Blame for economic hardship focused on federal protective tariffs. Rising expenses and declining income, along with escalating hostility to slavery coming mostly from the North and increasingly voiced in the U.S. Congress, fanned the movement in southern states to find a way to thwart federal law.[12]

By the end of the 1820s, these resentments found expression and focus in the theory of nullification, authored by former senator and then-vice president John C. Calhoun. Rejecting his earlier fealty to "expansive nationalism," Calhoun now formulated a theory and system of minority veto, explicated as the right of a state to veto any federal law that it concluded encroached on a state's sovereignty. Such encroachment, Calhoun argued, was incompatible with the federal Constitution, as the latter, by Calhoun's reckoning, was formulated and based on "the sovereignty of the states," not on the "unrestrained will of a majority."[13] That is, because the Constitution was in effect created by the states, according to Calhoun, the states were the ultimate sovereigns. The state veto was properly exercised by state nullification conventions. The Supreme Court, Calhoun further argued, had no power to block the action of a state's "sovereign convention."[14] In the pre-Civil War era, the nullification crisis came to a head in 1832 when a South Carolina state convention voted to nullify a federal tariff. That crisis was averted in 1833 only after Congress passed a "Force bill" authorizing President Andrew Jackson to employ the army to compel compliance with the tariff along with a second bill that lowered tariff rates. The South Carolina convention then met and repealed its tariff nullification but also voted to nullify the Force bill, even though its need no longer existed. In addition to the hated tariff, Calhoun and his allies fully embraced nullification because they viewed it as the best way to ensure the perpetuation of "the tyranny of white men over the slaves" by forestalling "a reform-minded majority in Congress" from "passing antislavery legislation."[15]

Theorists James H. Read and Neal Allen define nullification theory this way:

each individual state is fully "sovereign" and as such the final judge
of its own constitutional rights and obligations . . . consequently it
may legitimately rule that any federal act—law, regulation, judicial
decision, executive action, or treaty—is unconstitutional; and, most
important . . . it may act on this judgment by blocking the implementation of that federal act within the state's boundaries.[16]

Without relitigating the dubious merits of nullification, suffice it to say
that it fails in three fundamental respects: first, it obliterates Article VI of
the Constitution, in effect returning the nation to an approximation of the
discredited and failed Articles of Confederation; second, it was defeated by
the federal government's justified use of force in the Civil War; and third, the
addition of the Thirteenth (1865), Fourteenth (1868), and Fifteenth (1870)
Amendments to the Constitution in the years after the Civil War specifically
vested Congress with enforcement powers over the states, and with the power
to protect the residents of states from state efforts to deprive persons within
them of privileges or immunities, liberty, due process, equal protection, or the
right to vote.[17] Despite all this, nullification is a doctrine that did not, and has
not, disappeared.

In the post-World War II South, defenders of racial segregation revived
their own versions of nullification to argue that the federal government had
no right to tell the states how to govern themselves with respect to race. This
rationale took off after the landmark 1954 Supreme Court decision of *Brown
v. Board of Education* (349 U.S. 294) which ordered the racial integration
of public schools. By 1957, four southern states had passed "interposition"
resolutions (treated as a synonym for nullification; its use dates to the pre-
Civil War rise of nullification, although its meaning then was more complicated[18]) seeking in various ways to block the implementation of *Brown*. In
the face of this refusal by southern states to abide by the desegregation order,
the Supreme Court stated with unanimity and categorical clarity in *Cooper
v. Aaron* (358 U.S. 1, 17; 1958) that "constitutional rights . . . can neither be
nullified openly and directly by state legislators or state executive or judicial
officers nor nullified indirectly by them through evasive schemes."

This was hardly the first time the high court came to such a conclusion. As
early as 1809, in the case of *U.S. v. Peters* (9 U.S. 115), for example, the court
stated flatly that:

The legislature of a state cannot annul the judgments, nor determine the
jurisdiction, of the courts of the United States . . . . If the legislatures of

the several states may, at will, annul the judgments of the courts of the United States, and destroy the rights acquired under those judgments, the constitution itself becomes a solemn mockery; and the nation is deprived of the means of enforcing its laws by the instrumentality of its own tribunals. So fatal a result must be deprecated by all.

The combined efforts of the federal courts, Congress and the president all beat back the scourge of *de jure* segregation in the post-World War II era, even as racism continues to besmirch the American experiment from then to the present.

In recent years, versions of nullification resolutions have been debated and at times enacted in a handful of states to thwart the federal Affordable Care Act of 2010, environmental regulations, land use laws, the Fourteenth Amendment's birthright citizenship provision, and gun laws.[19] As mentioned at the start of this chapter, the Second Amendment sanctuary movement took off around 2018. Yet it was predated by the actions of several states. By 2012, Alaska, Arizona, Idaho, Montana, South Dakota, Tennessee, Utah, and Wyoming had enacted so-called "Firearms Freedoms" laws. These state measures claimed a state right to ignore certain federal gun laws based on the arcane argument that Congress's power to regulate interstate commerce would apply to them only as of the date these states entered the Union at the end of the nineteenth century, when the commerce power was interpreted more narrowly.[20] None of these actions actually confronted federal gun laws.

The concept of federalism is relatively easy to define, but its application in the real world of politics and policy is anything but easy, clear, or simple. There is indeed a large gray area between national and state government powers that is in constant motion. As noted in Chapter 1, the Supreme Court has in recent years restricted federal power over the states as an overreach of the commerce power and a violation of states' rights under the Tenth Amendment. No court case to date has accepted the idea that the Second Amendment sanctuary movement might find approval under the expanded view of states' rights, but it is not beyond imagining given the more sharply conservative turn of federal courts outlined in Chapter 1. That notwithstanding, however, a very different relationship exists between state governments and local governments.

State Powers and Local Governments

The Second Amendment sanctuary movement has involved a handful of state government actions, but it has flowered most prolifically among local governments. Unlike the federal–state relationship, the relationship between state and local governments is very different. The roughly ninety thousand local governments in America[21] are entirely creatures of the states within which they are located. Indeed, "local government authority is limited to those powers enumerated in the states' constitution and laws, and this authority is quite limited."[22] Thus, state governments have broad latitude to curtail or sweep aside local laws, decisions, and actions that do not conform to state law, although most state governments grant "home rule" authority to local municipalities for some circumstances and purposes.[23] Yet home rule itself "is often of little practical significance"[24] because state governments can modify it as it sees fit. Stated another way: "In the federal system, local governments have long been viewed as 'convenient agencies' or 'political subdivisions' of the state without any inherent power to act."[25] This relationship was fortified in a Supreme Court decision from over a century ago, *Hunter v. City of Pittsburgh* (207 U.S. 161, 1907).[26]

This relationship between state governments and localities has served as the basis for state enactment of gun preemption laws that bar localities from enacting any gun laws at variance with existing state laws, although preemption efforts have been levied against a variety of both liberal and conservative issue causes.[27] With respect to gun laws, in America's first three hundred years, before the rise of the preemption movement, localities often enacted their own gun laws regardless of existing state laws, without prompting any notable state government backlash.[28] But starting in the 1980s, the NRA began a concerted lobbying effort in state capitals to push the enactment of state preemption laws specifically to keep localities from enacting their own stricter gun laws. That effort proved remarkably successful, for three key reasons: state governments tend to be more politically conservative, therefore receptive to the idea; state politics is relatively low visibility, meaning that opponents were often left unaware of the effort, as was the public at large; and because the idea of preemption itself, while important, is little-known and arcane in the annals of governance.[29] At the start of the 1980s, only a handful of states had gun preemption laws in place. As of 2020, forty-five states had partial or full preemption measures restricting the enactment of local gun laws.[30] I mention preemption in the context of this consideration of Second Amendment sanctuaries not because of any effort to use preemption to thwart such measures—not that such a move might not occur in the future—but to emphasize and illustrate the one-sided legal relationship between states and localities. In one ironic twist, after Arizona enacted a sanctuary law in April 2021, the city of Tucson enacted a measure two months later saying that it would continue to enforce federal gun laws, contrary to the state law. Court action was expected.[31]

The Second Amendment Sanctuary Legislative Tide

The term Second Amendment sanctuary is said to have been coined in 2013 by the Board of Commissioners in Carroll County, Maryland in reaction to a new gun law in that state.[32] But the contemporary Second Amendment sanctuary movement dates to 2018 when Effingham County, Illinois (a rural county in southern Illinois with a population of about thirty-five thousand) enacted the first such resolution that expressly borrowed the language of the immigration sanctuary movement. According to Effingham County board member David Campbell, he had heard about another county in Illinois that had enacted a gun rights resolution but thought it might be useful to employ language that was "a little more provocative . . . . I said, well, they're creating sanctuary counties for illegals up in Chicago, why don't we just steal their word and make Effingham County a sanctuary county for firearms?" Campbell further explained that "It's not a binding law, it's to get the attention of legislators. I think there is a big disconnect—our lawmakers down here really don't have a say, they're overwhelmed by the Democrats."[33] The movement spread rapidly to other conservative counties in Illinois, all of whom sought to express their dismay at pending gun legislation then being considered by the state legislature, and in other states with Democratic-controlled legislatures, although conservative states saw similar resolution efforts. The gun measures that provoked such ire included universal background checks for gun purchases, extreme risk protection order or "red flag" laws, and assault weapons bans.[34] While this has been a grassroots movement, it has also received help from the NRA.[35]

After some paralysis in the Second Amendment sanctuary movement during the height of the COVID-19 pandemic in 2020 and early 2021, when many state and local governments stopped holding meetings, the movement again picked up momentum. By mid-2021, local governments around the country had enacted sanctuary-type provisions, although estimates vary (partly for reasons to be discussed). One count reports that about three hundred counties have adopted such measures.[36] Counts that encompass all local governments peg the number at about one thousand to twelve hundred.[37]

An advocacy website called SanctuaryCounties.com says it is "dedicated to the law-abiding, Constitution loving citizens who refuse to simply give up their Second Amendment rights." It includes counts of various conservative sanctuary-type efforts in addition to those related to the Second Amendment including opposition to abortion, to critical race theory, to COVID vaccine mandates, and support for free speech and various other constitutional rights. It also purports to maintain a rolling count of Second Amendment sanctuary counties and states, although a perusal of the site suggests that its tabulations are less than reliable. For example, a June 20, 2021 story on the site proclaims that over sixty-one percent of U.S. counties "are now Second Amendment Sanctuaries." A story adjacent to that one, dated March 24, 2021, proclaims that a "Staggering 1,188 2A Sanctuary Counties" had adopted such measures (in a different place on the website it tallies 1073 sanctuary counties). But when the larger number of 1188 is divided by the total number of counties in the country, 3141, it yields 37.8 percent. The sixty-one percent number might be calculated by including all of the counties within states that have enacted state-wide sanctuary resolutions; the difficulty here, however, is that all counties within these states may not agree with (or may be indifferent to) these resolutions. Under the aegis of state law, proponents may indeed claim that they are "covered," but that is not the same thing as an affirmative expression of support.

The entry on the SanctuaryCounties website for New York State lists four entities enacting such resolutions: three counties and one town. One of them is Wyoming County, but the accompanying narrative for the county, dated January 8, 2019, says this: "There is nothing in Resolution No. 19-021 that protects the citizens of its county or discourages legislatures from passing unconstitutional laws. To be frank it is less than the bare minimum at best." Lewis County is another of the four. The account on the website, dated February 5, 2020, describes a Lewis County board meeting where the matter was discussed, but from then until at least the middle of 2021 no such resolution was enacted.[38] This all suggests that these aggregate counts lump together a variety of resolutions and enactments that range from pledges deemed inadequate or too weak to general pledges to support the Second Amendment to specific commitments to violate existing or future gun laws with penalties for any who do not comply—and apparently even municipalities that proposed but failed to enact them.

A New Sheriff in Town

Aside from the significant number of counties with such resolutions, supporters have taken great pains to note that some county sheriffs have also embraced the idea. For example, in 2018 Washington State voters approved by initiative gun policy measures to raise the minimum age to purchase a semiautomatic rifle to twenty-one, and to increase background checks and the gun purchase waiting period to ten days. That action prompted a majority of sheriffs of the state's thirty-nine counties to declare that they would not enforce the new law, although they voiced differing perspectives on whether or how this would affect their duties.[39] During this time, the state attorney general warned the sheriffs that they could be held liable for failure to carry out the laws.[40] In a letter dated July 15, 2021, thirty-seven of thirty-nine Washington sheriffs signed a statement saying in part: "As your elected Sheriffs, we individually and collectively pledge to do everything within our power to steadfastly protect the Second Amendment and all other individual rights guaranteed by the Constitution."[41] Nowhere did the letter say or suggest that the signers would flout the law.

A 2019 Nevada law that required uniform background checks for all gun purchases prompted all seventeen elected Nevada county sheriffs to sign a letter saying that gun crime is a multi-pronged problem requiring "a myriad of approaches" to address. It further said:

> The Sheriffs of the State of Nevada are here to enforce the laws and uphold the Constitutions of this state and this country. We will do so with all persons, while still protecting our Second Amendment freedoms. The Second Amendment is important to us, and we as Sheriffs will uphold all that it stands for. We will work within the law and not succumb to perceived threats, rumor, false or malicious information to weight our decision-making process. We as Nevada Sheriffs support The Right to Bear Arms, and we will do all within our power to uphold and defend its principles.[42]

The sheriffs' statement is notable because it did not say that the sheriffs would refuse to endorse or enforce the new law, even though various outlets claimed that it did (the state background checks law was even erroneously dubbed a "gun registration law," which it is not).[43]

A letter signed by all twenty-nine sheriffs in Utah in 2021 proclaimed: "We hereby recognize a significant principle underlying the Second Amendment: the right to keep and bear arms is indispensable to the existence of a free people."[44] Beyond claiming fealty to the Second Amendment, however, the letter did not suggest any intention to violate or ignore the law. Again, a closer examination of these efforts reveals far less uniformity and zealotry regarding sanctuary-type measures than is often repeated.

Two significant cautions bracket the statements of these sheriffs. First, the statements and actions of these and other sheriffs cannot be taken as somehow representative of sheriffs throughout the country, or of law enforcement more generally. The country employs roughly 800,000 law enforcement officers, incorporating about eighteen thousand police agencies. They include personnel spanning federal law enforcement, state police, city and municipal police departments, and about three thousand county sheriffs.[45] Police in general are, politically speaking, more conservative than the population at large, owing in part (although not entirely) to the fact that they are overwhelmingly white and male, who demographically tend to be more conservative (party identification varies widely by occupation). For example, police are twice as likely to identify as Republicans than as Democrats.[46] Nevertheless, sheriffs who have aligned themselves with the sanctuary movement places them ideologically at the extreme right wing even within America's police community as a whole.

Second, county sheriffs are different from the other segments of the police community in one critical respect: in forty-six states they win office by election,[47] as opposed to other law enforcement personnel who gain their positions by appointment or hiring, often by competitive examination. No law enforcement background is normally required to run for sheriff. Thus, sheriffs by definition are political positions obtained by election subject to reelection most commonly on a four-year cycle (although occasionally two, three, or six years). In forty states, sheriff candidates run on political party labels rather than on a non-partisan basis.[48] Without question, sanctuary-embracing sheriffs see political and electoral benefit in embracing that position.

Moreover, police other than sheriffs function within an administrative hierarchy where nonpartisanship is a norm of the job. Police, after all, are charged with administering the law and public policy, not making it. Sheriffs cannot make law either, aside from the discretion and relative autonomy that comes with the job (all police retain some on-the-job discretion), but on the other hand they may find reward from voters at election time for staking out high profile, controversial, or even questionable issue positions, such as embrace of the Second Amendment sanctuary idea. One analysis notes: "the sheriff is less insulated from the public than the police chief, lacking the administrative buffer from the general public that most municipal departments have in the mayor, police commission, or city board who oversee them and appoint their chief executive."[49]

The greater conservatism of sheriffs compared to others in law enforcement is enforced by their districts and constituencies. Most counties encompass rural and small-town areas, bearing in mind that counties represent geography, not people. Indeed, "it is the unincorporated areas within those counties" that get particular attention from sheriffs because they would "otherwise be without police coverage if it were not for the sheriff's office" because "municipal police agencies are responsible for providing police services only within their incorporated municipal limits. . . . This is true even in reasonably urbanized counties, since the sheriff has sole responsibility for police services in areas of the county outside the incorporated city limits."[50] There are a few exceptions to the rural orientation of sheriffs' county jurisdictions: a handful of very large metropolitan counties like Cook County, Illinois (including Chicago) and Los Angeles County in California. But these are "anomalies in many ways from the traditional picture of the sheriff's office as it commonly exists in most counties."[51] Demographically speaking, then, sheriffs tend to represent the most politically conservative (and gun friendly) election districts in the country. It should come as no surprise, then, that they would reflect more conservative political values, even when compared with other police, and that some stake out politically inflammatory positions that are otherwise at odds with enforcing existing law.

These traits are key to understanding the extreme end point of politicized sheriffing: the so-called "Constitutional" sheriff movement. The most prominent and organized element of that movement, the Constitutional Sheriffs and Peace Officers Association (CSPOA), was founded by Richard Mack, a former Arizona sheriff. Mack gained notoriety in the 1990s when he and a sheriff from Montana, Jay Printz, sued the federal government in a challenge to the 1993 federal Brady law that required sheriffs to run background checks on prospective gun purchasers. They prevailed in the Supreme Court case of Printz v. U.S. (521 U.S. 898; 1997), in which the court ruled that the federal government cannot "commandeer" (i.e., require) states or their officials to carry out a federal program or law, although this does not prevent federal officials from carrying out gun laws in localities. Formed around 2010, the CSPOA claims about five thousand members (a different source reported the number of sheriff members as about four hundred[52]), although, as there are only about three thousand sheriffs in the country, membership is obviously open to anyone who pays the $99 annual membership fee.[53]

Sheriffs and others who adhere to the Constitutional sheriff movement believe that "in any given county, no state or federal official's interpretation .

of state or federal law is superior to that of the local sheriff."[54] Their justification for this is predicated on their own reading and interpretation of the Constitution. As Mack said, "Sheriffs standing for freedom have the responsibility to interpose—it's the 'doctrine of interposition'—whenever anybody is trying to diminish or violate the individual rights of our counties."[55] (Note the resurrection of the idea of "interposition" from the pre-Civil War era discussed earlier.) Within their counties, in other words, these sheriffs believe that their personal authority and interpretation of the Constitution countermands that of any other law enforcement entity, level or branch of government—that they reign supreme. That extends not just to gun laws of which they disapprove, but land use laws, wildlife protection laws, environmental laws, mask mandates, or any other matters they decide justify their exercise of authority.[56] They have also voiced support for the January 6, 2021 Capitol Hill rioters.[57]

The Constitutional sheriff movement traces back to the 1970s and a World War II army veteran, William Potter Gale, a self-styled "Christian Identity" minister who preached that the Constitution was a divinely inspired document designed to elevate Christian white people above Jews and Blacks. He advanced the "Posse Comitatus" movement, which perverted the old idea of law enforcement organizing civilian, deputized posses to help enforce the law, to instead organize citizens as a paramilitary group to use violence to promote armed insurrection against the government. Gale was also a founder of the "Christian Patriot" movement in the 1980s. These ideas spread to a Salt Lake City police chief, W. Cleon Skousen, who advanced the idea that the Constitution was a Christian document and that the founders were disciples of God. Mack embraced Skousen's teachings. Mack's Constitutional sheriffs idea also helped inspire a similar "county supremacy" movement where some counties have claimed control over federal lands (an obvious parallel to the Second Amendment sanctuary movement).[58]

While noting that the unique nature and traits of county sheriffs make them something of a breeding ground for these radical ideas, including the Second Amendment sanctuary movement, nothing discussed here supports the idea that most or even many sheriffs support fringe political ideas like these. Still, as a part of the American law enforcement community, when sheriffs speak up on behalf of the sanctuary movement or similar ideas, it lends them a morsel of legitimacy and a degree of attention much sought by advocates. Among such attention-getting sheriffs, former longtime Arizona sheriff Joe Arpaio is probably the most prominent. Arpaio is widely known for harsh treatment of inmates, immigrants, and persons of Latino heritage.

In 2017, he was convicted of flouting a court order to cease the racial profiling of Latinos. That same year, President Donald Trump pardoned him.

The Sanctuary Movement Comes to Upstate New York

At the start of 2019, two municipalities in New York State—Wyoming County (a rural county east of Buffalo) and the town of Grand Island (an island township in the middle of the Niagara River located between Buffalo and Niagara Falls)—enacted resolutions expressing opposition to state gun laws. The Wyoming resolution said, "the Wyoming County Board of Supervisors stands in strong opposition to any and all legislation that would intentionally violate the rights of lawful citizens that are guaranteed in the Constitution, the supreme cause of the land."[59] Even though this sentence did not mention gun rights specifically, it was said to be aimed at the prospect of new gun laws. The Grand Island resolution voiced opposition to possible new gun measures including long gun registration, social media and search engine history background checks for prospective gun buyers, and requiring liability insurance for gun owners.[60] Neither resolution suggested non-compliance with state laws, but they helped embolden those pursuing stronger and more confrontational statements, and spurred debate elsewhere upstate.

Among the earliest leaders to speak out against the idea of sanctuary resolutions were the sheriffs of upstate Montgomery and Fulton Counties. In early 2020, both sheriffs expressed unhappiness with the SAFE Act and support for Second Amendment rights, but as one said, "Under my Oath as the Fulton County Sheriff. . . I can't refuse to enforce any duly passed law which has been found Constitutional by the Courts. To do so would make myself or any other Sheriff derelict in their duties and subject to removal." The sheriff of Montgomery County said:

> Declaring the county as a Sanctuary County is basically encouraging people to not obey the law. Although there is the ability for police to use discretion, this type of behavior could become very problematic. At what point and time do others ask us to ignore other laws, for example property crimes, or sex crimes or any other law on the books that some people are not in favor of? It is simply a double-edged sword. I cannot ignore the law, nor can I turn a blind eye to others who do so. This would be considered a dereliction of my duties, and something that I would hope you would not stand for.[61]

In March 2020, the small, rural township of Solon, located in Cortland County, went further than Wyoming County and Grand Island to become the first municipality in New York to enact a resolution refusing to enforce unnamed future state gun laws.[62] Later that month, the Cortland County town of Truxton enacted a similar defiant resolution. That June, a third Cortland township, Cincinnatus, followed suit. (The population of all three townships is just over one thousand each.) When asked his reaction, Cortland County Sheriff Mark Helms said, "I understand where all these people are coming from, and I don't have an issue with it by any means . . , . But these [sanctuary] laws don't affect me . . . . It would affect local law enforcement. But they don't have local law enforcement."[63] (Helms is noting here that these local townships have no town police forces of their own to which such enactments might apply.)

Cortland County is a mostly rural county found in the geographic center of the state. Situated about thirty miles due south of Syracuse along north-south interstate Route 81, this county of about forty-seven thousand leans conservative and Republican, but thanks in large part to its one city, Cortland (population about nineteen thousand), known as the Crown City, it has been competitive at times for Democrats. In 2008 and 2012, the county voted for Barack Obama for President, but in 2016 and 2020, it went for Donald Trump. County-wide offices are usually won by Republicans, but Democrats can and do sometimes break through. Among the county's notable residents were Baseball Hall of Fame player and coach John McGraw, the 1904 Democratic presidential candidate Alton B. Parker, and rocker Ronnie James Dio.

Cortland County was established in 1808 by its separation from Onondaga County to the north. It was named after Pierre Van Cortlandt (although he never lived in the area), who served as president of the first state constitutional convention in 1777 and was the state's first lieutenant governor. Timber and agriculture were the mainstays of the county in its early years, but as water and rail transportation developed, heavy industry emerged. As with so many communities in the Northeast, its economic fortunes rose and fell with once-thriving heavy industries, although agriculture persisted and continues as an important, if declining part of the county's economic base. In the 1870s, brothers Chester and Theodore Wickwire opened a factory to produce wire cloth—think window screening—as well as nails, wire, and fencing, which rapidly became the county's largest employer. Their patent innovations helped make them enormously wealthy, and the mansions they built and occupied still line one of the city's main thoroughfares. The Wickwire Co. remained in business for almost a century.[64] Its eclipse coincided with the growth of

Smith-Corona, a division of SCM Corporation, maker of widely used typewriters. At its height in the 1970s and early 1980s, it was the area's largest employer, earning the area the title of "Typewriter Capital of the World."[65] Predictably, it was done in by international competition and the computer. Today, its largest employer is a state university campus, SUNY Cortland, my long-time employer.

Nothing in Cortland County's profile suggests that it would be a hotbed of Second Amendment sanctuary activity, except that the three townships are very rural, low population entities where a few determined voices can exert great influence. A half-dozen surrounding counties have mounted similar efforts,[66] but none has resulted in the adoption of such resolutions as of the end of 2021. In nearby Steuben County, a resolution copied after the Solon resolution was introduced in the county legislature in early 2021, but it died in committee and never came to a full vote. The county attorney called it a "non-starter."[67]

As has been true in other states, this movement was a response to debate over, and the enactment of, new gun laws in New York in 2020 and 2021, including an extreme risk protection order law, also referred to as a "red flag" law that allows family members or police to temporarily take guns from individuals deemed at imminent risk of harming themselves or others; restrictions on "ghost guns," referring to firearms without identifying serial numbers that are assembled from unmarked gun parts; and a bill to make it easier to file lawsuits against gun manufacturers who sell guns to dealers that in turn wind up in criminal hands.[68]

The other, backdrop factor for these activists is a major gun law enacted in New York in early 2013, the SAFE Act. Passed in the weeks after the 2012 Sandy Hook elementary school massacre, the SAFE Act imposed new restrictions on assault weapons, ammunition magazines, extended background checks to private gun sales, instituted a record-keeping and background check system for ammunition sales, established a five-year renewal for pistol permits, set new requirements for mental health professionals to report to authorities any persons under their care who they believe might cause serious harm to themselves or others; strengthened criminal penalties for firearms-related violations and crimes; allowed for revocation or suspension of gun licenses for those under a court-ordered order of protection; required safe gun storage in homes where anyone with a criminal background lives; and required gun owners to report stolen guns within twenty-four hours. Passage of the law provoked fury from many in the state's gun community, and "Repeal the SAFE Act" lawn signs sprung up all over. Yet the effort to repeal or weaken the law failed at every turn. Repeal efforts in the state legislature went nowhere; the law was upheld in successive federal court challenges; and polls showed consistently that a large majority of New Yorkers supported the law. Even in more conservative upstate, support and opposition split evenly.[69]

The resolutions enacted by the three Cortland County townships were nearly identical in content and form (although re-titled "Second Amendment Preservation" resolutions). All drew from a model resolution written by the Gun Owners of America,[70] a gun group formed in the 1970s by those who considered the NRA to be insufficiently hardline.[71] The resolutions expressly "recognize" the legality of the 2013 SAFE Act, but then insist that they will not recognize or abide by any future gun laws, some of which they list. They state that "all further and future Local, State, and Federal . . . Regulations regarding firearms, firearms accessories, and ammunition are a violation of the Second Amendment." They then bar any official within their jurisdictions from participating in the enforcement of any new or future gun laws. The resolutions of two of the three towns (not Truxton) allow local residents to sue anyone for violating the local laws for "declaratory and injunctive relief, damages, and attorney fees" as well as for civil fines from $500 to $2000.[72] This thoroughly odd enforcement mechanism received national attention when it appeared in the anti-abortion law enacted by Texas in 2021 that allows any citizen to file a civil suit against anyone who performs, or aids a woman seeking an abortion, with the prospect of winning at least $10,000, plus legal fees, for the action (if the defendant in such cases prevails, that person receives nothing). This private suit mechanism is "part of an emerging trend in Republican-dominated governments that find it difficult to constitutionally prohibit cultural grievances."[73]

This theory granting everyone in a jurisdiction the standing to sue as the method for enforcing law was formulated by Texas lawyer Jonathan F. Mitchell and appeared in full form in a 2018 law journal article. Echoing the path of Second Amendment sanctuary resolutions, Mitchell engineered an anti-abortion civil litigation provision that was approved by the town of Waskom, Texas in 2019. Over thirty localities adopted similar anti-abortion measures before Texas acted; the local enactments received virtually no attention.[74] The federal Justice Department immediately moved to invalidate the law. Subsequent to enactment of the Texas law, at least three states (California, Illinois, and New York) proceeded with efforts to enact laws using the same enforcement mechanic constitutionalism as the Texas anti-abortion law, but to enforce gun laws.[75]

The Sanctuary Philosophy

On September 15, 2020, SUNY Cortland's Institute for Civic Engagement hosted a panel discussion in honor of Constitution Day (September 17) on the Second Amendment sanctuaries movement. Three local government officials participated, as did I. Two of the participants were architects of the local resolutions: Solon Town Supervisor Stephen A. Furlin, and Truxton Town Councilperson Gus Wehbe. Neither are lawyers or constitutional scholars, but both offered very thoughtful and detailed expressions of their philosophy and are thus worthy of extended examination.[76]

Mr. Furlin began by identifying the Second Amendment as "a God-given constitutional right," and also invoked the Fourth and Fourteenth Amendments, all of which, he said, are "important to our freedom." The idea of a "God-given constitutional right" would seem to be something of a contradiction because civil law is made by political leaders, not clerics, but it echoes the belief of some that the founders were divinely inspired or that the document itself somehow came from God (for example, this is a key tenet of the Latter-Day Saints, also known as the Mormon religion[77]). He then said that the New York Constitution "reads the same way" as the U.S. Constitution, but that is not so, in that the state constitution does not have a Second Amendment-type provision (one of six states that does not). It does include provisions pertaining to the state militia. Furlin then said: "Every time you turn around New York State has yet another law infringing on our rights . . . . The state spends millions of dollars of taxpayers' money restricting legal law-abiding gun owners." These gun laws, he said, "are written with New York City in mind with no consideration for anyone outside of New York City." This reflects two fundamental arguments of state gun rights activists: that any gun law is a violation of gun rights, and that state gun laws are written to address city problems that do not fit upstate gun habits, needs, or problems. The rural–urban/upstate–downstate split has been a defining feature of state politics for well over a century, as is true for states across the country from California to Florida to Illinois (where upstate is urban and downstate rural) to Oregon and Washington State (where the urban–rural divide is west versus east). Just as there are upstaters dissatisfied with state gun laws, so too are there downstaters no less unhappy with other state laws. Gun laws, of course, are obviously not per se unconstitutional; state gun laws have withstood legal challenges[78]; and the idea that gun laws and gun rights are somehow incompatible or mutually exclusive is an artifact of the hyper-charged gun politics of the last few decades. As our own history shows, in most of American history gun laws and gun rights were perfectly compatible.[79] Furlin then echoes Thomas Jefferson when he says that "local governments can play a huge role in protecting the rights of the people" because that "is where your voice can and does get heard—not Albany [the state capital]," sidestepping the fact that state governments are elected as well. He proceeds to argue that he is upholding the oath of office that he and all state and local government officials are required to take by "refus[ing] to participate in the enforcement of unconstitutional restrictions on the Second Amendment." Furlin then quotes the oath of office required of all officials: "I do solemnly swear (or affirm) that I will support the constitution of the United States, and the constitution of the State of New York, and that I will faithfully discharge the duties of the office of ___, according to the best of my ability." Furlin wants to have his cake and eat it too: claiming he is upholding his oath of office by pledging to violate valid state and federal law in refusing to enforce it.

Gus Wehbe's statement reflected similar "rights talk" themes. His motivating concern: "the fear of losing our Second Amendment altogether." The familiar slippery slope argument animates his concern that the right is being whittled away "one little chip at a time" with "the ultimate goal . . . the abolishment of the Second Amendment." Wehbe sees the solution to gun violence as consisting only of increasing punishments for those who commit crimes with guns—measures that already exist in law. "Gun laws on law abiding citizens," he added, "is not the solution. Criminals by definition do not go through background checks . . . You cannot stop an evil person, intent on harm, with more gun laws." Here Wehbe restates one of the most frequently repeated slogans of the gun movement—yet it is an exemplar of how gun laws are criticized for traits inherent in the nature of all law and policy that are not questioned for any other kind of law. One might similarly argue, for example, that mandatory seat belt laws penalize good drivers. Yet that law, like any, is predicated on the fundamental proposition that the law must apply to everyone, good and reckless drivers alike. Even though most people will never suffer a serious accident, possible harm cannot be foreseen, and seat belt laws are a vanishingly small price to pay for fewer highway injuries and deaths. The same can be said of gun laws, or any laws designed to protect the health, safety, and welfare of citizens. Wehbe also contemplates a world that can be neatly divided into "law abiding citizens" and "evil persons." But that bears no relationship to the world in which we live. Good people do bad things; bad people do good things; and how, exactly, can mere mortals divine, before the fact, good versus evil people? And what of people unidentifiable as "evil" who wind up doing bad things, whether by mistake, accident, momentary rage, or calculation? Such judgments incorporate a task far beyond any government. Its goal is far more limited: to craft public policies that deter, proscribe, and sanction behavior deemed inimical to society. As for background checks, nearly four million gun purchases have been blocked since the federal Brady background check law was enacted in 1993.[80] Obviously, people who want guns but shouldn't have them do try to obtain them legally. When they pursue illegal means, at least they must pursue a path that is outside of the law and therefore more risky, less certain, and more precarious. Finally, Wehbe says that New York's gun laws "go above the Constitution." And why, he asks, do New Yorkers "have less [gun] rights than the residents, let's say, of Ohio?" The answer, to return to an earlier theme in this chapter, is federalism. State gun laws do indeed vary widely among the states, as is true of much state policy. In the absence of stricter, standardized federal law, it is all but inevitable.

Finally, dissatisfied local government leaders like Furlin and Wehbe in New York might seek legal shelter for their efforts in the fact that the state Constitution assigns local governments seemingly expansive "home rule" authority to enact home rule legislation that protects "government, protection, order, conduct, safety, health and well-being of persons or property therein."[81] Nevertheless, the state maintains full authority to supervise and preempt any such local regulations, a power endorsed by state court rulings.[82]

Conclusion: Why Second Amendment Sanctuary Laws Matter

The gun laws that have provoked the ire of sanctuary adherents, including red flag laws, uniform background checks, and restrictions on assault weapons and large capacity magazines, have existed for years, are widely popular, and have withstood past legal challenges. One might argue, with no little irony, that the anger and extreme reaction of the sanctuary movement exists, in part or whole, precisely because of the relative modesty of these measures. It has indeed led sanctuary adherents to embrace the absolutist (and absolutely unfounded) notion that any and all gun laws violate the Second Amendment. At bottom, sanctuary adherents have mounted a movement based on the simple fact that they just don't like gun laws. Beyond that, one recent study concludes that this movement has an identifiable race basis, meaning that these resolution carve out what the researchers label a "White sanctuary.... an imagined safe space—a space of impunity—that legitimizes and normalizes White prerogatives."[83]

The evaluation of nullification by theorists Read and Allen is a no less appropriate diagnosis of the sanctuary movement: "Nullification's seductive appeal is that it promises faster results than the long, patient work of winning national elections and convincing national majorities. Rather than persuading those who live and vote in other states, one can ignore them and simply act— but in ways that nevertheless affect those whom one has ignored."[84]

Many have argued that Second Amendment sanctuary measures are largely political theater—resolutions that are only symbolic expressions of unhappiness with gun laws, even those resolutions that seek to penalize those who might try to enforce federal or state gun laws. Symbolism is of course very much a part of this movement, but it is far more than that. As one advocate said in 2019, "We've gotten past the symbolic stage. We're standing up for ourselves."[85]

First, the movement has undergone statutory and political escalation. Initial resolutions that were limited to expressions of disapproval have yielded to increasingly aggressive measures that create the conditions for an eventual legal if not actual confrontation between dueling authorities. One town supervisor in Truxton who voted against the sanctuary resolution noted that while his town did not have a police force, it did have a town judge. Supervisor Lloyd Sutton, who voted against the resolution, worried that this local law could put a local judge in an impossible position: having to uphold state law but also a contradictory local sanctuary law. That, in turn, could breed confusion about what laws apply and under what circumstances.[86]

A more extreme example of this escalation comes from Missouri, where its governor, Republican Mike Parson, signed into law the Second Amendment Preservation Act, which took effect at the end of August 2021. It bars police in the state from enforcing federal gun laws. Officers violating the law can be fined up to $50,000. Alarms were immediately raised that the law would keep police officers from testifying in federal court against gun offenders, using federal resources to solve local gun crimes, or even coordinating with federal authorities to interdict illegal gun trafficking. One city police chief was so appalled that the new law would keep officers from seizing weapons during arrests or interceding to stop suicides that he resigned from his position. A 1996 federal law allows authorities to take guns from those under a restraining order for stalking or threatening an intimate partner or those convicted of domestic violence. Many states have equivalent state laws, but Missouri does not, meaning that the new state law penalizes officers trying to protect victims under the federal law. (In 2018, Missouri had the second highest rate of domestic violence homicide in the nation.) State and local law enforcement who traditionally worked with the federal Bureau of Alcohol, Tobacco, Firearms and Explosives, the FBI, the U.S. Marshals Service, and the Drug Enforcement Administration ended their collaborations, including those involving gun and drug crimes. State and local access to federal crime-related data, police reports, and investigative records was also shut down. In the city of Columbia, the local police department ended access to a federal gun tracing national ballistics system that it had used by local law enforcement agencies over six thousand times in criminal investigations in the previous three years. The state attorney general withdrew from over twenty federal violent crime cases, and the state Highway Patrol stopped working with a joint task force with the ATF.[87]

Some traditionally supportive groups were put off by the law. The Missouri Sheriffs' Association worked against the bill's enactment. Even though the NRA has been a booster of Second Amendment sanctuary measures, it did not support the Missouri law, although the legislation did receive major backing from a far-right political activist, Aaron Dorr. Dorr and his family run a group of far-right non-profit organizations based in Iowa that are known for their embrace of causes including opposition to abortion and to COVID-19 regulations. Dorr and his groups are widely known for fiery rhetoric and extremist positions that are key to its fundraising activities.[88] Responding to numerous criticisms of the law, Governor Parson conceded a few months after signing the law that it needed work and "corrections."[89]

Second, law enforcement and judicial confusion is not the end point. In states where anti-government zealots hold more local sway, the prospect of armed confrontations between state or national law enforcement and local law officials, perhaps with armed civilians in the mix, are not merely hypothetical.

The Constitutional sheriffs movement described in this chapter epitomizes a template for intergovernmental violence. Perhaps none of these sheriffs will ever directly confront contrary state or federal law or authority, despite their bellicose rhetoric. They surely do, however, contribute to the energizing of extremist anti-government groups who have openly and even violently challenged the legitimacy of the government and its authority,[90] such as extremist rancher Cliven Bundy who has successfully bullied the federal Bureau of Land Management over his illegal cattle grazing on federal lands despite an armed standoff against federal agents in 2014.[91] In 2016, armed extremists took over the Malheur National Wildlife Refuge in southeast Oregon after a long-simmering conflict with federal authorities, insisting that control of the federal refuge be given to local authorities. One of the armed protestors was killed by federal agents as he reached for his gun. In 2018, President Trump pardoned the two men whose earlier conviction of arson had sparked the protest.[92] These incidents did not directly involve elected sheriffs but are the logical consequence of the escalating and emboldened claims of the Second Amendment sanctuary movement.

Third, as if it needs to be said, the political system offers abundant legal and peaceful means to register objections to, or seek change in, existing laws and policies. The underlying argument of and cases in the other chapters in this book examine legal, if questionable efforts to expand the definition of gun rights through institutional means. The key feature of this chapter that distinguishes it from the rest is that the sanctuary movement, in at least some of its forms, is that it crosses the rule of law line, as did its antecedent nullification movement from early in the country's history. Obviously, states and localities have every right to endorse support for the Bill of Rights, or to register policy objections to existing or proposed law. A bright line is crossed, however, when localities insist through enactment that they will ignore or flout law that otherwise applies to them or punishes those who try to follow existing gun laws.

Fourth, as if it needs to be said, officeholders who so openly flout the law, even if only in rhetoric, subvert the idea of law. Several state attorneys general have responded to sanctuary resolutions in their states by announcing that they expect gun laws to be enforced and that they would act appropriately toward any non-complying localities. Under federalism, states like Missouri may have adequate legal grounds to enact at least some sanctuary-type measures, although the Missouri law was immediately challenged in court. But as noted, local governments, where the sanctuary movement has mostly flowered, do not possess any similar constitutional standing. Shibboleths about the rule of law abound, but one among many bears repeating. As Supreme Court Justice Louis Brandeis wrote nearly a century ago, "In a government of laws, existence of the government will be imperiled if it fails to observe the law scrupulously. Our Government is the potent, the omnipresent teacher. For good or for ill, it teaches the whole people by its example. Crime is contagious. If the Government becomes a lawbreaker, it breeds contempt for law; it invites every man to become a law unto himself; it invites anarchy."[93]

6

Conclusion

NAVIGATING THE GUN FORK IN THE ROAD

ON THE MORNING of August 9, 1910, New York City Mayor William J. Gaynor boarded the steamship liner Kaiser Wilhelm der Grosse, moored at the Hoboken dock, to embark on a month-long vacation to Europe. He had little more than stepped on board when a disgruntled former city docks employee, James J. Gallagher, shot the mayor once in the neck with a concealed pistol, seriously wounding him. Gallagher fired three times, also wounding a second person. By his own account, Gallagher held the mayor responsible for the loss of his dockworker job two months earlier.[1] Gaynor survived the assassination attempt, but never fully recovered his health, dying in 1913.

A photographer chanced to take a photo of the stricken mayor seconds after the shooting. Standing directly behind the mayor in the photo was Robert Todd Lincoln, the only surviving child of Abraham Lincoln, who was infamously struck down by an assassin's bullet in 1865 (the son was not in the theater at the time). In 1881, Lincoln was entering Washington D.C.'s Baltimore and Potomac train station trying to catch up with President James A. Garfield, under whom he was serving as Secretary of War. Lincoln was about forty feet away when the president was shot by assassin Charles Guiteau, a frustrated office-seeker. After lingering more than two months, Garfield died. In 1901, as he was traveling back to Chicago, Lincoln stopped in Buffalo to pay a visit to the Pan-American Exposition. As he was exiting the train, Lincoln was handed a telegram saying that President William McKinley had been shot earlier that day at the Exposition while shaking hands in a receiving line. The assassin was an anarchist named Leon Czolgosz. Lincoln immediately paid a visit to the private home where the wounded president was resting after surgery.[2] McKinley died a week later. One might say that the specter of assassination seemed to haunt the president's son. All were killed by concealed handguns.

The assassination attempt against Gaynor heightened already growing calls for the enactment of a state handgun law. New York City, in particular, had witnessed rising gun violence since around the turn of the century, as did cities around the country. Newspapers regularly printed stories of gun-fueled mayhem, including a bloody tong war among the city's Chinese population and violence tied to the Black Hand (forerunner of the Mafia) in the Italian community.[3]

In January 1911, a noted novelist, David Graham Phillips, was shot by Fitzhugh Coyle Goldsborough, a "demented violinist," in the area of Gramercy Park in New York City.[4] The shooter then turned his gun on himself. Both died.[5] A few days later, the city Coroner's Office reported that gun homicides had increased by half in the previous year, and the calls for a tough new pistol law increased.[6]

Within weeks, the State Legislature began hearings on what would become known as the Sullivan Law, named after the bill's sponsor, State Senator Timothy Sullivan, a Tammany Hall politico who had staked out a position in favor of a new state gun law the previous year.[7] Sullivan's bill passed by lopsided margins in both houses of the State Legislature and took effect on September 1, 1911. It established statewide regulation for the purchase, ownership, and carrying of pistols and other concealed weapons by requiring that handguns be licensed to own and carry. Gun dealers were required to sell pistols only to those with a valid permit.[8] Unlicensed carrying was made a felony under an amendment enacted in 1913. This amendment also established the "good cause/proper cause" standard for issuing licenses.[9]

As some have noted, suspicion and hostility toward recent immigrant communities was undoubtedly part of the motivation for this early twentieth century handgun law reform.[10] Racism and ethnic animus was woven into the fabric of the time, but by itself does not explain the adoption of the Sullivan law for two reasons. First, the State Legislature enacted a different gun law that was aimed squarely at immigrants in 1905 that made it illegal for non-citizens to own guns. The law said: "No person not a citizen of the United States, shall have or carry firearms or dangerous weapons in any public place at any time."[11] Second, the Sullivan law applied uniformly and statewide to all prospective and actual pistol owners. If the law was applied more harshly against members of ethnic or immigrant communities, as it likely was, nothing in the law itself bore responsibility for discriminatory implementation. The law itself, however, cannot be denigrated or dismissed as a mere artifact of racism. The lesson of this period was the same as that of the modern era: particularly heinous crimes and assassinations focused public attention and heightened calls for legislative action addressing the gun problem.

The Sullivan law, today found in Section 400 of the state penal code,[12] has survived court challenges and efforts to repeal. It made New York one of nine states as of 2021 to have a "may issue" handgun permit law,[13] meaning that applicants must state affirmative reasons ("proper cause") for wanting to own and carry a handgun. Local authorities then gather information and evaluate the reasons offered. They have the discretion to reject the application based on discretionary factors like character. After more than a century on the books, it is long fully integrated into the fabric of handgun ownership in the state. It is also a law with which I have personal acquaintance.[14]

But that status quo was abruptly disrupted in April 2021 when the Supreme Court agreed to take up a challenge to the state law in *New York State Rifle & Pistol Association (NYSRPA) v. Bruen*. Even though the law had been upheld in federal court as recently as 2012 (the Supreme Court declined to hear an appeal of that lower court ruling),[15] as I argue in this book, everything is different in 2021, at least with respect to gun policy.

On its face, the high court is simply addressing a question many consider importantly unanswered: whether Second Amendment gun rights apply to public gun carrying (aside from transportation, law enforcement, the military, etc.). As I argued in Chapter 1, lower federal court rulings have come to a reasonable balance on this general question, having established that every state must provide for some kind of public gun carrying (even though that contradicts America's gun law history, when gun carrying was strictly regulated or barred in every state but three by the start of the twentieth century[16]), but that the states may retain discretion as to the degree to which that carrying can be regulated, with states like New York among those that have stricter standards.

The overriding significance of the Supreme Court's decision to hear this case is the fact that it decided to do so. In principle, the court could uphold the law, rule narrowly against it, or rule more broadly to strike it down, implicating other "may issue" state laws.[17] Any prudent court observer would agree that making predictions about court outcomes is a fraught enterprise. In this instance, however, given the makeup of the current court and the argument of this book, the chances that it agreed to hear the case in order to uphold it are, frankly, zero. Put another way, the mere existence of this case is stark testimony to the vitality and zealotry of the effort to significantly expand gun rights beyond the standard set out in the 2008 *Heller* case in the manner examined in this book, even when that includes upending New York's long settled state gun license policy. To be clear, this is not an argument against disturbing the law simply because it has existed for more than a century. Rather, the law is eminently defensible because if its viability, practicality, and sensibility, all of which have long been established.[18] And no coherent understanding of America's gun past offers any justification for overturning it now. History aside, considerable research and evidence supports the efficacy of stricter gun permitting laws. For example, states with weaker pistol permitting laws have higher rates of handgun homicides[19] and higher rates of violent crime (finding a thirteen to fifteen percent rise in violent crime when states moved from strict to permissive gun carry laws)[20] than those with stronger laws. States with carry laws like that of New York's were found to have a seventeen percent lower gun homicide rate in large cities.[21] Higher public gun ownership is correlated with a three times higher homicide rate of law enforcement officers.[22] Weak permit states also have higher incidents of gun thefts, accidental gun injuries, and deaths, including suicides.[23] A study of Illinois found that firearm homicide rates increased sharply after it passed a permissive carry law in 2014.[24] Purely as a matter of public policy, the government has an abiding interest in weeding out people who simply ought not to have pistol permits.

Consistent with the arguments in this book, on June 23, 2022, the Supreme Court struck down New York state's concealed gun carry law in NYSRPA v. Bruen (https://www.supremecourt.gov/opinions/slipopinion/21). In a sweeping 6-3 decision authored by Justice Clarence Thomas, along with the votes of the five other conservative court justices, it ruled that the Second Amendment protects "an individual's right to carry a handgun for self-defense outside the home." It also said that states "may continue to require licenses for carrying handguns for self-defense," but that this licensing must follow the "shall issue" rules found in many states, meaning that the license must be granted unless the applicant falls into the narrow categories of applicants barred from gun ownership, including felons, those adjudged mentally incompetent, and similar restrictions. The majority based its conclusion on its reading of gun law history, asserting that there was "little evidence of an early American practice of regulating public carry by the general public." As discussed throughout this book, the court again badly distorts history in order to justify its Originalist orientation. In the dissent authored by Justice Stephen Breyer, joined by Justices Sotomayor and Kagan, he takes the majority opinion to task for failing to examine the actual operation of the New York carry law, for focusing solely on history and therefore failing to consider contemporary government and public policy interest in gun laws, and for "ignoring an abundance of historical evidence supporting regulations restricting the public carriage of firearms."

Gun Policy is No Anomaly

We have examined a single policy issue: gun policy. But the concerted press by conservative gun rights activists in law and politics to significantly broaden the definition of those rights is indeed part of a larger movement from the political right to push or redefine rights in many areas in a more conservative direction. This book can thus be taken as a case study, if not exemplar, of that larger movement. Abundant writing has examined similar sharp right turns in law, policy, and politics in areas including abortion, civil rights and the right to vote, expansions of religious rights, restrictions on the right of individuals to sue corporations or other entities, and efforts to curtail if not dismantle governmental administrative structures and powers.[25]

Some of these efforts to push the law to the right have received extensive national attention, including abortion and voting rights. Others fall below the radar screens of most Americans, even though their consequences for the direction of the country are no less profound. As for the specific subjects covered in this book, most of what is examined here has received scant public attention. For example, even though the Second Amendment sanctuary movement has been active for several years in forty states, precious little attention has been given to it or to the emergent enforcement mechanism of inviting and allowing private citizens to sue government officials who attempt to enforce existing state or federal gun laws. This mechanism received sudden national attention when it was incorporated in the Texas anti-abortion law enacted in 2021 that allowed private citizens to sue anyone connected with an effort to help a woman obtain an abortion (discussed in Chapter 5). In an explainer article appearing in the *New York Times* at the time of the law's enactment, it posed the question: "Are there other laws that use the same mechanism?" The article's misplaced reply to its own question: "Not really."[26]

The Lessons of Our Gun Law Past

An additional and primary theme and methodology of this book centers on a close excavation and examination of our gun law history—not for the sake of constitutional Originalism, a notion that, as I argued in Chapter 1, collapses of its own dead weight—but because history always matters. We cannot, and should not, be ruled by the past, yet we must understand our past as best we can discern it, to both know ourselves and to inform the present. These goals are both necessary and noble. The other, related methodology has been to examine each case from the lens of public policy.

The debate over restricting assault weapons and large capacity ammunition magazines dissected in Chapter 2, perhaps the most contentious contemporary gun policy idea examined here, has a little-known past that long predates the assault weapons controversy that emerged in the 1980s. While it is well known that fully automatic weapons were regulated by the federal government in the National Firearms Act of 1934, less well known is that a majority of the states enacted their own measures actually barring such weapons throughout the 1920s and early 1930s. Less well known still is the fact that between eight and eleven states similarly restricted or barred semi-automatic weapons during this same period. Contrary to the sophistic claims of some gun rights advocates that semi-automatic weapons were somehow common or widely known, and by inference available, hundreds of years ago, reliable multishot hand-held firearms did not achieve anything like meaningful circulation until after the Civil War, thanks to Samuel Colt, his competitors, and the war that brought millions of men under arms. As multi-shot firearms, and people carrying them, spread in the South and frontier West, so did laws barring or restricting their concealed (and sometimes open) carrying.[27] As handguns became more common in the population toward the end of the nineteenth century in urban areas, crime rose, as did political pressure to restrict both civilian gun carrying and various weapons through changes in public policy. In other words, gun regulations emerged when new weapons or new weapons technologies emerged posing a threat or danger to public safety. As this and the rest of the chapters show, this cycle is not new or limited to the last few decades but has existed throughout our country's gun history. Commenting on the history of the regulation of fully automatic weapons, for example, an article in the *Commercial Law Journal* observed: "When machine guns came to play a prominent part in gang warfare, it was apparent that new legislative prohibitions would have to be set up."[28] That article appeared in 1932.

A similar pattern revealed itself regarding restrictions on ammunition magazines. In data compiled and presented here for the first time in Chapter 2, roughly half of the states regulated or even barred multi-shot ammunition feeding devices (and sometimes any weapons that could accommodate them) as they began to filter into criminal and civilian hands after World War I. The widespread enactment of these regulations was accompanied by virtually no controversy. Surely the political leaders of the time would be dumbstruck by the fierce vituperation that accompanies any contemporary discussion over the enactment of similar regulations that, as the chapter shows, were common a century ago.

The story of gun silencers presents a more compressed, but comparable, example of the relationship between changing gun technology and public policy. Calls to keep them out of civilian hands came almost as soon as the Maxim silencer became available. And the cause for concern was justified, as Chapter 3 details from an examination of the historical record. The sampling of abundant contemporaneous news stories reporting on criminal silencer use in the early 1900s underscores the safety problem posed by silencers. Here, too, early regulatory efforts were mounted. From the first through fourth decades of the twentieth century, roughly a third of the states outlawed silencers, with the federal government regulating them nationwide in 1934. Modern gun activists seeking to roll back the existing federal regulation of silencers in the name of protecting shooters' hearing mostly reflect historical amnesia concerning silencers' problematic past. Gun owners have a legitimate interest in protecting their hearing. Yet the noise produced by firearms serves an essential de facto safety function. Fortunately, in the modern era other remedies exist for those gun owners disinclined to file the necessary paperwork to obtain a silencer under current federal law.

The arming and militarization of some political protests within the past decade has been framed by its defenders as the simple public expression of Second Amendment rights, insofar as many states allow for such carrying. But public gun carrying during demonstrations, rallies, and other similar events is barely about that. The Chapter 4 excavation, compilation, and analysis of early laws restricting public weapons brandishing and display demonstrates that such acts do violence to, and are a direct assault on, peaceful assembly, public order, and safety. The legal record from Middle Ages Britain to early American colonies up through the twentieth century leaves no doubt on that score. Contemporary advocates of gun carrying at public demonstrations have met considerable success at reframing this criminal behavior as a matter of constitutional right, or at best an ambiguous interface between the First and Second Amendments. But reframing cannot obliterate hundreds of years of legal history and criminal law. Make no mistake: public gun carrying at demonstrations is all about intimidation. It has little to nothing to do with real constitutional gun rights, and everything to do with disruption of the public order. Pretending it to be otherwise changes nothing, except maybe political optics.

Speaking of political optics, the Second Amendment sanctuary movement on its face seems an entirely new movement—scarcely a decade old, apparently unconnected to America's legal past. Yet Chapter 5 excavates the clear line from this current movement back to the nullification doctrine of the pre-Civil War era. Even though one might have thought that nullification was put to rest by the Civil War, this is one zombie that will not die. Yes, nullification and its twentieth century civil-rights-era equivalent were about preserving slavery and racial segregation, whereas the Second Amendment sanctuary movement is—its advocates would claim—about preserving or enhancing gun rights. But their commonality is their shared defective methodology. Don't like some existing law? Let's just call it null and void, then. Skeptics of this movement who dismiss its nullification tactics as nothing more than political theater or symbolic politics misjudge the full consequences of this still-evolving movement.

A "Disfavored" Right?

Chapter 1 examined the claim coming from some members of the Supreme Court, led by Justice Clarence Thomas, and a growing chorus of supporters, that the Second Amendment in the post-*Heller* era had been treated "cavalierly," as "a disfavored right," a "second class right," or as a "constitutional orphan," especially as compared with other Bill of Rights protections. I argued against that claim and argued further that Thomas and others had not offered any evidence to support this proposition, aside from the fact that courts had mostly upheld existing gun laws—an outcome with which they obviously disagreed. The analysis offered in this book examining in detail the history, law, and policy of the regulation of assault weapons, ammunition magazines, silencers, brandishing laws, and the Second Amendment sanctuary movement, provide testimony and evidence that refutes the "disfavored right" argument. If these chapter case studies demonstrate anything, it is that governance and policymaking is all about the balancing of rules and rights; that the rough balances struck in each instance in our own gun history vindicate the regulatory regimes of each (with the brandishing and sanctuaries movements new efforts to disrupt that balance); and that dissatisfaction with the current state of gun policy from gun rights advocates is a matter of policy unhappiness, not the deprivation or denigration of rights.

The Gun Policy Fork in the Road

The first chapter in this book set out the gun dilemma facing the country: the swelling of federal judicial ranks with extremely conservative jurists whose fealty to an expansive interpretation of gun rights was virtually a prerequisite for nomination to the courts. This means not merely upholding the Supreme Court's gun rights definition as set out in *D.C. v. Heller* in 2008 (Gun Rights 1.0), but also expanding it far beyond the court's definition in that case into what is dubbed here Gun Rights 2.0. As we have seen, that expansion is also occurring outside of the courts, spilling into extremist grassroots behavior seen in armed escalations of brandishing and into local government jurisdictions around the country in the Second Amendment sanctuary movement. Yet the country at large abhors gun violence, supports stronger gun laws, and has little relative awareness of much that is examined in this book.

There is reason to believe that this divergence between public opinion and court behavior is starting to take a toll on court legitimacy and prestige, although the treatment of gun policy is likely only a small part of this larger trend. A September 2021 Gallup poll reported the lowest approval rating for the Supreme Court—forty percent—it had ever recorded since it began polling on the subject in 2000.[29] Another poll taken at about the same time noted a similar significant drop, in this case from sixty percent approval in July 2021 to forty-nine percent in September.[30] To be sure, this dip may be short-term. In the aftermath of the disputed 2000 presidential election and the Supreme Court's controversial decision ending the Florida presidential election recount process, the court also took a public beating for what was seen as a nakedly partisan ruling, and some predicted that the court's prestige would never recover. Yet it did recover.[31] In that instance, however, the drop in public confidence was keyed to a single court decision, not a longer and more systematic ideological shift across many areas of law and policy. Current members of the court seemed sufficiently concerned about this drop in confidence and charges that the court is motivated more by politics than by law that three members spoke out in defense of the court during this time.[32]

The goal of the post-*Heller* gun rights movement has been to expand the parameters of gun rights by redefining Second Amendment rights as existing, in effect, whenever a gun, or gun accessory, comes into contact with a human hand. Assault weapons' ownership? Covered by the Second Amendment. Large capacity ammunition magazine possession? Covered by the Second Amendment. Gun silencer ownership? Ditto. Public gun brandishing and display? Merely a benign expression of Second Amendment rights. Second Amendment sanctuary resolutions? Same thing.

Perhaps the high court will not ultimately press ahead with a major expansion of gun rights in the way or to the degree suggested in this book, whether because of concerns over court legitimacy, or lack of supporting evidence, or lack of will. But this new gun rights movement is much broader than, and extends far beyond, the Supreme Court alone, and the wheels of this movement, in all the areas examined in the earlier chapters, continue to turn.

Gun rights activists advancing these respective causes recognize that the legal environment has changed in a direction favorable to them, thanks to the rightward shift in the courts chronicled in Chapter 1, and of course a similar shift in the Republican party where the movement has made its home. As Tammany Hall politician and philosopher George Washington Plunkitt noted more than a century ago to explain his career pursuit of what he called "honest graft": "I seen my opportunities and I took 'em."[33] The clearest explanation and justification for this post-*Heller* gun rights push isn't history, constitutional law, or sound public policy, all of which contradict the professed basis of their efforts. The historical lesson in each case is a story of regulation, not opposition to it. Rather, it is old fashioned political opportunism, gussied up in an imagined constitutional indignity. Mr. Plunkitt would certainly have understood.

About the Author

ROBERT J. SPITZER (PhD Cornell, 1980) is Distinguished Service Professor Emeritus of Political Science at the State University of New York at Cortland. He is the author of sixteen books, including *The Presidency and Public Policy*, *The Right to Life Movement and Third Party Politics*, *The Presidential Veto*, *The Bicentennial of the U.S. Constitution*, *President and Congress*, *Media and Public Policy*, *Politics and Constitutionalism*, *The Right to Bear Arms*, *The Presidency and the Constitution*, *Saving the Constitution from Lawyers*, *Gun Control*, *The Encyclopedia of Gun Control and Gun Rights*, *We the People: Essentials Edition*, *The Politics of Gun Control* (8th ed.), and *Guns across America* (Oxford University Press). He is also Series Editor for the book series *American Constitutionalism* for SUNY Press, and the *Presidential Briefing Book* series for Routledge. In 2003, he received the SUNY Chancellor's Award for Excellence in Scholarship. Spitzer is the author of over seven hundred articles, papers, and op-eds appearing in many books, journals, newspapers, and websites on a variety of American politics subjects. He served as President of the Presidents and Executive Politics Section of the American Political Science Association and as a member of the New York State Commission on the Bicentennial of the U.S. Constitution. He has testified before Congress on several occasions. Spitzer is often quoted and interviewed by American and international news outlets, including *The Today Show*, *Good Morning America*, *ABC Nightly News*, the *PBS News Hour*, MSNBC's *All In with Chris Hayes*, CNN, NPR's *Fresh Air with Terry Gross*, *The Diane Rehm Show*, and *1A*; the documentary films *Guns and Mothers* (PBS, 2003), *Under the Gun* (Katie Couric Film Company, Epix, 2016), and *The Price of Freedom* (Flatbush Pictures/Tribeca Films, 2021); and media outlets in over twenty countries. His articles have appeared in such publications as the *New York Times*, *The Washington Post*, the *Los Angeles Times*, *CNN.com*, the *New York Daily News*, the *Chicago Tribune*, *Time Magazine*, *Newsweek*, *U.S. News and World Report*, and *Salon*, among others. He was also a visiting professor at Cornell University for thirty years.

Notes

CHAPTER I

1. While criminals took to sawing off most of the barrel of a traditional shotgun for its devastating spray effect, such weapons were at one time manufactured, such as by Winchester in 1898 when it was dubbed a "riot gun." These weapons also appeared in World War I as useful in trench warfare. Lee Kennett and James LaVerne Anderson, *The Gun in America* (Westport, CT: Greenwood Press, 1975), 202.

2. Kennett and Anderson, *The Gun in America*, 192–193; Patrick J. Charles, *Armed in America* (Amherst, NY: Prometheus Books, 2018), 194–199; Adam Winkler, *Gunfight* (New York: W.W. Norton, 2011), 208–210.

3. Robert J. Spitzer, *The Politics of Gun Control*, 8th ed. (New York: Routledge, 2021), 194–195. The 1927 federal law was limited in scope because it did not regulate the mailing of firearms by private express services.

4. In addition to the eight states enacting restrictions three more included statutory language that might have had the effect of restricting semi-automatic weapons in addition to fully automatic ones. Robert J. Spitzer, "Gun Law History in the United States and Second Amendment Rights," *Law and Contemporary Problems* 80 (2017): 67–71.

5. Genesa C. Cefali and Jacob D. Charles, "An Overview of Gun Registration in U.S. History?" Unpublished manuscript. Some states enacted registration and permitting laws before the 1920s. According to the authors, when added together over two-thirds of the states at one point or another enacted either or both types of measures.

6. I use the term "ultra-conservative" here to indicate that this new generation of lawyers, jurists, and other allied gun rights political activists have pushed the boundary of traditional conservatism significantly beyond its defined meaning in the post-Reagan (much less pre-Reagan) era. Evidence offered in this chapter provides empirical support for this claim. The fact that the post-*Heller* gun rights movement examined in this book is seeking to expand the definition of gun rights

far beyond the standard set out in the 2008 *Heller* Supreme Court case—a phenomenon examined in and throughout this book—questions whether in fact the label "conservatism" as it is traditionally used is even appropriate or accurate. Despite this, however, I will simply use the term "conservative" henceforth.

7. Spitzer, *The Politics of Gun Control*, 170–171.

8. Frank Newport, "American Public Opinion and Gun Violence," *Gallup*, April 2, 2021, https://news.gallup.com/opinion/polling-matters/343649/american-pub lic-opinion-gun-violence.aspx.

9. Leigh Paterson, "Poll: Americans, Including Republicans And Gun Owners, Broadly Support Red Flag Laws," *NPR*, August 20, 2019, https://www.npr.org/ 2019/08/20/752427922/poll-americans-including-republicans-and-gun-owners- broadly-support-red-flag-law; Mike DeBonis and Emily Guskin, "Americans of Both Parties Overwhelmingly Support 'Red Flag' Laws, Expanded Background Checks for Gun Buyers, Washington Post–ABC News poll finds," *Washington Post*, September 9, 2019, https://www.washingtonpost.com/politics/americans- of-both-parties-overwhelmingly-support-red-flag-laws-expanded-gun-backgro und-checks-washington-post-abc-news-poll-finds/2019/09/08/97208916-ca75- 11e9-a4f3-c081a126de70_story.html.

10. Spitzer, *The Politics of Gun Control*, 170–176.

11. The new conservative legal movement has succeeded in advancing its agenda in many areas, including the dismantling of campaign finance laws, weakening of voting rights, expansion of religious liberty rights, undercutting the power of unions, and much more. Ian Millhiser, *The Agenda: How a Republican Supreme Court is Reshaping America* (New York: Columbia Global Reports, 2021).

12. Carrie Johnson, "Wave Of Young Judges Pushed By McConnell Will Be 'Ruling For Decades To Come'," *NPR*, July 2, 2020, https://www.npr.org/2020/07/02/ 886285772/trump-and-mcconnell-via-swath-of-judges-will-affect-u-s-law-for-deca des; Jonathan N. Katz and Matthew L. Spitzer, "What's Age Got to Do With It? Supreme Court Appointees and the Long Run Location of the Supreme Court Median Justice," *Arizona State Law Journal* 46 (Spring 2014): 41–88.

13. Nancy Scherer and Banks Miller, "The Federalist Society's Influence on the Federal Judiciary," *Political Research Quarterly* 62 (June 2009): 366–367.

14. Ian Millhiser, "Trump Says He Will Delegate Judicial Selection To The Conservative Federalist Society," *ThinkProgress*, June 15, 2016, https://archive.thinkprogress.org/ trump-says-he-will-delegate-judicial-selection-to-the-conservative-federalist-soci ety-26f622b10c49/.

15. Scherer and Miller, "The Federalist Society's Influence on the Federal Judiciary," 368.

16. Neal Devins and Allison Orr Larsen, "Weaponizing En Banc," *New York University Law Review* 96 (2021, forthcoming). They report that forty-three of Trump's first fifty-one appellate nominees were Federalist Society members (amounting to eighty-four percent). It is impossible to imagine any other single group having had such sway over federal court nominations in modern history.

17. "On the Bench: Federal Judiciary," *American Constitution Society*, January 14, 2021, https://www.acslaw.org/judicial-nominations/on-the-bench/. Of the 234, seventy-six percent are male, and eighty-four percent are white. Three of the courts of appeal have now tipped ideologically in a more conservative direction: the Second, Third, and Eleventh. Other circuits also have a larger number of conservative judges. "Courting Change," *Reuters*, January 14, 2021, https://fingfx.thomsonreut ers.com/gfx/rngs/TRUMP-EFFECT-COURTS/010080E30TG/index.html.

18. This applies to federal courts of appeal, but not to federal district court seats, where Democrats from states where district court seats are located still maintained some ability to slow nominations from the opposing party. A couple of late court vacancies did occur. Carl Hulse, "With Wilson Confirmation, Trump and Senate Republicans Achieve a Milestone," *New York Times*, June 24, 2020, https://www. nytimes.com/2020/06/24/us/trump-senate-judges-wilson.html. During the Trump years, majority leader McConnell engineered the end of the "blue slip" process whereby home-state senators could block judicial nominations of the opposing party from their home state, ended the filibuster for Supreme Court nominees, and reduced debate time on nominees.

19. Devins and Larsen, "Weaponizing En Banc"; John Gramlich, "How Trump Compares with Other Recent Presidents in Appointing Federal Judges," *Pew Research Center*, January 13, 2021, https://www.pewresearch.org/fact-tank/2021/ 01/13/how-trump-compares-with-other-recent-presidents-in-appointing-fede ral-judges/. The number of active judicial positions changes regularly owing to resignations, retirements, deaths, or other reasons.

20. Susan Davis and Richard Wolf, "U.S. Senate Goes 'Nuclear,' Changes Filibuster Rules," *USA Today*, November 21, 2013, https://www.usatoday.com/story/news/ politics/2013/11/21/harry-reid-nuclear-senate/3662445/.

21. Nate Raymond, "Biden Finishes 2021 With Most Confirmed Judicial Picks Since Reagan," *Reuters*, December 28, 2021, https://www.reuters.com/legal/governm ent/biden-finishes-2021-with-most-confirmed-judicial-picks-since-reagan-2021-12-28/.

22. Katz and Spitzer, "What's Age Got to Do With It?"

23. Micah Schwartzman and David Fontana, "Trump Picked the Youngest Judges to Sit on the Federal Bench. Your Move, Biden." *Washington Post*, February 21, 2021, https://www.washingtonpost.com/outlook/2021/02/16/court-appointments-age-biden-trump-judges-age/; Russell Wheeler, "Judicial Appointments in Trump's First Three Years: Myths and Realities," *Brookings*, January 28, 2020, https://www. brookings.edu/blog/fixgov/2020/01/28/judicial-appointments-in-trumps-first-three-years-myths-and-realities/.

24. This is the society's standard disclaimer. For example, "Supreme Silence: A Decade of Second Amendment Litigation in the Circuits," *The Federalist Society*, October 28, 2020, https://fedsoc.org/commentary/fedsoc-blog/supreme-silence-a-decade-of-second-amendment-litigation-in-the-circuits.

25. Kenneth L. Manning, Robert A. Carp, and Lisa M. Holmes, "The Decision-Making Ideology of Federal Judges Appointed by President Trump," (2020), UMass Dartmouth Working Paper, https://ssrn.com/abstract=3716378).

26. Devins and Larsen, "Weaponizing En Banc." The authors note that partisanship "occasionally plays a role in en banc decisions," but "not in any predictable pattern." The Trump-era partisan turn is thus an anomaly.

27. Lee Epstein, William M. Landes, and Richard A. Posner, "Revisiting the Ideological Rankings of Supreme Court Justices," *Journal of Legal Studies* 44 (January 2015): 313–314.

28. Jill Abramson, "It's the Thomas Court Now," *New York Times*, October 16, 2021.

29. 521 U.S. 898 (1997).

30. Robert J. Spitzer, *The Right to Bear Arms* (Santa Barbara, CA: ABC-CLIO, 2001), 90–96.

31. That case was *U.S. v. Lopez*, 541 U.S. 549 (1995).

32. 521 U.S. 898, 938. Emphasis in original.

33. Ralph A. Rossum, *Understanding Clarence Thomas* (Lawrence, KS: University Press of Kansas, 2014), 218.

34. Adam Winkler, *Gunfight: The Battle Over the Right to Bear Arms in America* (New York: W.W. Norton, 2011), 6–8, 60–61. Winkler dubbed Thomas, as of 2011, as "the most conservative justice to sit on the Court since the 1930s" (130). See also Brian Doherty, *Gun Control on Trial* (Washington, D.C.: Cato Institute, 2008), xxiii.

35. 561 U.S. 742 (2010).

36. 561 U.S. 742, 809, 858.

37. 137 S. Ct. 1995 (2017). See also Thomas's dissent in denial of certiorari in *Friedman v. City of Highland Park*, 577 U.S. 1039 (2015).

38. 137 S. Ct. 1995, 1999.

39. 138 S. Ct. 945 (2018).

40. 138 S. Ct. 945.

41. 138 S. Ct. 945. Emphasis in original.

42. 138 S. Ct. 945, 952.

43. 140 S. Ct. 1865 (2020).

44. 140 S. Ct. 1865, 1868.

45. 140 S. Ct. 1865, 1875.

46. Corey Robin, *The Enigma of Clarence Thomas* (New York: Henry Holt, 2019), 15, 169–170.

47. Robin, *The Enigma of Clarence Thomas*, 184.

48. Ibram X. Kendi, *Stamped from the Beginning* (New York: Nation Books, 2017); Bobby Seale, *Seize the Time* (Baltimore, MD: Black Classic Press, 1991).

49. Robert J. Spitzer, *Guns across America: Reconciling Gun Rules and Rights* (New York: Oxford University Press, 2015), 10–28; Joshua Horwitz and

Casey Anderson, *Guns, Democracy, and the Insurrectionist Idea* (Ann Arbor, MI: University of Michigan Press, 2009).

50. Sally E. Hadden, *Slave Patrols: Law and Violence in Virginia and the Carolinas* (Cambridge, MA: Harvard University Press, 2001), 205.

51. Hadden, *Slave Patrols*, 204–209.

52. Saul Cornell, "The Right to Regulate Arms in the Era of the Fourteenth Amendment: The Emergence of Good Cause Permit Schemes in Post-Civil War America," *U.C. Davis Law Review Online* 55 (September 2021): 70–71, https://lawreview.law.ucdavis.edu/online/55/files/55-online-Cornell.pdf.

53. Cornell, "The Right to Regulate Arms in the Era of the Fourteenth Amendment." See also William J. Novak, *The People's Welfare: Law and Regulation in Nineteenth-Century America* (Chapel Hill, NC: University of North Carolina Press, 1996).

54. The Colfax massacre arose over the disputed election of 1872. When the governor declared the Republicans the winners, a group of armed Black men, including armed Black Militiamen, along with the newly elected sheriff and judge, entered the Colfax courthouse to claim office. After brief and unsuccessful negotiations between the occupants and the opposition white Democrats, whites surrounded the courthouse, set it on fire, and killed over one hundred Blacks (and perhaps many more). Robert M. Goldman, *Reconstruction and Black Suffrage* (Lawrence, KS: University Press of Kansas, 2001), 42–51; Joan Burbick, *Gun Show Nation* (New York: The New Press, 2006), 20–23. The Tulsa massacre was set off by an unfounded rumor of a Black man accosting a white woman operating an elevator. Armed Blacks mobilized to protect the accused man but were quickly overwhelmed by a far larger group of whites, some of whom were also armed. The net result was the burning of the prosperous and predominantly Black Greenwood section of Tulsa. Hundreds were killed and many more were left homeless and out of business. Tim Madigan, *The Burning: Massacre, Destruction, and the Tulsa Race Riot of 1921* (New York: St. Martin's 2003); "Tulsa Race Massacre," *History.com*, March 18, 2021, https://www.history.com/topics/roaring-twenties/tulsa-race-massacre; Yuliya Parshina-Kottas et al., "What Was Lost in the Tulsa Race Massacre," *New York Times*, May 30, 2021.

55. Caroline E. Light, *Stand Your Ground: A History of America's Love Affair with Lethal Self-Defense* (Boston: Beacon Press, 2017), 50.

56. For example, Rebecca Onion writes of armed Black resistance and the inevitable depiction of armed Blacks as perpetrators: "This was one of the drawbacks of self-defense, which, in a racist society, put those who resisted in perilous positions, vulnerable to further violence and legal prosecution." "Red Summer," *Slate*, March 4, 2015, https://slate.com/news-and-politics/2015/03/civil-rights-movement-history-the-long-tradition-of-black-americans-taking-up-arms-to-defend-themselves-against-racial-violence.html. Historians and researchers have pointed out that arming was in fact a part of the twentieth century civil rights movement. For example, Light, *Stand Your Ground*, 108–132.

57. For example, Donald L. Carper et al., *Understanding the Law* (St. Paul, MN: West Pub. Co., 1990), 252–253; William C. Sprague, *Blackstone's Commentaries*, abridged, 5th ed. (Detroit, MI: Sprague Correspondence School of Law, 1899), 289; Darrell A.H. Miller, "Self-Defense, Defense of Others, and the State," *Law and Contemporary Problems* 80 (2017): 85–102.

58. Matthew Lacombe, *Firepower: Hoe the NRA Turned Gun Owners Into a Political Force* (Princeton, NJ: Princeton University Press, 2021), 39.

59. 561 U.S. 742, 780.

60. 140 S. Ct. 1525 (2020).

61. Ian Millhiser, "The Supreme Court Is About To Hear the Biggest Guns Case in Over a Decade," *Vox*, November 29, 2019, https://www.vox.com/policy-and-polit ics/2019/11/25/20974025/supreme-court-guns-second-amendment-new-york-state-rifle. This case was first brought in 2013, when gun law opponents thought they might achieve an incremental victory by prevailing against the city law. But the retirement of Justice Anthony Kennedy, considered more moderate on gun rights despite his vote for *Heller*, and his replacement with the more gun-rights-zealous Kavanaugh, emboldened the opponents of gun laws.

62. 140 S. Ct. 1525, 1527.

63. According to *Black's Law Dictionary*, mootness is "the principle that when the matter in dispute has already been resolved [in this case by the repeal of the New York law], there is no actual controversy that would be affected by a judicial decision, and federal courts will not exercise their jurisdiction over such matters." (St. Paul, MN: West Publishing Co., 1991), 697.

64. 140 S. Ct. 1525, 1527.

65. 140 S. Ct. 1525, 1544.

66. Ian Millhiser, "The Fight to Expand Gun Rights May Have Hit a Snag in the Supreme Court," *Vox*, December 2, 2019, https://www.vox.com/2019/12/2/20991 785/supreme-court-second-amendment-guns-roberts-new-york-state-rifle.

67. 670 F.3d 1244 (D.C. Cir. 2011).

68. 670 F.3d 1244, 1269.

69. "Assault Weapons: Summary of State Law," *Giffords Law Center*, https://giffords. org/lawcenter/gun-laws/policy-areas/hardware-ammunition/assault-weapons/; "Large Capacity Magazines," *Giffords Law Center*, https://giffords.org/lawcen ter/gun-laws/policy-areas/hardware-ammunition/large-capacity-magazines/. Washington State became the tenth state to enact a large capacity magazine restriction in 2022.

70. National Firearms Act of 1934 (48 *Stat.* 1236).

71. Cefali and Charles, "An Overview of Gun Registration in U.S. History?"

72. 919 F.3d 437 (7th Cir. 2019).

73. 919 F.3d 437, 451.

74. 919 F.3d 437, 451.

75. 919 F.3d 437, 469.
76. Joseph Blocher, "The Breadth of Judge Barrett's 'Dangerousness' Principle," *Duke Center for Firearms Law*, October 2, 2020, https://firearmslaw.duke.edu/2020/10/ the-breadth-of-judge-barretts-dangerousness-principle/.
77. Marcia Coyle, "Amy Coney Barrett's Broad View of 2nd Amendment Could Energize Gun Rights Challenges," *The National Law Journal*, September 28, 2020, https://www.law.com/nationallawjournal/2020/09/28/amy-coney-barretts-broad-view-of-2nd-amendment-could-energize-gun-rights-challenges/.
78. "Little Nell" was a frail and sickly child who died in Charles Dickens' 1840's novel, *The Old Curiosity Shop*.
79. This sort of counter-factual labeling is not confined to these jurists' views of the Second Amendment. In a recent speech Justice Alito said that "religious liberty is fast becoming a disfavored right." Adam Liptak, "An Extraordinary Winning Streak for Religion at the Supreme Court, *New York Times*, April 6, 2021. The irony of his comment is that nothing could be further from the truth, as Alito no doubt knows. A contemporaneous study reported that religious liberty has become a more and more favored right in the courts. According to Lee Epstein and Eric A. Posner, the Supreme Court has become ever more likely to rule in favor of re-ligious rights, according to their study of cases spanning seventy years. Over that time, rulings in favor of religious liberty have increased thirty-five percent, with the Roberts court hitting a high of eighty-one percent success. "The Roberts Court and the Transformation of Constitutional Protections for Religion: A Statistical Portrait," *Supreme Court Review* (2021, forthcoming).
80. Helen E. Veit, Kenneth R. Bowling, and Charlene Bangs Bickford, *Creating the Bill of Rights* (Baltimore, MD: The Johns Hopkins University Press, 1991), ix–xiii.
81. *Palko v. Connecticut*, 302 U.S. 319 (1937).
82. Andrea L. Bonnicksen, *Civil Rights and Liberties* (Palo Alto, CA: Mayfield Publishing, 1982), ix. The preferred freedoms doctrine traces back at least to *Palko v. Connecticut*, 302 U.S. 319 (1937).
83. Quoted in Kermit L. Hall, ed., *The Oxford Companion to the Supreme Court of the United States* (New York: Oxford University Press, 1992), 664.
84. Spitzer, *The Politics of Gun Control*, Ch. 2.
85. Spitzer, *The Politics of Gun Control*, 55–65; Spitzer, *Guns across America: Reconciling Gun Rules and Rights*, 65–76.
86. 554 U.S. 570, 626–627.
87. 554 U.S. 570, 625.
88. 554 U.S. 570, 626–627, 632.
89. "Post-Heller Second Amendment Jurisprudence," *Congressional Research Service*, R44618, March 25, 2019, 12–15.
90. "Post-Heller Second Amendment Jurisprudence."

Notes to pages 18–20

91. "Protecting Gun Safety Laws in Appellate Courts," *Giffords Law Center*, https://lawcenter.giffords.org/protecting-strong-gun-laws-the-supreme-court-leaves-lower-court-victories-untouched/. Kristin A. Goss and Matthew J. Lacombe conclude that the impact of Heller on existing gun laws up to the end of the 2010s has indeed been minimal. "Do Courts Change Politics? Heller and the Limits of Policy Feedback Effects," *Emory Law Journal* 69 (2020): 881–918.

92. For more on this argument see Spitzer, *Guns across America*.

93. Antonin Scalia, "Constitutional Interpretation the Old Fashioned Way," Remarks Delivered at the Woodrow Wilson International Center for Scholars, Washington, DC, March 14, 2005, http://www.cfif.org/htdocs/freedomline/current/guest_commentary/scalia-constitutional-speech.htm. See also Antonin Scalia, "Originalism: The Lesser Evil," *University of Cincinnati Law Review* 57 (1989): 849–865.

94. Stephen Breyer, *Active Liberty: Interpreting Our Democratic Constitution* (New York: Knopf, 2005), 115–132; Joseph J. Ellis, "Immaculate Misconception and the Supreme Court," *Washington Post*, May 7, 2010, https://www.washingtonpost.com/wp-dyn/content/article/2010/05/02/AR2010050202446.html.

95. Daniel A. Farber and Suzanna Sherry, *Desperately Seeking Certainty* (Chicago: University of Chicago Press, 2002), 14.

96. Farber and Sherry, *Desperately Seeking Certainty*, 10–54. See also Steven M. Teles, *The Rise of the Conservative Legal Movement* (Princeton, NJ: Princeton University Press, 2008); Amanda Hollis-Brusky, *Ideas with Consequences: The Federalist Society and the Conservative Counterrevolution* (New York: Oxford University Press, 2015). Amanda Hollis-Brusky and Joshua C. Wilson examine the role of the Christian Right on the conservative legal movement in *Separate but Faithful: The Christian Right's Radical Struggle to Transform Law and Legal Culture* (New York: Oxford University Press, 2021). Ken I. Kersch traces the roots of the conservative movement that emerged in the 1980s, including Originalism, dating it back several decades, in *Conservatives and the Constitution: Imagining Constitutional Restoration in the Heyday of American Liberalism* (New York: Cambridge University Press, 2019). Jack Balkin argues that originalist and living Constitution perspectives are compatible with each other. See *Living Originalism* (Cambridge, MA: Harvard University Press, 2011). There is, to be sure, greater complexity to this debate than the simple Originalist–Living dichotomy presented here. See for example Corey Brettschneider, *Constitutional Law and American Democracy* (Frederick, MD: Wolters Kluwer, 2012), 135–237.

97. Jeffrey Toobin, *The Oath* (New York: Doubleday, 2012), 105–115.

98. Bruce Allen Murphy, *Scalia: A Court of One* (New York: Simon and Schuster, 2014), 397.

99. Quoted in Murphy, *Scalia*, 403.

100. Jonathan Gienapp, "Constitutional Originalism and History," *Process: A Blog for American History*, March 20, 2017, http://www.processhistory.org/originalism-history/.
101. John O. McGinnis and Michael B. Rappaport, *Originalism and the Good Constitution* (Cambridge, MA: Harvard University Press, 2013), 8.
102. Gienapp, "Constitutional Originalism and History."
103. Jack Rakove, "The Framers of the Constitution Didn't Worry About 'Originalism,'" *Washington Post*, October 16, 2020, https://www.washingtonpost.com/outlook/originalism-constitution-founders-barrett/2020/10/16/1906922e-0f33-11eb-8a35-237ef1eb2ef7_story.html.
104. Rakove, "The Framers of the Constitution Didn't Worry About 'Originalism.'"
105. Murphy, *Scalia*, 398. Murphy reports that the thick-skinned Scalia was "particularly stung" by the many criticisms leveled against his ahistorical historicism in *Heller*, which included criticisms from noted conservative jurists like Judges Richard Posner and Harvie Wilkinson, (392–394).
106. Paul L. Murphy, "Time to Reclaim: The Current Challenge of American Constitutional History," *The American Historical Review* 69 (October 1963): 77. Murphy traces the term back to Howard Jay Graham. See "The Fourteenth Amendment and School Desegregation," *Buffalo Law Review* 3 (December 1953): 1–24. In a widely cited article from 1965 historian Alfred H. Kelly described lawyers' practice of "the selection of data favorable to the position being advanced without regard to or concern for contradictory data or proper evaluation of the relevance of data proffered." Quoted in Robert J. Spitzer, *Saving the Constitution from Lawyers: How Legal Training and Law Reviews Distort Constitutional Meaning* (New York: Cambridge University Press, 2008), 28. As I argue in this book, the distortion of history by lawyers is not limited to Originalists, but the Originalist singular reliance on history opens the door wide to wayward constitutional theorizing.
107. Richard A. Posner, "In Defense of Looseness," *The New Republic,* August 27, 2008, https://newrepublic.com/article/62124/defense-looseness
108. Theodore J. Lowi, *The End of Liberalism: The Second Republic of the United States* (New York: W.W. Norton, 1979). Others have made similar arguments, for example Bruce Ackerman, *We the People: Transformations* (Cambridge, MA: Harvard University Press, 1998).
109. Susan P. Liebell, "Sensitive Places?: How Gender Unmasks the Myth of Originalism in *District of Columbia v. Heller,*" *Polity* 53 (April 2021): 207.
110. Brandon L. Bartels and Christopher D. Johnston, *Curbing the Court: Why the Public Constrains Judicial Independence* (New York: Cambridge University Press, 2020).
111. Michael W. McConnell, "Textualisn and the Dead Hand of the Past," *George Washington Law Review* 66(June/August 1998): 1127–1140.

CHAPTER 2

1. Fred Barbash, "Gun Rights Groups Celebrate Win as Judge Rejects California's Ban on High-Capacity Magazines," *Washington Post*, April 1, 2019, https://www.washingtonpost.com/world/national-security/gun-rights-groups-celebrate-win-as-judge-cuts-down-californias-ban-on-high-capacity-magazines/2019/04/01/odc5830e-549d-11e9-9136-f8e636f1f6df_story.html?utm_term=.487f87caf9bf.

2. *Fyock v. Sunnyvale*, 779 F.3d 991 (9th Cir. 2015).

3. *Duncan v. Becerra*, 366 F.Supp. 3d 1131 (S.D. Cal. 2019).

4. *Duncan v. Becerra*, e.g., 1141, 1147, 1153, 1155, 1156.

5. For example, *Heller v. District of Columbia*, 670 F.3d 1244 (D.C. Cir. 2011); *New York State Rifle and Pistol Association v. Cuomo*, 804 F.3d 242 (2nd Cir. 2015); *Kolbe v. Hogan*, 849 F.3d 114 (4th Cir. 2017); *Association of New Jersey Rifle and Pistol Clubs Inc. v Attorney General of New Jersey*, 910 F.3d 106 (3rd Cir. 2018); *Worman v. Healey*, 922 F.3d 26 (1st Cir. 2019). See also Barbash, "Gun Rights Groups Celebrate Win as Judge Rejects California's Ban on High-Capacity Magazines."

6. *Duncan v. Becerra*, 366 F.Supp. 3d 1131, 1142.

7. *Duncan v. Becerra*, 366 F.Supp. 3d 1131, 1149.

8. *Duncan v. Becerra*, 970 F.3d 1133 (9th Cir. 2020).

9. *Duncan v. Becerra*, 970 F.3d 1133, 1150.

10. Robert J. Spitzer, *Guns across America: Reconciling Gun Rules and Rights* (New York: Oxford University Press, 2015), 77–79. See also Ellen Stephano, "Living *Heller*: Large-Capacity Magazine Bans and the Circuit Courts' Search for Clarity on Second Amendment Constitutional Scrutiny," *Suffolk University Law Review* 54 (2021): 573–598.

11. Spitzer, *Guns across America*, Ch. 2; Adam Winkler, *Gunfight* (New York: W.W. Norton, 2011).

12. The term "bullet magazine" is often used but, strictly speaking, is incorrect, in that the term bullet refers to that portion of a cartridge that leaves the barrel of a gun when it is fired, whereas magazines hold an entire cartridge. But the term bullet is more clearly understood in general parlance as a synonym for round.

13. Larry Kahaner, *AK-47: The Weapon That Changed the Face of War* (New York: Wiley, 2007).

14. "America's Gun—the Rise of the AR-15," *CNBC*, April 25, 2013, http://www.youtube.com/watch?v=OCvjoFPD5Kg.

15. Laura Bult, "Inventor of the AR-15 Would be 'Sickened' By Its Use in Mass Shootings, Family Says," *New York Daily News*, June 16, 2016, https://www.nydailynews.com/news/national/inventor-ar-15-sickened-mass-shootings-article-1.2676028. The family of the man credited with the original design of the AR-15, Eugene Stoner, who died in 1997, said that he "would have been horrified" at its appeal to mass shooters and that "he designed it as a military rifle."

16. Kyle Mizokani, "The Army's M4 Carbine Can Fire Even If You Don't Pull the Trigger," *Popular Mechanics*, June 1, 2018, https://www.popularmechanics.com/military/weapons/a21052857/army-m4-carbine-firing-defect/.

17. According to Phillip Peterson, the first assault weapon marketed to civilians was the Colt AR-15, introduced in 1964. *Buyer's Guide to Assault Weapons* (Iola, WI: Gun Digest Books, 2008), 4. Peterson says that the poor sales of these weapons, along with imported versions, was attributable at least in part to the fact that they were "too expensive to appeal to the average shooter."

18. Jay Mathews, "AK47 Rifles Flood Into U.S. from Chinese Sales War," *Washington Post*, February 2, 1989, A1.

19. Tom Diaz, *Making a Killing* (New York: The New Press, 1999), 125.

20. Peter Ferrara, "'Assault Weapon' is Just a PR Stunt Meant to Fool the Gullible," *Forbes*, December 28, 2012, http://www.forbes.com/sites/peterferrara/2012/12/28/assault-weapon-is-just-a-pr-stunt-meant-to-fool-the-gullible/.

21. Bruce H. Kobayashi and Joseph E. Olson, "In Re 101 California Street: A Legal and Economic Analysis of Strict Liability for the Manufacture and Sale of 'Assault Weapons,'" *Stanford Law & Policy Review* 8 (Winter 1997): 43.

22. Violence Policy Center, *The Militarization of the U.S. Civilian Arms Market*, June 2011, http://www.vpc.org/studies/militarization.pdf#page=33; see also Violence Policy Center, *Assault Weapons and Accessories in America*, 1988, http://www.vpc.org/studies/awacont.htm and http://www.vpc.org/studies/thatintr.htm. An ad appearing in the NRA magazine *American Rifleman* in its June 1961 issue advertises an "FN Browning Semi-Auto Assault Rifle" sold by The Gun Shop of Lancaster, California.

23. Diaz, *Making a Killing*, 124–128, 230–231; Tom Diaz, *The Last Gun* (New York: The New Press, 2013), 142–143.

24. Erica Goode, "Even Defining 'Assault Rifles' Is Complicated," *New York Times*, January 17, 2013, A1.

25. Peterson, *Buyer's Guide to Assault Weapons*, 11.

26. Diaz, *The Last Gun*, 144.

27. http://www.nssf.org/msr/.

28. John Haughey, "Five Things You Need to Know About 'Assault Weapons,'" *Outdoor Life*, March 19, 2013, http://www.outdoorlife.com/blogs/gun-shots/2013/03/five-things-you-need-know-about-assault-weapons.

29. Phillip Peterson, *Gun Digest Buyer's Guide to Assault Weapons* (Iola, WI: Gun Digest Books, 2008).

30. Goode, "Even Defining 'Assault Rifles' Is Complicated."

31. Phillip Peterson, *Gun Digest Buyer's Guide to Tactical Rifles* (Iola, WI: Gun Digest Books, 2010).

32. According to Blake Brown, Canadian newspapers ran ads from gun companies selling weapons like the "AR-15 semi-automatic assault rifle," the "Colt AR-15 Semi Auto Assault Rifle," and the "SKS Assault Rifle" among others, in 1976, 1982,

1983, 1985, and 1986 from dealers and companies including MilArm, Colt, and Ruger. "Gun Advocates' Changing Definition of 'Assault Rifles' is Meant to Sow Confusion," *Toronto Globe and Mail*, May 21, 2020, https://www.theglobeandm ail.com/opinion/article-gun-advocates-changing-definition-of-assault-rifles-is-meant-to-sow/.

33. Robert J. Spitzer, *The Politics of Gun Control*, 8th ed. (New York: Routledge, 2021), 205–211. The definition of large capacity magazines as those holding more than ten rounds dates back at least to the 1994 law.

34. Christopher S. Koper et al., "An Updated Assessment of the Federal Assault Weapons Ban: Impacts on Gun Markets and Gun Violence, 1994–2003," Report to the National Institute of Justice, U.S. Department of Justice, Jerry Lee Center of Criminology, University of Pennsylvania, June 2004, 2–3, https://www.ncjrs. gov/pdffiles1/nij/grants/204431.pdf; Charles DiMaggio et al., "Changes in US Mass Shooting Deaths Associated with the 1994–2004 Federal Assault Weapons Ban," *Journal of Trauma and Acute Care Surgery* 86 (January 2019): 11–19; John Donohue and Theodora Boulouta, "That Assault Weapons Ban Worked," *New York Times*, September 5, 2019, https://www.nytimes.com/2019/09/04/opinion/assa ult-weapon-ban.html. Christopher S. Koper cites five additional studies that found the 1994 law to have reduced public mass shooting deaths and injuries from as-sault weapons: "Assessing the Potential to Reduce Deaths and Injuries from Mass Shootings Through Restrictions on Assault Weapons and Other High-Capacity Semiautomatic Firearms," *Criminology & Public Policy* 19 (February 2020): 157.

35. Giffords Law Center, "Assault Weapons," https://lawcenter.giffords.org/gun-laws/ policy-areas/hardware-ammunition/assault-weapons/#state.

36. Giffords Law Center, "Large Capacity Magazines," https://lawcenter.giffords.org/ gun-laws/policy-areas/hardware-ammunition/large-capacity-magazines/.

37. David Kopel, "The History of Magazines Holding 11 or More Rounds: Amicus Brief in 9th Circuit," *Washington Post*, May 29, 2014, https://www.washingtonp ost.com/news/volokh-conspiracy/wp/2014/05/29/the-history-of-magazines-holding-11-or-more-rounds-amicus-brief-in-9th-circuit/.

38. Mike Markowitz, "The Girandoni Air Rifle," *DefenseMediaNetwork*, May 14, 2013, https://www.defensemedianetwork.com/stories/the-girandoni-air-rifle/. The rifles never caught on as they proved to be impractical even on the battlefield, much less for civilian use. Roughly 1500 were made: "Leather gaskets needed to be constantly maintained and swelled with water to sustain pressure. Once empty the reservoirs required a significant effort and 1500 strokes to restore full power. A supply wagon was subsequently outfitted with a mounted pump to readily supply soldiers but this negated one of the key features—mobility. The rudimen-tary fabrication methods of the day engineered weak threading on the reservoir neck and this was the ultimate downfall of the weapon. The reservoirs were delicate in the field and if the riveted brazed welds parted the weapon was rendered into an awkward club as a last resort." John Paul Jarvis, "The Girandoni Air Rifle: Deadly

Under Pressure," *GUNS.com*, March 15, 2011, https://www.guns.com/news/2011/03/15/the-girandoni-air-rifle-deadly-under-pressure.

39. "The Puckle Gun: Repeating Firepower in 1718," December 25, 2016, https://www.youtube.com/watch?v=GPC7KiYDshw. The term "celerity of fire" references the rate at which rounds can be fired from a gun.

40. Jim Rasenberger, *Revolver: Sam Colt and the Six-Shooter That Changed America* (New York: Scribner, 2021), 3.

41. Rasenberger, *Revolver*, 54.

42. Rasenberger, *Revolver*, 401.

43. Kopel, "The History of Magazines Holding 11 or More Rounds"; Lee Kennett and James LaVerne Anderson, *The Gun in America* (Westport, CT: Greenwood Press, 1975), 112–113.

44. Rasenberger, *Revolver*, 3–5, 401.

45. Pamela Haag, *The Gunning of America* (New York: Basic Books, 2016), 24.

46. Rasenberger, *Revolver*, 136.

47. Haag, *The Gunning of America*, 34–37, 46–64. As Haag said, "the Civil War saved" the gun industrialists (65).

48. *Duncan v. Becerra*, 970 F.3d 1133, 1147.

49. Dickinson D. Bruce, *Violence and Culture in the Antebellum South* (Austin, TX: University of Texas Press, 1979); Randolph Roth, *American Homicide* (Cambridge, MA: Belknap Press, 2012).

50. Robert J. Spitzer, "Gun Law History in the United States and Second Amendment Rights," *Law and Contemporary Problems* 80 (2017): 63–67.

51. Spitzer, "Gun Law History in the United States and Second Amendment Rights," 67. Historic laws from https://law.duke.edu/gunlaws/. This database only includes laws up to 1934, so it is possible that other states enacted laws like the ones discussed here after 1934.

52. 48 Stat. 1236.

53. 1927 Mass. Acts 413, 413–14.

54. 1927 R.I. Pub. Laws 256, 256.

55. Act of June 2, 1927, no. 372, 1927 Mich. Pub. Acts 887, 888; Mich. Pub. Acts 1929, Act No. 206, Sec. 3, Comp. Laws 1929.

56. Act of Apr. 10, 1933, ch. 190, 1933 Minn. Laws 231, 232.

57. Act of Apr. 10, 1933, ch. 190, 1933 Minn. Laws 231, 232.

58. Act of Apr. 8, 1933, no. 64, 1933 Ohio Laws 189, 189.

59. Act of Apr. 8, 1933, no. 64, 1933 Ohio Laws 189, 189.

60. Uniform Machine Gun Act, ch. 206, 1933 S.D. Sess. Laws 245, 245.

61. Act of Mar. 7, 1934, ch. 96, 1934 Va. Acts 137, 137.

62. Act of July 8, 1932, ch. 465, §§ 1, 8, 47 Stat. 650, 650, 652 (District of Columbia).

63. Act of July 2, 1931, 1931 Ill. Laws 452, 452; Act of July 7, 1932, no. 80, 1932 La. Acts 336; Act of Mar. 2, 1934, no. 731, 1934 S.C. Acts 1288.

64. 1920 N.J. Laws 67, ch. 31, Section 9.

65. 1917 N.C. Sess. Laws 309, ch. 209, Sec. 1.

66. 1931 Ill. Laws 452–453, An Act to Regulate the Sale, Possession and Transportation of Machine Guns, §§ 1–2; 1927 N.J. Laws 180–181, A Supplement to an Act Entitled "An Act for the Punishment of Crimes," ch. 95, §§ 1–2; 1931 N.D. Laws 305–306, An Act to Prohibit the Possession, Sale and Use of Machine Guns, Sub-Machine Guns, or Automatic Rifles and Defining the Same . . . , ch. 178, §§ 1–2; 1933 Or. Laws 488, An Act to Amend Sections 72-201, 72-202, 72-207; 1929 Pa. Laws 777, §1; 1933 Tex. Gen. Laws 219–220, 1st Called Sess., An Act Defining "Machine Gun" and "Person"; Making It an Offense to Possess or Use Machine Guns . . . , ch. 82, §§ 1–4, § 6; 1923 Vt. Acts and Resolves 127, An Act to Prohibit the Use of Machine Guns and Automatic Rifles in Hunting, § 1; 1933 Wis. Sess. Laws 245, 164.01.

67. 1927 Cal. Stat. 938.

68. 1933 Haw. Sess. Laws 117; 1929 Mo. Laws 170; Wash. 1933 Sess. Laws 335.

69. "National Firearms Act," Hearings Before the Committee on Ways and Means, House of Representatives, on H.R. 9066, April 16, 18, and May 14, 15, and 16, 1934 (Washington, D.C.: GPO, 1934), 52.

70. *D.C. v. Heller*, 554 U.S. 570, 627.

71. Diaz, *The Last Gun*, 156–157.

72. Christopher S. Koper et al., "Criminal Use of Assault Weapons and High-Capacity Semiautomatic Firearms," *Journal of Urban Health* 95 (2018): 314; also Luke Dillon, "Mass Shootings in the United States: An Exploratory Study of the Trends from 1982–2012," Mason Archival Repository Service, George Mason University, May 22, 2014, http://mars.gmu.edu/xmlui/handle/1920/8694.

73. Brad Plumer, "Everything You Need to Know About the Assault Weapons Ban, In One Post," *Washington Post*, December 17, 2012, https://www.washingtonpost. com/news/wonk/wp/2012/12/17/everything-you-need-to-know-about-banning-assault-weapons-in-one-post/?utm_term=.6244243b2e1c.

74. Spitzer, *Guns across America*, 93.

75. Justin Peters, "The NRA Claims the AR-15 Is Useful for Hunting and Home Defense. Not Exactly," *Slate.com*, June 12, 2016, https://slate.com/news-and-polit ics/2016/06/gun-control-ar-15-rifle-the-nra-claims-the-ar-15-rifle-is-for-hunting-and-home-defense-not-exactly.html.

76. John W. Schoen, "Owned by Five Million Americans, AR-15 Under Renewed Fire After Orlando Massacre," *CNBC.com*, June 13, 2016, https://www.cnbc.com/2016/ 06/13/owned-by-5-million-americans-ar-15-under-renewed-fire-after-orlando-massacre.html.

77. Alex Yablon, "How Many Assault Weapons Do Americans Own?" *The Trace*, September 22, 2018, https://www.thetrace.org/2018/09/how-many-assault-weap ons-in-the-us/; "NSSF Releases Most Recent Firearm Production Figures," *NSSF*, November 16, 2020, https://www.nssf.org/nssf-releases-most-recent-firearm-pro duction-figures/.

78. "What Makes the AR-15 Style Rifle the Weapon of Choice for Mass Shooters?" *60 Minutes*, June 23, 2019, https://www.cbsnews.com/news/ar-15-used-mass-shootings-weapon-of-choice-60-minutes-2019-06-23/.

79. David Heath et al., "How an 'Ugly,' Unwanted Weapon Became the Most Popular Rifle in America," *CNN.com*, December 14, 2017, https://www.cnn.com/2017/12/14/health/ar15-rifle-history-trnd/index.html.

80. Koper et al., "Criminal Use of Assault Weapons and High-Capacity Semiautomatic Firearms," 319. The 1994 assault weapons ban also limited bullet magazines to those that could hold up to ten rounds.

81. Spitzer, *The Politics of Gun Control*, 85.

82. Koper et al., "Criminal Use of Assault Weapons and High-Capacity Semiautomatic Firearms," 319.

83. The FBI definition, set in the 1980s, is by no means universally accepted by researchers, for several reasons, including the simple fact that expeditious police and medical intervention may succeed in reducing the number of deaths to below four, even if many people are injured or are targeted for injury. Surely such an event is no less a mass shooting than one where four or more are killed. "Mass Shootings: Definitions and Trends," *RAND Corporation*, n.d., https://www.rand.org/research/gun-policy/analysis/supplementary/mass-shootings.html.

84. "Assault Weapons and High-Capacity Magazines," *Everytown for Gun Safety*, March 22, 2019, https://everytownresearch.org/assault-weapons-high-capacity-magazines/.

85. "Large Capacity Magazines," Giffords Law Center, https://giffords.org/lawcenter/gun-laws/policy-areas/hardware-ammunition/large-capacity-magazines/

86. Paige Williams, "American Vigilante," *The New Yorker*, July 5, 2021, 32.

87. Jaclyn Schildkraut, "Assault Weapons, Mass Shootings, and Options for Lawmakers," Rockefeller Institute of Government, March 22, 2019, https://rockinst.org/issue-area/assault-weapons-mass-shootings-and-options-for-lawmakers/. See also Schildkraut, *Mass Shootings: Media, Myths, and Realities* (Santa Barbara, CA: Praeger, 2016).

88. Mark Follman, Gavin Aronsen, and Deanna Pan, "A Guide to Mass Shootings in America," *Mother Jones*, February 19, 2019, https://www.motherjones.com/politics/2012/07/mass-shootings-map/.

89. Mark Follman, "Why Mass Shootings Deserve Deeper Investigation," *Mother Jones*, January 30, 2013, http://www.motherjones.com/politics/2013/01/mass-shootings-james-alan-fox; Mark Follman, "More Guns, More Mass Shootings—Coincidence?" *Mother Jones*, December 15, 2012, http://www.motherjones.com/politics/2012/09/mass-shootings-investigation.

90. William J. Krouse and Daniel J. Richardson, "Mass Murder with Firearms," *CRS Report*, July 30, 2015, 29, https://fas.org/sgp/crs/misc/R44126.pdf; Michael S. Rosenwald, "Why Banning AR-15s and Other Assault Weapons Won't Stop Mass Shootings," *Washington Post*, June 16, 2016, https://www.washingtonpost.com/

news/local/wp/2016/06/16/why-banning-ar-15s-and-other-assault-weapons-wont-stop-mass-shootings/?utm_term=.7dffcadbb47b.

91. Alex Yablon, "Most Active Shooters Use Pistols, Not Rifles, According to FBI Data," *The Trace*, August 28, 2018, https://www.thetrace.org/rounds/mass-shoot ing-gun-type-data/.

92. Polly Mosendz, "Assault Rifles Aren't the Weapon of Choice for 'Active Shooters,'" Bloomberg, September 11, 2018, https://www.bloomberg.com/news/articles/ 2018-09-11/semi-autos-aren-t-the-weapon-of-choice-for-active-shooters.

93. Adam Lankford and James Silver, "Why Have Public Mass Shootings Become More Deadly?" *Criminology & Public Policy* 19 (February 2020): 37–60.

94. Rosanna Smart and Terry L. Schell, "Mass Shootings in the United States," *RAND*, April 15, 2021, https://www.rand.org/research/gun-policy/analysis/ess ays/mass-shootings.html.

95. "Officer Down," *Violence Policy Center*, May 2003.

96. See "New Data Shows One in Five Law Enforcement Officers Slain in the Line of Duty in 2016 and 2017 Were Felled by an Assault Weapon," September 25, 2019, https://vpc.org/press/new-data-shows-one-in-five-law-enforcement-officers-slain-in-the-line-of-duty-in-2016-and-2017-were-felled-by-an-assault-weapon/. Of 109 officers slain, twenty-five were killed by assault weapons fire.

97. Lori Robertson, "Biden Wrong on Police Deaths," *FactCheck.org*, January 30, 2013, http://www.factcheck.org/2013/01/biden-wrong-on-police-deaths/. The FBI data categorizes shootings by types of guns (handguns, rifles, shotguns) but does not have a separate category for assault weapons, meaning that the data must be reanalyzed or obtained in some other way.

98. Koper et al., "Criminal Use of Assault Weapons and High-Capacity Semiautomatic Firearms," 319.

99. John J. Donohue III, "Stanford's John Donohue on One Tragic Week, Two Mass Shootings, and the Uniquely American Gun Problem," *SLS Blogs*, March 25, 2021, https://law.stanford.edu/2021/03/25/stanfords-john-donohue-on-one-tragic-week-with-two-mass-shootings-and-the-uniquely-american-gun-problem/.

100. "Firearms Policy Position Statement," International Association of Chiefs of Police, n.d., https://www.theiacp.org; "What Law Enforcement Says About Assault Weapons," The Coalition to Stop Gun Violence, https://www.csgv.org/ what-law-enforcement-says-about-assault-weapons/.

101. International Association of Chiefs of Police, "Taking a Stand," 2007, http://www.theiacp.org/Portals/0/pdfs/GVR_A-page-iii_IACP-Taking-A-Stand.pdf.

102. Police Executive Research Forum, "Guns and Crime," May 2010, 2, http:// www.policeforum.org/assets/docs/Critical_Issues_Series/guns%20and%20cr ime%20-%20breaking%20new%20ground%20by%20focusing%20on%20 the%20local%20impact%202010.pdf.

103. Spitzer, *Guns across America*, 164. The law was upheld in *New York State Rifle and Pistol Association v. Cuomo*.

104. Statement by John F. Walsh, U.S. Attorney for the District of Colorado, testimony before the U.S. Senate Committee on the Judiciary, Washington, D.C., February 27, 2013, 3. See also Police Executive Research Forum, *Guns and Crime: Breaking New Ground By Focusing on the Local Impact*, May 2010; "Target: Law Enforcement," *Violence Policy Center*, February 2010; Statement of Kristen Rand, Legislative Director, Violence Policy Center Before the Committee on Oversight and Government Reform, U.S. House of Representatives, Hearing on Firearms Trafficking on the U.S.–Mexico Border, June 30, 2011, https://democrats-oversi ght.house.gov/sites/democrats.oversight.house.gov/files/migrated/images/user _images/gt/stories/MINORITY/630%20gun%20forum/VPC--Kristen%20R and%20Testimony%206-30-11.pdf; Arindrajit Dube, Oeindrila Dube, and Omar Garcia-Ponce, "Cross-Border Spillover: U.S. Gun Laws and Violence in Mexico," *American Political Science Review* 107 (August 2013): 397–417.

105. George W. Knox et al., "Gangs and Guns," National Gang Crime Research Center (2001), 35, 36, https://cops.usdoj.gov/html/cd_rom/solution_gang_crime/ pubs/gangsandgunsataskforcereport2001.pdf. According to the Report: "Four social contexts were used for the survey: eight county jails from the farmland to the urban central area (891 inmates), matched pair design samples from a Chicago public high school and an inner city program, and a sample of gang members in a private suburban probation program" (2).

106. Diaz, *Making a Killing*, 131; Philip J. Cook and Kristin A. Goss, *The Gun Debate* (New York: Oxford University Press, 2014), 13.

107. Violence Policy Center, "Assault Weapons and Accessories in America," https:// www.vpc.org/studies/awacont.htm.

108. Wayne King, "In California, the 'Private Societies' Flaunt Firepower," *New York Times*, December 17, 1980, 17. Several of the groups described in the article were breakaway or fringe sects from larger groups bearing the same name but not sharing the interest in weaponry or extremist views.

109. "Military Extremists," Federal Bureau of Investigation, December 8, 2011.

110. Melissa K. Merry, *Warped Narratives* (Ann Arbor, MI: University of Michigan Press, 2020), 8.

111. "Armed and Dangerous," *Everytown for Gun Safety*, September 30, 2020, https:// everytownresearch.org/report/extreme-right/.

112. Ryan Busse, *Gunfight: My Battle Against the Industry that Radicalized America* (New York: Public Affairs, 2021), 9, 15.

113. "The Role of Guns & Armed Extremism in the Attack on the U.S. Capitol," *Everytown for Gun Safety*, January 28, 2021, https://everytownresearch.org/rep ort/armed-extremism-us-capitol/; Zoe Tillman, "An Oath Keeper Admitted His Group Stashed Guns Outside DC For Jan. 6," *Buzzfeed*, June 30, 2021, https:// www.buzzfeednews.com/article/zoetillman/oath-keepers-guns-jan-6-capitol- riots?utm_source=The%2BTrace%2Bmailing%2Blist&utm_campaign=edeb7bc 663-EMAIL_CAMPAIGN_2019_08_29_06_04_COPY_03&utm_medium= email&utm_term=0_f76c3ff31c-edeb7bc663-69360165; Mark Follman et al.,

"Trump Extremists Brought Numerous Guns on January 6, Evidence Shows," *Mother Jones*, September 30, 2021, https://www.motherjones.com/crime-just ice/2021/09/trump-extremists-guns-january-6-insurrection-congress-domestic-terrorism/.

114. Josh Meyer, "Antifa, White Supremacists Exploit Loose Gun Laws," *Politico*, September 11, 2017, https://www.politico.com/story/2017/09/11/antifa-white-supremacists-exploit-gun-laws-242506.

115. Matt Cohen, "A More Extreme Gun Rights Movement Is Emerging in the NRA's Wake," *Mother Jones*, December 2, 2020, https://www.motherjones.com/polit ics/2020/12/a-more-extreme-gun-rights-movement-is-emerging-in-the-nras-wake/.

116. Craig Timberg, Elizabeth Dwoskin, and Souad Mekhennet, "Men Wearing Hawaiian Shirts and Carrying Guns Add a Volatile New Element to Protests," *Washington Post*, June 4, 2020, https://www.washingtonpost.com/technology/2020/06/03/white-men-wearings-hawaiian-shirts-carrying-guns-add-volat ile-new-element-floyd-protests/; "COVID-19, Conspiracy and Contagious Sedition: A Case Study on the Militia-Sphere," Network Contagion Research Institute, Rutgers University, n.d., https://networkcontagion.us/reports/covid-19-conspiracy-and-contagious-sedition-a-case-study-on-the-militia-sphere/.

117. "U.S. Crisis Monitor," The Armed Conflict Location & Event Data Project, Princeton University, https://acleddata.com/special-projects/us-crisis-monitor/.

118. "Updated Armed Demonstration Data Released A Year After the 6 January Insurrection Show New Trends," The Armed Conflict Location & Event Data Project, Princeton University, https://acleddata.com/2022/01/05/updated-armed-demonstration-data-released-a-year-after-the-6-january-insurrection-show-new-trends/?utm_source=The+Trace+mailing+list&utm_campaign=589 479c541-EMAIL_CAMPAIGN_2019_09_24_04_06_COPY_01&utm_med ium=email&utm_term=0_f76c3ff31c-589479c541-69360165.

119. Elzerie de Jager et al., "Lethality of Civilian Active Shooter Incidents With and Without Semiautomatic Rifles in the United States," *JAMA Network*, September 11, 2018, https://jamanetwork.com/journals/jama/fullarticle/2702134.

120. Yasser S. Selman, "Medico-legal Study of Shockwave Damage by High Velocity Missiles in Firearm Injuries," *Journal of the Faculty of Medicine, Baghdad* 53 (October 2011): 401–405.

121. Jon Schuppe, "America's Rifle: Why So Many People Love the AR-15," *NBCNews. com*, December 27, 2017, https://www.nbcnews.com/news/us-news/america-s-rifle-why-so-many-people-love-ar-15-n831171.

122. Selman, "Medico-legal Study of Shockwave Damage by High Velocity Missiles in Firearm Injuries."

123. Leana Wen, "What Bullets Do To Bodies," *New York Times*, June 15, 2017, https://www.nytimes.com/2017/06/15/opinion/virginia-baseball-shoot

ing-gun-shot-wounds.html?_r=0; Ryan Hodnick, "Penetrating Trauma Wounds Challenge EMS Providers," *Journal of Emergency Medical Services*, March 30, 2012, http://www.jems.com/articles/print/volume-37/issue-4/patient-care/ penetrating-trauma-wounds-challenge-ems.html.

124. Sarah Zhang, "What an AR-15 Can Do to the Human Body," *Wired*, June 17, 2016, https://www.wired.com/2016/06/ar-15-can-human-body/.

125. Tom Avril, "Doctors: High-velocity Orlando Rifle Inflicts 'Devastating' Wounds," *Philadelphia Inquirer*, June 16, 2016, http://www.philly.com/philly/health/scie nce/20160616_Doctors__High-velocity_Orlando_rifle_inflicts__quot_devas tating_quot__wounds.html; Hodnick, "Penetrating Trauma Wounds."

126. Dina Fine Maron, "Data Confirm Semiautomatic Rifles Linked to More Deaths, Injuries," *Scientific American*, September 11, 2018, https://www.scientificamerican. com/article/data-confirm-semiautomatic-rifles-linked-to-more-deaths-injuries/.

127. "Colin Ferguson," *Crime Museum*, n.d., https://www.crimemuseum.org/crime-library/mass-murder/colin-ferguson/.

128. With the help of a friend, I participated in the process of altering an AR-15 so that the magazine was affixed in place permanently. The weapon would now be loaded by dropping in rounds from the top of the gun. We accomplished this relatively simple procedure to make it compliant with New York's gun laws. Spitzer, *Guns across America*, 143–146.

129. Mark Follman and Gavin Aronsen, "'A Killing Machine': Half of All Mass Shooters Used High-Capacity Magazines," *Mother Jones*, January 30, 2013, http:// www.motherjones.com/politics/2013/01/high-capacity-magazines-mass-shooti ngs/; Ashley Cannon, "Mayhem Multiplied: Mass Shooters and Large-Capacity Magazines," Citizens Crime Commission of New York City, May 2014; Martha Bellisle, "High-Capacity Magazines Get New Scrutiny as Congress Returns," *AP*, September 2, 2019, https://apnews.com/article/b080391f0da34f6ca0cc47848 3370e1a.

130. "Assault Weapons and High-Capacity Magazines," *Everytown for Gun Safety*, March 22, 2019, https://everytownresearch.org/report/assault-weapons-and-high-capacity-magazines/; also "Mass Shootings in America," *Everytown for Gun Safety*, November 21, 2020, https://everytownresearch.org/maps/mass-shooti ngs-in-america-2009-2019/.

131. Sam Petulla, "Here is 1 Correlation Between State Gun Laws and Mass Shootings," *CNN.com*, October 5, 2017, https://www.cnn.com/2017/10/05/politics/gun-laws-magazines-las-vegas/index.html. The study covers years from 2012 to 2016.

132. Louis Klarevas, Andrew Conner, and David Hemenway, "The Effect of Large-Capacity Magazine Bans on High-Fatality Mass Shootings, 1990–2017," *American Journal of Public Health* 109 (December 2019): 1754–1761. They defined high-fatality mass shootings as those that resulted in six or more deaths.

133. Koper, "Assessing the Potential to Reduce Deaths and Injuries from Mass Shootings," 147.

134. Daniel W. Webster et al., "Evidence Concerning the Regulation of Firearms Design, Sale, and Carrying on Fatal Mass Shootings in the United States," *Criminology & Public Policy* 19 (February 2020): 171–212.

135. Michael Rocque et al., "Policy Solutions to Address Mass Shootings," Regional Gun Violence Research Consortium of the Rockefeller Institute of Government, August 2021, 11, https://rockinst.org/issue-area/policy-solutions-to-address-mass-shootings/.

136. Matt Pearce, "Gun's Magazine Shaped the Pace of Colorado Theater Massacre," *Los Angeles Times*, July 22, 2012, https://www.latimes.com/nation/la-xpm-2012-jul-22-la-na-nn-theater-shooting-magazine-20120722-story.html; Ben Kesling and Zusha Elinson, "Mass Shootings Draw Attention to 'Drum Magazines,'" *Wall Street Journal*, August 16, 2019, https://www.wsj.com/articles/mass-shootings-draw-attention-to-drum-magazines-11565962690.

137. "Senate Judiciary Committee Hearing on Gun Violence," January 30, 2013, http://articles.washingtonpost.com/2013-01-30/politics/36628109_1_gun-viole nce-gabby-giffords-senator-grassley.

138. For example, Jacob Paulsen, "Why Magazine Capacity Limitations Are A Bad Idea," *Concealedcarry.com*, December 4, 2015, https://www.concealedcarry.com/law/magazine-capacity-limitations/.

139. Jim Barrett, "Assault Weapons Bans: Are You Ready?" *TheTruthAboutGuns.com*, June 8, 2012, http://www.thetruthaboutguns.com/2012/06/jim-barrett/assault-weapons-bans-are-you-ready/.

140. Robert J. Spitzer, "There's No Second Amendment Right to Large-Capacity Magazines," *New York Times*, August 5, 2019, https://www.nytimes.com/2019/08/05/opinion/dayton-gun-laws-shooting.html.

141. Everytown for Gun Safety, "Mass Shootings," https://www.everytown.org/iss ues/mass-shootings/; Alain Stephens, "The Gun Industry Is Betting on Bigger High-Capacity Magazines," *The Trace*, June 19, 2019, https://www.thetrace.org/2019/06/gun-industry-high-capacity-magazine-size/.

142. Koper et al., "Criminal Use of Assault Weapons and High-Capacity Semiautomatic Firearms," 318.

143. Stephens, "The Gun Industry Is Betting on Bigger High-Capacity Magazines."

144. Peters, "The NRA Claims the AR-15 Is Useful for Hunting and Home Defense."

145. David Keene, "The AR-15: The Gun Liberals Love to Hate," *Human Events*, January 2, 2013, https://humanevents.com/2013/01/02/the-ar-15-the-gun-liber als-love-to-hate/.

146. *Miller v. Bonta*, Case No.: 19-cv-1537-BEN (JLB), 2021.

147. *Miller v. Bonta*, 35.

148. *Miller v. Bonta*, 8.

149. *Miller v. Bonta*, 33.

150. "2019 Crime in the United States," U.S. Department of Justice, https://ucr.fbi. gov/crime-in-the-u.s/2019/crime-in-the-u.s.-2019/topic-pages/burglary.

151. National Crime Victimization Survey, U.S. Department of Justice, September 2010, https://bjs.ojp.gov/content/pub/ascii/vdhb.txt.

152. *Miller v. Bonta*, 32–33.

153. Noah Woods, "AR-15s: The Choice of Hypocrisy or Rationality," *Rambler Magazine*, September 26, 2019, http://www.ramblermagazine.net/news/ar-15s-the-choice-of-hypocrisy-or-rationality.

154. *D.C. v. Heller*, 629.

155. Peters, "The NRA Claims the AR-15 Is Useful for Hunting and Home Defense."

156. Lucy P. Allen, Declaration submitted in the case of *Kolbe et al. v. O'Malley et al.*, Case No. 1:13-cv-02841-CCB, U.S. District Court for the District of Maryland, filed February 14, 2014. The data reported in this Declaration did not include the maximum number of rounds fired in incidents reported and compiled from 1997 to 2001. It also did not report the number of incidents on which the 1997–2001 study was based but did report that the 2011–2013 study was based on 279 incidents.

157. Declaration of Lucy P. Allen (19-cv-1537 BEN-JLB), *Miller v. Becerra*, in the United States District Court for the Southern District of California, filed January 23, 2020, http://publicfiles.firearmspolicy.org/miller-v-becerra/2020-1-23-miller-mpi-opp-decs-exhibits.pdf. In her document, Allen readily admits the limitations of her data sources, yet they are the best available because no systematic such data is gathered by law enforcement or the government.

158. *Duncan v. Becerra*, 366 F.Supp. 3d 1131.

159. Paul Pinkham, "Have Gun, Will Not Fear It Anymore," *Jacksonville Times-Union*, July 18, 2000; reprinted in the *Palm Beach Post*, July 30, 2000.

160. Robin Reese, "Georgia Mom Shoots Home Invader, Hiding With Her Children," *ABC News*, January 8, 2013, https://abcnews.go.com/US/georgia-mom-hiding-kids-shoots-intruder/story?id=18164812.

161. Lindsey Bever, "Armed Intruders Kicked In the Door. What They Found Was a Woman Opening Fire," *Washington Post*, September 24, 2016, https://www.washingtonpost.com/news/true-crime/wp/2016/09/24/armed-intruders-kicked-in-the-door-what-they-found-was-a-woman-opening-fire/?noredirect=on.

162. "Americans Against Gun Violence Condemns District Court Judge's Ruling in *Duncan v. California State Attorney General* Invalidating High Capacity Magazine Ban," *Americans Against Gun Violence*, April 2, 2019, https://aagunv.org/americans-against-gun-violence-condemns-district-court-judges-ruling-in-duncan-v-becerra-invalidating-california-high-capacity-magazine-ban/.

163. Emily Lane, "Why Do Police Shoot So Many Times? FBI, Experts Answer On Officer-Involved Shootings," *New Orleans Times-Picayune*, March 9, 2016, https://www.nola.com/news/crime_police/article_ae82835c-0212-5e50-a175-85601a1ed8bb.html; Scottie Andrew, "Why Police Shoot So Many Times to Bring Down a Suspect," *CNN.com*, August 26, 2020, https://www.cnn.com/2020/08/26/us/why-police-shoot-so-many-rounds-trnd/index.html.

164. *Miller v. Bonta*, 36.
165. *Duncan v. Becerra*, 366 F.Supp. 3d 1131, 1142.
166. Saul Cornell, "The Right to Regulate Arms in the Era of the Fourteenth Amendment: The Emergence of Good Cause Permit Schemes in Post-Civil War America," *U.C. Davis Law Review Online* 55 (September 2021): 68–69, https://lawreview.law.ucdavis.edu/online/55/files/55-online-Cornell.pdf.

CHAPTER 3

1. I am indebted to Teresa Spitzer for suggesting the title of this chapter.
2. A similar bill was introduced in both houses in 2015, but the 2017 bill received more attention including the plan for hearings and a scheduled floor vote. "Firearm Silencers Threaten Public Safety, New VPC Study Finds," *Violence Policy Center*, February 11, 2016, http://www.vpc.org/press/firearm-silencers-threaten-public-safety-new-vpc-study-finds/.
3. I use the term "silencer" here rather than "suppressor" as it was the term used by the device's inventor, and it is the universally known term referencing devices added to the end of gun barrels to reduce the noise of firing. The devices were also sometimes called "mufflers." Silencer expert Patrick Sweeney wrote about these differences in terminology, "Don't get wrapped up in semantics.... And for god's sake don't correct someone else's usage. That's just rude." Patrick Sweeney, *The Suppressor Handbook* (Zephyr Cove, NV: Gun Digest Books, 2017), 18.
4. Silencers also come under the regulatory rubric of The Gun Control Act of 1968.
5. http://americansuppressorassociation.com/education/.
6. "Sen. Lee Introduces SHUSH Act," April 14, 2021, https://www.lee.senate.gov/public/index.cfm/2021/4/sen-lee-introduces-shush-act.
7. "Hearing Protection Act Would Declassify Silencers So They're No Longer Considered 'Firearms' Under Federal Law," *GovTrack Insider*, January 20, 2021, https://govtrackinsider.com/hearing-protection-act-would-declassify-silencers-so-theyre-no-longer-considered-firearms-under-538019260506.
8. *U.S. v. Cox*, 187 F. Supp. 3d 1282 (2016).
9. *U.S. v. Cox*, 235 F. Supp. 3d 1221, 1227 (2017).
10. *U.S. v. Cox*, 906 F.3d 1170 (2018).
11. *Cox v. U.S.*, 139 S. Ct. 2690 (2019).
12. "Gun Owners of America Funds Challenge to National Firearms Act in U.S. Supreme Court," Gun Owners of America, January 14, 2019, https://gunowners.org/gun-owners-of-america-funds-challenge-to-national-firearms-act-in-u-s-supreme-court/. Given a now more conservative and potentially gun friendly Supreme Court majority, gun rights activists clearly see a new opportunity to expand the scope of gun rights. Stephen P. Halbrook also suggests the same. "Firearm Sound Moderators: Issues of Criminalization and the Second Amendment," *Cumberland Law Review* 46, no. 33 (2015–2016), 75.

13. Awr Hawkins, "Eight Attorneys General to SCOTUS: Second Amendment Protects Suppressors Too," *Breitbart*, February 21, 2019, https://www.breitbart. com/politics/2019/02/21/eight-attorneys-general-to-scotus-second-amendment-protects-suppressors-too/. The basis for silencer regulations, the National Firearms Act of 1934, was upheld in a Second Amendment-based challenged in the 1939 case of *U.S. v. Miller*, 307 U.S. 174. Two years earlier the Supreme Court upheld the right of Congress to impose a regulatory tax in the 1934 law in *Sonzinsky v. U.S.*, 300 U.S. 506 (1937).

14. "Firearms Verification," ATF, 18 U.S.C., § 921(A)(24), https://www.atf.gov/firea rms/firearms-guides-importation-verification-firearms-gun-control-act-definit ion-silencer.

15. Paul A. Clark, "Criminal Use of Firearm Silencers," *Western Criminology Review* 8 (2007): 47.

16. Bureau of Alcohol, Tobacco, Firearms, and Explosives, "Firearms Commerce in the United States, Annual Statistical Update 2020," https://www.atf.gov. Texas alone accounts for 400,000, or twenty percent, of all silencers owned. "Silencer Registration Soars in 2016, Despite Gun Lobby Claim That Regulations Are Burdensome," *Giffords.org*, August 30, 2017, https://giffords.org/2017/08/atf201 7report/.

17. "Silencers," *Giffords Law Center*, n.d., https://giffords.org/lawcenter/gun-laws/pol icy-areas/hardware-ammunition/silencers/.

18. Bureau of Alcohol, Tobacco, Firearms, and Explosives, "Firearms Commerce in the United States: Annual Statistical Update 2021," https://www.atf.gov/firearms/ docs/report/2021-firearms-commerce-report/download.

19. Michael Marinaro, "A Diversified Mind: Hiram Percy Maxim," https://connect icuthistory.org/hiram-percy-maxim/; Maxim, Hiram Percy. Patent Number 916,885–Silent Firearm. 916885. Hartford, CT, issued March 30, 1909, https:// docs.google.com/viewer?url=patentimages.storage.googleapis.com/pdfs/US916 885.pdf.

20. Representatives of England, France, Russia, Germany, and Italy all purchased silencers and sent them back for testing to the militaries of their respective coun-tries. "To Try Maxim's Silencer," *New York Times*, March 11, 1909. The American military also tested the silencer. "Maxim Silencer Tests Successful," *New York Times*, July 4, 1909.

21. Alice Clink Schumacher, *Hiram Percy Maxim* (Greenvile, NH: The Ham Radio Publishing Group, 1970), 61. While Maxim was a prolific inventor, virtually the en-tirety of this biography is devoted to his work developing radio. According to the book, he was dubbed the "Father of Amateur Radio" (123).

22. "The Menace of the Noiseless Gun," *Scientific American* 100, no. 12 (March 20, 1909), 218.

23. "The 'Silencer' for Firearms," *New York Times*, March 18, 1909.

24. 1909 Me. Laws 141.

25. "Bars Maxim Silent Gun," *New York Times*, March 8, 1909.
26. 1911 N.J. Laws 185.
27. "Would Suppress Silencers," *New York Times*, February 3, 1916.
28. William T. Hornaday, *Our Vanishing Wild Life* (New York: New York Zoological Society, 1913), 146, 287.
29. "Would Suppress Silencers," *New York Times*, February 3, 1916.
30. Lee Kennett and James LaVerne Anderson, *The Gun in America* (Westport, CT: Greenwood Press, 1975), 202.
31. See § 1543, 1936 Ariz. Sess. Laws at 204; Act of Mar. 29, 1927, ch. 169, 35 Del. Laws 516 (1927); Act of July 1, 1933, no. 36, 1933 Haw. Sess. Laws 38, 38–39; Act of July 3, 1918, no. 88, § 3, 1918 La. Acts 131, 132; Act of Mar. 24, 1909, ch. 129, 1909 Me. Laws 141; Act of Apr. 16, 1926, ch. 261, 1926 Mass. Acts 256; Act of May 7, 1913, no. 250, 1913 Mich. Pub. Acts 472; Act of Mar. 13, 1913, ch. 64, 1913 Minn. Laws 55; Act of Mar. 7, 1925, ch. 460, § 4, 1925 N.C. Sess. Laws 529, 530; Act of Apr. 7, 1911, ch. 128, 1911 N.J. Laws 185; Act of Apr. 6, 1919, ch. 137, 1916 N.Y. Laws 338, 338–39; Act of May 24, 1923, no. 228, § 704, 1923 Pa. Laws 359, 386; Act of Apr. 22, 1927, ch. 1052, § 8, 1927 R.I. Pub. Laws 256, 259; Act of Nov. 14, 1912, no. 237, 1912 Vt. Acts & Resolves 310; § 97, ch. 83, 1921 Wyo. Sess. Laws 112-13.
32. See § 1543, 1936 Ariz. Sess. Laws at 204; ch. 169, 35 Del. Laws, 516 (1927); no. 88, § 3, 1918 La. Acts at 132; ch. 460, § 4, 1925 N.C. Sess. Laws at 530 (applying to both hunting and general use); ch. 128, 1911 N.J. Laws at 185; no. 228, § 704, 1923 Pa. Laws at 386; § 97, ch. 83, 1921 Wyo. Sess. Laws 112-113.
33. "Silent Gun Kills a Family of Four," *New York Times*, February 1, 1915.
34. 1916 N.Y. Laws 338–339.
35. "Trace Lewis's Movements," *New York Times*, January 6, 1917.
36. "Slayers Escape Police Net," *New York Times*, December 17, 1920.
37. "Motorist Shoots Holes in Glass Store Fronts," *Syracuse Post-Standard*, March 28, 1920. According to the account, one person was injured, and "pistol muffled with Maxim silencer."
38. "$80,000 Robbery Just Off 5th Av.," *New York Times*, March 17, 1921; "Murderer Decoys Victim By Phone," *New York Times*, December 11, 1921; "Slain with Own Gun, Say Veasey's Friends," *New York Times*, January 12, 1930.
39. "Other Cities Want Omaha Sniper," *New York Times*, February 24, 1926.
40. This account is based on stories found at newspapers.com. According to its website, it includes over twenty thousand newspapers in its archives. A search of the terms "Maxim silencer" and "silencer" yielded thousands of articles across the three decades examined. A systematic empirical study of these thousands of stories is beyond the scope of this project.
41. "Silent Guns in Taxi War; Special Orders to Police," *St. Louis Post-Dispatch*, December 19, 1911.
42. "Big Murder Plot in San Diego?" *Syracuse Journal*, May 24, 1912.
43. "Shoot at Militia on the Texas Border," *New York Times*, February 27, 1912.

44. "San Diego Mystery in Navy Man's Death," *Oxnard Daily Courier*, January 13, 1921.

45. "A Dangerous Device," *The Brooklyn Times*, February 28, 1912.

46. "Aids to Criminals," *Yonkers Statesman*, January 4, 1921.

47. "Crank Slays Young Boys," *St. Joseph (Mich.) Herald-Press*, June 23, 1921.

48. "Says He's Sorry He 'Has to Rob'," *The Daily Telegram (Long Beach)*, August 5, 1921.

49. "Ugly Giant and Arsenal Captured in Lagrange," *Bangor Daily News*, August 10, 1921.

50. "Gangsters Kill 2 At Stag Party in Gravesend Bay," *Brooklyn Daily Times*, May 12, 1925.

51. "Crime in Chicago," *The Great Falls Tribune*, July 18, 1926.

52. "Wounded by One of Two Burglars He Finds in Home," *St. Louis Post-Dispatch*, January 30, 1928.

53. "Phantom Sniper Wounds Three," *Lancaster (Pa.) New Era*, February 3, 1928.

54. "Bullet Crashes Through Window," *The Daily Times*, New Philadelphia, Ohio, June 16, 1928.

55. "Will Crooks Return Mr. Levy's License?" *Paterson (N.J.) Evening News*, June 22, 1928.

56. "Gangster Gives Grim Details in Capone's Flight," *Sunday Courier-Post*, Camden, N.J., May 19, 1929.

57. "Winklewads," *Rutland (Vt.) Daily Herald*, January 2, 1911.

58. "Daily Greeting," *The Long Beach (Cal.) Press*, January 16, 1912.

59. "Paragraphers' Shots," *Daily Press (Newport News, Va.)*, March 8, 1912.

60. "Maxim Bans Gun Silencer," *New York Times*, May 8, 1930.

61. "Hearings Before the Committee on Ways and Means, National Firearms Act, H.R. 9066," U.S. House of Representatives, April 16, 18, May 14, 15, and 16, 1934 (Washington, D.C.: GPO, 1934), 111.

62. Halbrook, "Firearm Sound Moderators," 41.

63. Adam C. Paulson, *Silencers: History and Performance* (Boulder, CO: Paladin Press, 1996), 10.

64. Clark, "Criminal Use of Gun Silencers," 48.

65. David Kopel, "The Hearing Protection Act and 'Silencers,'" *Washington Post*, June 19, 2017, https://www.washingtonpost.com/news/volokh-conspiracy/wp/2017/06/19/the-hearing-protection-act-and-silencers/.

66. Alexander Zaitchik, "Silencers: The NRA's Latest Big Lie," *Salon*, December 30, 2012, https://www.salon.com/2012/12/30/silencers_the_nras_latest_big_lie/.

67. Carl Brent Swisher, ed., *Selected Papers of Homer Cummings* (New York: Charles Scribner's Sons, 1939), 88.

68. According to one firearms expert who shoots AR-15s with silencers attached and with whom I spoke, a disadvantage of their use is that the trapped gas blows back to the person firing the weapon, leaving a carbonized firing powder taste and some black soot on the face, even when the weapon is regularly cleaned.

69. "Silencers Do More Than Save Your Hearing," *Gemtech Suppressors*, n.d., https://www.gemtech.com/silencers-do-more.

70. "Benefits of Using Suppressors for Hunting and Shooting Sports," National Shooting Sports Foundation, June 2016. The NSSF later removed this post.

71. Knox Williams, "Why I Formed the American Suppressor Association," November 26, 2019, https://americansuppressorassociation.com/why-i-formed-the-american-suppressor-association/. According to Williams, the initial meeting to establish the ASA included representatives from Williams' then-employer, the Advanced Armament Corp., and gun companies Gemtech, Gun Trust Lawyer, M3—Major Malfunction, SilencerCo, SWR, and the NRA. By the end of the meeting, three of the companies had pledged start-up money.

72. Nick Wing and Jessica Carro, "What If Millions of People Get Gun Silencers?" *The Huffington Post*, March 13, 2017, http://www.huffingtonpost.com/entry/gun-silencers-hearing-protection-act_us_58c6b59fe4b0ed71826e1be0; Glenn Kessler, "Are Firearms with a Silencer 'Quiet'?" *Washington Post*, March 20, 2017, https://www.washingtonpost.com/news/fact-checker/wp/2017/03/20/are-firearms-with-a-silencer-quiet/.

73. Scott E. Brueck et al., *Measurement of Exposure to Impulsive Noise at Indoor and Outdoor Firing Ranges During Tactical Training Exercises*, Health Hazard Evaluation Report No. 2013-0124-3208, June 2014, U.S. Department of Health and Human Services.

74. James K. Williamson, "How Easy Should It Be to Buy a Silencer for a Gun?" *The Trace*, June 14, 2017, https://www.thetrace.org/2017/06/gun-silencer-deregulation-congress/.

75. Kessler, "Are Firearms with a Silencer 'Quiet'?"

76. Sean Davis, "Progressives Don't Understand How Gun 'Silencers' Work," *The Federalist*, January 9, 2017, http://thefederalist.com/2017/01/09/progressives-dont-understand-how-gun-silencers-work-here-are-some-facts-to-help-them/.

77. Kessler, "Are Firearms with a Silencer 'Quiet'?"

78. See, for example, the full-page ad by Hornady marketing its "Sub-X Bullets" in *America's 1st Freedom*, December 2021, 3. As the ad says, "For ammunition that delivers big results without a big bang."

79. "NHCA Position Statement, Recreational Firearm Noise," National Hearing Conservation Association, March 16, 2017, 5.

80. Michael Stewart, "Recreational Firearm Noise Exposure," American Speech-Language-Hearing Association, n.d., http://www.asha.org/public/hearing/Recreational-Firearm-Noise-Exposure/.

81. Such "electronic hearing protection" earmuffs can be found on the internet for under $40. See for example "First Gear," *America's 1st Freedom,* March 2022, 45. I tried out such a set at a shooting range and found them remarkably effective at blocking out noise yet also allowing the wearer to hear sound in the immediate area.

82. Sweeney, *The Suppressor Handbook*, 13.

83. "Firearm Justifiable Homicides and Non-Fatal Self-Defense Gun Use," *Violence Policy Center*, June 2015, http://www.vpc.org/studies/justifiable15.pdf.

84. Rich Morin and Andrew Mercer, "A Closer Look at Police Officers Who Have Fired Their Weapon on Duty," *Pew Research Center*, April 8, 2017, https://www.pewresearch.org/fact-tank/2017/02/08/a-closer-look-at-police-officers-who-have-fired-their-weapon-on-duty/; Tim Stelloh, "Most Officers Never Fire Their Guns. But Some Kill Multiple People—And Are Still on the Job." *NBC News*, April 22, 2021, https://www.nbcnews.com/news/us-news/most-officers-never-fire-their-guns-some-kill-multiple-people-n1264795.

85. Sari Horwitz and Cleve R. Wootson, Jr., "'There Was a trail of blood': Ari Fleischer Was Nearly Caught in the Fort Lauderdale Shooting," *Washington Post*, January 7, 2017, https://www.washingtonpost.com/news/post-nation/wp/2017/01/07/there-was-a-trail-of-blood-ari-fleischer-was-nearly-caught-in-the-fort-lauderdale-shooting/.

86. Robert J. Spitzer, "The NRA Wants to Suppress One of Guns' Most Important Safety Features," *Washington Post*, January 22, 2017, https://www.washingtonpost.com/opinions/the-nra-wants-to-suppress-one-of-guns-most-important-safety-features/2017/01/22/5a7140fc-dcd7-11e6-ad42-f3375f271c9c_story.html?utm_t erm=.3f3e6a0dae3e. I do not mean to suggest that guns are somehow deliberately manufactured to make more noise than they would otherwise as a safety feature.

87. "Quiet Hybrid and Electric Cars Must Make Noise under New U.S. Safety Rule," *PBS Newshour*, November 14, 2016, http://www.pbs.org/newshour/rundown/quiet-hybrid-electric-cars-must-make-noise-new-u-s-safety-rule/; Stephen Edelstein, "EVs and Hybrids Get an Extension to Meet US Noise-Making Requirements," *Green Car Reports*, September 1, 2020, https://www.greencarreports.com/news/1129448_evs-and-hybrids-get-an-extension-to-meet-us-noise-making-requirements.

88. Ronald Turk, "Federal Firearms Regulations: Options to Reduce or Modify Firearms Regulations," Bureau of Alcohol, Tobacco, Firearms, and Explosives, January 20, 2017, 6–7. This document was marked "White Paper" and "Not for public distribution."

89. Williamson, "How Easy Should It Be to Buy a Silencer for a Gun?"

90. https://www.atf.gov/docs/undefined/typesbystatecy2017xlsx/download, Firearm Types Recovered and Traced in the United States and Territories, 2017.

91. Clark, "Criminal Use of Firearm Silencers," 48.

92. Lisa Marie Pane, "Did 'Silencer' Make a Difference in Virginia Beach Carnage?" *APnews.com*, June 2, 2019, https://www.apnews.com/1cfdc645dbd54592b685b 977e211c99b. A 2013 mass shooter, Christopher Dorner, employed silencers in a mass shooting in California that killed four and wounded three, including police officers. Claudia Koerner and Alejandra Molina, "Dorner Amassed Arsenal for Rampage," *Orange County Register*, February 28, 2013, https://www.ocregister.com/2013/02/28/dorner-amassed-arsenal-for-rampage/.

93. Gary A. Harki, Marie Albiges, and Peter Coutu, "The Silencer Used in Virginia Beach Was Legal. A Survivor Says It Was Lethal." *The Virginian-Pilot*, June 3, 2019, https://www.pilotonline.com/news/virginia-beach-mass-shooting/artic le_5f0bde4e-8660-11e9-b20e-9ff07af186a9.html.

94. These studies are summarized in: Michael Siegel and Claire Boine, "What Are the Most Effective Policies in Reducing Gun Homicides?" Rockefeller Institute of Government, March 29, 2019, https://rockinst.org/issue-area/what-are-the-most-effective-policies-in-reducing-gun-homicides/; Rosanna Smart et al., "The Science of Gun Policy: A Critical Synthesis of Research Evidence on the Effects of Gun Policies in the United States," 2nd ed. (Santa Monica, CA: RAND Corporation, 2020), https://www.rand.org/pubs/research_reports/RR2088-1.html; Chelsea Parsons and Rukmani Bhatia, "Dangerous Gaps in Gun Laws Exposed by the Coronavirus Gun Sale Surge," *Center for American Progress*, July 8, 2020, https://www.americanprogress.org/issues/guns-crime/reports/2020/07/08/486292/dangerous-gaps-gun-laws-exposed-coronavirus-gun-sale-surge/; Cassandra K. Crifasi, Alexander D. McCourt, and Daniel W. Webster, "The Impact of Handgun Purchaser Licensing on Gun Violence," Center for Gun Policy and Research, Johns Hopkins Bloomberg School of Public Health, n.d.; Cassandra K. Crifasi et al., "The Initial Impact of Maryland's Firearm Safety Act of 2013 on the Supply of Crime Handguns in Baltimore," *The Russell Sage Foundation Journal of the Social Sciences* 3 (October 2017): 128–140; Michael Rocque et al., "Policy Solutions to Address Mass Shootings," Regional Gun Violence Research Consortium of the Rockefeller Institute of Government, August 2021, 11, https://rockinst.org/issue-area/policy-solutions-to-address-mass-shootings/.

95. "Silencers: A Threat to Public Safety," *Violence Policy Center*, July 2019, http://www.vpc.org/studies/silencers.pdf.

96. Abby Simons, "Minnesota House Panel Backs Legalizing Firearm 'Silencers,'" *Star Tribune*, March 13, 2015, http://www.startribune.com/minnesota-house-panel-backs-legalizing-firearm-silencers/296160971/.

97. Robin L. Barton, "Why Silencers Aren't Golden," *The Crime Report*, June 20, 2017, https://thecrimereport.org/2017/06/20/why-silenced-guns-arent-golden/.

98. Stephanie Mencimer, "Gunmakers and the NRA Bet Big on Silencers," *Mother Jones*, March 19, 2013, http://www.motherjones.com/politics/2013/03/guns-nra-national-rifle-association-wants-states-legalize-silencers-supressors/.

99. Wing and Carro, "What If Millions of People Get Gun Silencers?"

100. Wing and Carro, "What If Millions of People Get Gun Silencers?"

101. "Silencers: A Threat to Public Safety," 2.

102. Karsten Strauss, "Guns And Money: The Silencer Industry Seeks to Break Down Barriers," *Forbes*, March 29, 2015, https://www.forbes.com/sites/karstenstrauss/2015/03/29/guns-and-money-the-silencer-industry-seeks-to-break-down-barriers/?sh=2b7854615f50.

103. Caitlin McFaul, "House Dems to Investigate WH Move to End Ban on Some Gun-Silencer Sales," *Fox News*, July 28, 2020, https://www.foxnews.com/polit ics/house-dems-to-investigate-wh-move-to-end-ban-on-some-gun-silencer-sales; "Oversight Subcommittee Opens Investigation into Trump Administration Decision to Overturn Firearm Suppressor Export Ban," Committee on Oversight and Reform, U.S. House of Representatives, July 28, 2020, https://oversight. house.gov/news/press-releases/oversight-subcommittee-opens-investigation- into-trump-administration-decision-to.

104. Michael Daly, "Donald Trump Jr. Endorsed Gun Silencers His Father Claims to Hate," *The Daily Beast*, June 4, 2019, https://www.thedailybeast.com/donald- trump-jr-endorsed-gun-silencers-his-father-claims-to-hate.

CHAPTER 4

1. Nolan McCaskill, "'A Seismic Quake': Floyd Killing Transforms Views on Race," *Politico*, June 10, 2020, https://www.politico.com/news/2020/06/10/george-flo yds-death-transforms-views-on-race-307575.

2. Jacqueline Alemany, "Power Up: There's Been a Dramatic Shift in Public Opinion About Police Treatment of Black Americans," *Washington Post*, June 9, 2020, https://www.washingtonpost.com/news/powerpost/paloma/powerup/2020/ 06/09/powerup-there-s-been-a-dramatic-shift-in-public-opinion-over-police- treatment-of-black-americans/5edef042602ff12947e87b23/.

3. Hannah Fingerhut, "Wide Shift in Opinion on Police, Race Rare in US Polling," *Associated Press*, July 2, 2020, https://apnews.com/8a0269689d3f981e8db1620ad bde4b95.

4. Teo Armus and Kim Bellware, "St. Louis Couple Point Guns at Crowd of Protesters Calling for Mayor to Resign," *Washington Post*, June 29, 2020, https:// www.washingtonpost.com/nation/2020/06/29/st-louis-protest-gun-mayor/.

5. Armus and Bellware, "St. Louis Couple"; Rachel Rice and Kim Bell, "Couple Points Guns at Protesters Marching to St. Louis Mayor's Home to Demand Resignation," *St. Louis Post Dispatch*, June 29, 2020, https://www.stltoday. com/news/local/crime-and-courts/couple-points-guns-at-protesters-march ing-to-st-louis-mayor-s-home-to-demand-resignation/article_9edc57ed-c307- 583f-9226-a44ba6ac9c03.html; Adam Weinstein, "Standing Their Ground in Well-Manicured Yards," *The New Republic*, June 29, 2020, https://newrepublic. com/article/158328/mark-patricia-mccloskey-st-louis-lawyers-guns-protesters; "Private Streets in Saint Louis," *urbanSTL*, n.d., https://urbanstl.com/private- streets-in-saint-louis-t2397.html.

6. Tom Jackman, "St. Louis Couple Who Aimed Guns at Protesters Charged with Felony Weapons Count," *Washington Post*, July 20, 2020, https://www.washing tonpost.com/nation/2020/07/20/st-louis-couple-who-aimed-guns-protesters- charged-with-felony-weapons-count/.

7. Joel Currier, "Grand Jury Indicts Gun-Waving St. Louis Couple on Gun, Tampering Charges," *St. Louis Post-Dispatch*, October 6, 2020, https://www. stltoday.com/news/local/crime-and-courts/mccloskeys-lawyer-says-st-louis-cou ple-indicted-on-gun-tampering-charges/article_4b967366-e448-53fc-b718-c2741 e45dc5d.html?utm_source=The+Trace+mailing+list&utm_campaign=d9dc14f a19-EMAIL_CAMPAIGN_2019_09_24_04_06_COPY_01&utm_medium= email&utm_term=0_f76c3ff31c-d9dc14fa19-69360165.

8. Jim Salter, "St. Louis Gun-Waving Couple Pleads Guilty to Misdemeanors," *AP*, June 17, 2021, https://apnews.com/article/michael-brown-st-louis-5d8codd118abe f6df4a4214becd2f30a.

9. "Missouri Revised Statutes Title XXXVIII. Crimes and Punishment; Peace Officers and Public Defenders § 571.030. Unlawful use of weapons—exceptions— penalties," *FindLaw*, https://codes.findlaw.com/mo/title-xxxviii-crimes-and-punishment-peace-officers-and-public-defenders/mo-rev-st-571-030.html; Chip Brownlee, "What Counts as Brandishing? When Is It Illegal?" *The Trace*, July 2, 2020, https://www.thetrace.org/2020/07/armed-st-louis-missouri-couple-threat-brandishing-self-defense/.

10. Brownlee, "What Counts as Brandishing?"

11. Heath Druzin and Leigh Paterson, "Guns Are an Increasing Danger at Already Tense Protests," *Guns & America*, July 30, 2020, https://gunsandamerica.org/ story/20/07/30/guns-anti-police-violence-protests-aurora-colorado/?utm_sou rce=The+Trace+mailing+list&utm_campaign=b6fd14fa42-EMAIL_CAMPAI GN_2019_09_24_04_06_COPY_01&utm_medium=email&utm_term=0_ f76c3ff31c-b6fd14fa42-69360165; Joshua Partlow, "Politics at the Point of a Gun," *Washington Post*, July 28, 2020, https://www.washingtonpost.com/politics/2020/ 07/28/conservative-armed-militias-protests-coronavirus/?arc404=true.

12. Alex Yablon, "The 36 States Where Local Officials Can't Ban Guns at Protests," *The Trace*, September 11, 2017, https://www.thetrace.org/2017/09/35-states-local-offici als-cant-ban-guns-protests/.

13. Jennifer Carlson, *Citizen-Protectors* (New York: Oxford University Press, 2015), 129.

14. A 2019 nationwide survey of over two thousand gun owners reported that about eight percent of respondents said they owned guns "to exercise my constitutional rights, they give me a feeling of power." Michael B. Siegel and Claire C. Boine, "The Meaning of Guns to Gun Owners in the U.S.: The 2019 National Lawful Use of Guns Survey," *American Journal of Preventive Medicine*, July 28, 2020, https:// www.ajpmonline.org/article/S0749-3797(20)30239-7/fulltext?utm_source= The+Trace+mailing+list&utm_campaign=0c21f2aac5-EMAIL_CAMPAIGN_ 2019_08_29_06_04_COPY_01&utm_medium=email&utm_term=0_f76c3ff 31c-0c21f2aac5-69360165.

15. Mike Spies, "The Push to Allow Americans to Carry Concealed Guns Without Permits," *The Trace*, February 9, 2021, https://www.thetrace.org/2016/03/per mitless-carry-states-west-virginia/?utm_source=The+Trace+mailing+list&utm_

campaign=4426d2c5b4-EMAIL_CAMPAIGN_2019_09_24_04_06_COPY _01&utm_medium=email&utm_term=0_f76c3ff31c-4426d2c5b4-112434 573&utm_source=The+Trace+mailing+list&utm_campaign=4b1ed74690- EMAIL_CAMPAIGN_2019_09_24_04_06_COPY_01&utm_medium= email&utm_term=0_f76c3ff31c-4b1ed74690-112434573.

16. Leah Sottile, "The Chaos Agents," *The New York Times Magazine*, August 23, 2020, 42.

17. Gus Burns, "Soggy Protesters Demand Michigan Gov. Whitmer End the Coronavirus 'Lockdown,'" *LiveMichigan*, May 14, 2020, https://www.mlive.com/ public-interest/2020/05/soggy-protesters-demand-michigan-gov-whitmer-end- the-coronavirus-lockdown.html.

18. Luke Mogelson, "Nothing to Lose But Your Masks," *The New Yorker*, August 24, 2020, 38.

19. Interview posted on Twitter, August 26, 2020, https://twitter.com/RichieMcGinn iss/status/1298657958205820928?utm_source=The+Trace+mailing+list&utm_ campaign=bfeef019a1-EMAIL_CAMPAIGN_2019_09_24_04_06_COPY_ 01&utm_medium=email&utm_term=0_f76c3ff31c-bfeef019a1-69360165.

20. "17-Year-Old Arrested After 2 Killed During Unrest in Kenosha," *U.S. News and World Report*, August 27, 2020, https://www.usnews.com/news/us/articles/2020- 08-26/kenosha-police-3-shot-2-fatally-during-wisconsin-protests. Wisconsin also does not have a stand-your-ground law.

21. Glenn C. Altschuler, "Vigilantes Are Not Patriots," *The Hill*, November 28, 2021, https://thehill.com/opinion/criminal-justice/583255-vigilantes-are-not-patriots.

22. Robert J. Spitzer, *Guns Across America: Reconciling Gun Rules and Rights* (New York: Oxford University Press, 2015), Ch. 2.

23. Dahlia Lithwick and Olivia Li, "Can You Bring a Gun to a Protest?" *Slate*, October 17, 2017, https://slate.com/news-and-politics/2017/10/protests-might-be-one- place-you-cant-carry-guns.html.

24. Saul Cornell, "The Right to Keep and Carry Arms in Anglo-American Law," *Law and Contemporary Problems* 80 (2017): 14.

25. Saul Cornell, "History, Text, Tradition, and the Future of Second Amendment Jurisprudence," *Law and Contemporary Problems* 83 (2020): 82.

26. Lithwick and Li, "Can You Bring a Gun to a Protest?" Mark Anthony Frassetto cites a number of British treatises and court cases that all confirm that "the simple possession of weapons was sufficient to turn a lawful gathering into an un- lawful assembly." Neither violence nor the threat of violence need have occurred. "To the Terror of the People: Public Disorder Crimes and the Original Public Understanding of the Second Amendment," *Southern Illinois University Law Journal* 43 (2018): 79.

27. Stephen P. Halbrook, The Common Law and the Right of the People to Bear Arms: Carrying Firearms at the Founding and in the Early Republic," *Lincoln Memorial University Law Review* 7 (Spring 2020): 74.

28. Michael Dalton, *The Country Justice,* Chap. CXVI, Sect. LXVII, "Sureties for the Peace" (1727), 380. The original version of Dalton's work dates to the early 1600s.

29. William C. Sprague, *Blackstone's Commentaries,* abridged, 5th ed. (Detroit, MI: Sprague Correspondence, 1899), 460.

30. Dalton, *The Country Justice,* 380.

31. Cornell, "The Right to Keep and Carry Arms in Anglo-American Law," 18–21. Quoted in Cornell, 18.

32. Quoted in Frassetto, "To the Terror of the People," 82.

33. Frassetto, "To the Terror of the People," 82–83.

34. 1642 N.Y. Laws 33. This and the other colonial and state laws found at the Duke Center for Firearms Law digital archive of gun laws, https://firearmslaw.duke.edu/repository/search-the-repository/; *Young v. Hawaii,* 992 F.3d 765, 794–795 (9th Cir. 2021); Jonathan E. Taylor, "The Surprisingly Strong Originalist Case for Public Carry Laws," *Harvard Journal of Law & Public Policy* 43 (Spring 2020): 353.

35. 1786 Mass. Sess. Laws, § 1.

36. Taylor, "The Surprisingly Strong Originalist Case for Public Carry Laws," 353. See also Joseph Blocher and Reva B. Siegel, "When Guns Threaten the Public Sphere: A New Account of Public Safety Regulation Under Heller," *Northwestern University Law Review* 116 (2021): 164–172.

37. An Act against Swords, &c, 1686 N.J. Laws 289, 289, ch. IX. Quoted in *Young v. Hawaii,* 992 F.3d 765, 794 (9th Cir. 2021).

38. 1699 N.H. Laws, 1. Quoted in *Young v. Hawaii,* 794–795.

39. 1786 Va. Acts 33, ch. 21.

40. Francois Xavier Martin, *A Collection of Statutes of the Parliament of England in Force in the State of North Carolina,* 60–61 (Newbern 1792).

41. 1795 Mass. Acts 436, ch. 2. Quoted in *Young v. Hawaii,* 799. See also 1692 Mass. Acts 10, 11–12.

42. 1801 Tenn. Pub. Acts 260, ch. 22, § 6. Quoted in *Young v. Hawaii,* 798.

43. 1821 Me. Laws 285, ch. 73 § 1. Quoted in *Young v. Hawaii,* 798–799.

44. The Statutes of the State of Mississippi, 1840, § 55; 1854 Wash. Sess. Law 80, ch. 2, §30; Digest of the Laws of California, 1858; A Digest of the Laws of Pennsylvania, 1860, page 250; 1867 Ariz. Sess. Laws 21–22, § 1; 1868 Ark. Acts 218, § 12–13; 1870 Id. Sess. Laws 21; 1873 Nev. Stat. 118, ch. 62, § 1; A Digest of the Laws of Texas, 1873; 1875 Ind. Acts 62, § 1; The Revised Charter and Ordinances of the City of Boonville, MO., 1881, § 6; The General Laws of New Mexico, 1882 Page 313; The Revised Statutes of the State of Illinois, 1883; 1884 Wyo. Sess. Laws 114, ch. 67, § 1; 1885 Mont. Laws 74; 1897 Fla. Laws 59, chap. 4532, § 1; Annotated Code of the State of Iowa, 1897, Page 1898, § 4775; The Session Laws (Washington) of 1897, Page 1956; Annotated Statutes of the Indian Territory (Oklahoma), 1899; 1925 W.Va. Acts 25–30, ch. 3, § 7, pt. a; 1931 Mich. Pub. Acts 670, ch. 37, § 233.

45. The Statutes of the State of Mississippi, 1840, § 55.

46. Henry C. Black, *Black's Law Dictionary* (St. Paul, MN: West Publishing Co., 1991), 680.

47. 1642 N.Y. Laws 33; 1686 N.J. Laws 289, ch. IX; 1692 Mass. Acts 10, 11–12; 1786 Mass. Sess. Laws (included Maine); 1795 Mass. Acts 436, ch. 2; 1836 Mass. Acts 748, 750, ch. 134; 1699 N.H. Laws 1, 1–2; 1786 Va. Acts 33, ch. 21; Francois Xavier Martin, *A Collection of Statutes of the Parliament of England in Force in the State of North Carolina*, 60–61 (Newbern 1792): 1801 Tenn. Pub. Acts 260, ch. 22 § 6; 1821 Me. Laws 285, ch. 73 § 1; Revised Statutes of the State of Delaware, 1852, § 3; 1880 Ga. Laws 151; 1883 Ind. Acts 1712, chap. 87, § 6678; 1886 N.M. Laws 56, ch. 30, § 4; 1889 N.C. Sess. Laws 502, ch. 527, § 1; 1893 Or. Laws 29–30, § 1; The Code of Alabama, 1897, § 4342; Book of Ordinances of the City of Wichita, Kansas, 1899, § 1; Revised Statutes of Wyoming, 1899; 1910 S.C. Acts 694.

48. 1880 Ga. Laws 151.

49. Revised Statutes of Delaware, 1852, § 3.

50. 1893 Or. Laws 29–30, § 1.

51. 1889 N.C. Sess. Laws 502, ch. 527, § 1.

52. Robert J. Spitzer, "Gun Law History in the United States and Second Amendment Rights," *Law and Contemporary Problems* 80 (2017): 63–67. The list of states with anti-concealed carry laws found in this article did not include California (1917 Cal. Sess. Laws 221–225) which brings the total to forty-seven states.

53. Robert J. Spitzer, *The Politics of Gun Control*, 8th ed. (New York: Routledge, 2021), 98–99.

54. Spitzer, "Gun Law History in the United States and Second Amendment Rights," 58–68; Robert J. Spitzer, "Guns Don't Belong Near Polling Places. Right Wingers Want Them There Anyway," *Washington Post*, September 30, 2020, https://www.washingtonpost.com/outlook/2020/09/30/guns-polling-places-intimidation/.

55. Richard Franklin Bensel, *The American Ballot Box in the Mid-Nineteenth Century* (New York: Cambridge University Press, 2004), 292.

56. Bensel, *The American Ballot Box in the Mid-Nineteenth Century*, xiv.

57. Glenn C. Altschuler and Stuart M. Blumin, *Rude Republic: Americans and Their Politics in the Nineteenth Century* (Princeton, NJ: Princeton University Press, 2000), 175.

58. Jill Lepore, "Rock, Paper, Scissors," *The New Yorker*, October 6, 2008, https://www.newyorker.com/magazine/2008/10/13/rock-paper-scissors; Kate Keller, "Why Are There Laws That Restrict What People Can Wear to the Polls?" *Smithsonian*, June 15, 2018, https://www.smithsonianmag.com/history/why-are-there-laws-restrict-what-people-can-wear-polls-180969381.

59. Proceedings of The Conventions of the Province of Maryland, Held at the City of Annapolis in 1774, 1775, & 1776 185 (1836); Del. Const. art. 28 (1776); Act of Jan. 26, 1787, ch. 1, 1787 N.Y. Laws 345; Act of Dec. 1, 1869, ch. 22, sec. 2, 1869 Tenn. Pub. Acts 108; Act of Mar. 16, 1870, sec. 73, 1870 La. Acts 159; Ga. Code § 4528 (1873); Chief Justice LeBaron Bradford Prince, The General Laws of New

Mexico: Including All the Unrepealed General Laws from the Promulgation of the "Kearney Code" in 1846, to the End of the Legislative Session of 1880, with Supplement, Including the Session of 1882 Page 313, Image 313 (1882) available at The Making of Modern Law: Primary Sources; 1879 Tex. Crim. Stat. tit. IX, Ch. 4 (Penal Code); 1895 Tex. Crim. Stat. 93; 1883 Mo. Laws 76, An Act to Amend Section 1274, Article 2, Chapter 24 of the Revised Statutes of Missouri, Entitled "Of Crimes and Criminal Procedure," § 1; Terr. Okla. Stat. ch. 25, art. 47, § 7 (1890); 1901 Ariz. Acts 1252, Crimes and Punishments, §§ 387 and 391.

60. Md. Laws 216, §6 (1637). Maryland enacted a similar measure in 1650 extending the rule to the now-bicameral colonial legislature.

61. Del. Const., art. 28 (1776).

62. Act of Jan. 26, 1787, ch. 1, 1787 N.Y. Laws 345.

63. Act of Dec. 1, 1869, ch. 22, sec. 2, 1869 Tenn. Pub. Acts 108.

64. Robert J. Spitzer, "Guns Don't Belong Near Polling Places"; Mark Berman, "Guns at Voting Sites Emerge as Flash Point in Michigan amid Nationwide Election Tension," *Washington Post*, October 26, 2020, https://www.washingtonpost.com/national/guns-at-voting-sites-emerge-as-flash-point-in-michigan-amid-nationwide-election-tension/2020/10/26/27c72488-17ce-11eb-82db-60b15c874105_story.html; "Guns in Polling Places Make a Mockery of the American Ideal of Free and Open Elections," *Chicago Sun-Times*, October 27, 2020, https://chicago.suntimes.com/2020/10/27/21537018/election-day-guns-intimidation-poll-watchers-donald-trump-editorial.

65. For example, Darrell A.G. Miller, "Guns as Smut: Defending the Home-Bound Second Amendment," *Columbia Law Review* 109 (2009): 1278–1356; Eugene Volokh, "The First and Second Amendment," *Columbia Law Review Sidebar* 109 (October 27, 2009): 97–104; Darrell A.H. Miller, "A Short Reply to Professor Volokh," *Columbia Law Review* 109 (October 27, 2009): 105–106; Eric M. Rubin, "Justifying Perceptions in First and Second Amendment Doctrine," *Law and Contemporary Problems* 80, no. 2 (2017): 149–177; Katlyn E. DeBoer, "Clash of the First and Second Amendments," *Hastings Constitutional Law Quarterly* 45 (Winter 2018): 333–371; Eric Tirschwell and Alla Lefkowitz, "Prohibiting Guns at Public Demonstrations: Debunking First and Second Amendment Myths After Charlottesville," *UCLA Law Review*, April 5, 2018, https://www.uclalawreview.org/prohibiting-guns-at-public-demonstrations/; Joseph Blocher and Bardia Vaseghi, "True Threats and the Second Amendment," *The Journal of Law, Medicine & Ethics* (Forthcoming 2020); Michael C. Dorf, "When Two Rights Make a Wrong: Armed Assembly Under the First and Second Amendments," *Northwestern University Law Review* 116 (2021): 111–138.

66. Joseph Blocher et al., "Pointing Guns," *Texas Law Review* 99 (2021): 1173–2000.

67. Gregory P. Magarian, "Conflicting Reports: When Gun Rights Threaten Free Speech," *Law and Contemporary Problems* 83 (2020): 172.

68. Miller, "Guns as Smut," 1309–1310.

69. Volokh, "The First and Second Amendment," 102.

70. Christopher Ingraham, "3 Million Americans Carry Loaded Handguns with Them Every Single Day, Study Finds," *Washington Post,* October 19, 2017, https://www. washingtonpost.com/news/wonk/wp/2017/10/19/3-million-americans-carry-loa ded-handguns-with-them-every-single-day-study-finds/. Three million divided by roughly 270 million adult Americans is a little over one percent. The consequences of concealed gun carry, by definition, center on its relationship to crime and safety, which is beyond the scope of this essay. For more on that, see Spitzer, *The Politics of Gun Control,* 92–107.

71. David Frum, "The Chilling Effects of Openly Displayed Firearms," *The Atlantic,* August 16, 2017, https://www.theatlantic.com/politics/archive/2017/08/open-carry-laws-mean-charlottesville-could-have-been-graver/537087/.

72. Blocher and Vaseghi, "True Threats and the Second Amendment."

73. Garrett Epps, "Guns Are No Mere Symbol," *The Atlantic,* January 21, 2020, https:// www.theatlantic.com/ideas/archive/2020/01/guns-are-no-mere-symbol/605239/ ?fbclid=IwAR1bLACiL6GbBhegaTuhp6loxEycBbyoyU3JJZEK8YgCP_27ieEi 7zqTqos.

74. Julia Lurie, "The Human Brain Reacts to Guns as If They Were Spiders or Snakes," *Mother Jones,* October 26, 2015, https://www.motherjones.com/politics/2015/10/ psychology-gun-violence-brad-bushman-inquiring-minds/.

75. Quoted in Paige Williams, "American Vigilante," *The New Yorker,* July 5, 2021, 33. Emphasis in original.

76. David Hemenway, Mary Vriniotis, and Matthew Miller, "Is an Armed Society a Polite Society? Guns and Road Rage," *Accident Analysis and Prevention,* 38 (July 2006): 687–695.

77. *Miranda v. Arizona,* 384 U.S. 436 (1966), 455, 533.

78. Robert Jervis, "Cooperation Under the Security Dilemma," *World Politics* 30 (January 1978): 169.

79. John J. Mearsheimer, *The Tragedy of Great Power Politics* (New York: W.W. Norton, 2014), 36. See also Bruce Russett, *The Prisoners of Insecurity* (San Francisco, CA: W.H. Freeman, 1983).

80. Mearsheimer, *The Tragedy of Great Power Politics,* 129–130; Joseph S. Nye, *Understanding International Conflicts* (New York: Pearson, 2009), 61–63.

81. Guha Krishnamurthi and Peter Salib, *Small Arms Races,* University of Chicago Law Review Online (Forthcoming), https://papers.ssrn.com/sol3/papers. cfm?abstract_id=4007572

82. Siegel and Boine, "The Meaning of Guns to Gun Owners in the U.S."; Joan Burbick, *Gun Show Nation* (New York: The New Press, 2006), 91–93.

83. Tara D. Warner and Shawn Ratcliff, "What Guns Mean: Who Sees Guns as Important, Essential, and Empowering (and Why)?" *Sociological Inquiry* 20, no. 10 (2021): 20.

84. David Hemenway, Sara J. Skolnick, and Deborah R. Azrael, "Firearms and Community Feelings of Safety," *Journal of Criminal Law and Criminology* 86 (Fall 1995): 123; Carlson, *Citizen-Protectors*, 130.

85. "Guns," *Gallup.com*, n.d., https://news.gallup.com/poll/1645/guns.aspx.

86. Julia A. Wolfson et al., "US Public Opinion on Carrying Firearms in Public Places," *American Journal of Public Health* 107 (June 2017): 929–937. Similar polling results date back decades. See Spitzer, *The Politics of Gun Control*, 106–107.

87. Alexandra Filindra, "Americans Do Not Want Guns at Protests, This Research Shows," *Washington Post*, November 21, 2021, https://www.washingtonpost.com/politics/2021/11/21/americans-do-not-want-guns-protests-this-research-shows/?utm_source=The+Trace+mailing+list&utm_campaign=d5d8f25745-EMAIL_CAMPAIGN_2019_09_24_04_06_COPY_01&utm_medium=email. The survey was of 1500 respondents, one thousand white and five hundred Black. See Alexandra Filindra, et al., "American Identity, Guns, and Political Violence in Black and White: A Report Based on a New National Survey," University of Illinois Chicago, June 14, 2021, https://pols.uic.edu/wp-content/uploads/sites/273/2021/06/Guns-and-Violence-in-America-Report-6.17.21.pdf

88. Timothy Johnson, "Daily Caller Pushes Invented Psychological Disorder to Silence Victims of Gun Violence," *Media Matters*, May 2, 2013, https://www.mediamatters.org/national-rifle-association/daily-caller-pushes-invented-psychological-disorder-silence-victims-gun.

89. Dan Baum, *Gun Guys* (New York: Vintage books, 2013), 151–152.

90. Scott Melzer, *Gun Crusaders* (New York: New York University Press, 2009), 133–135.

91. Baum, *Gun Guys*, 151. With slight variations, these rules, sometimes expanded in number, are pretty much universal, such as: *NRA Guide to the Basics of Pistol Shooting* (Fairfax, VA: The National Rifle Association of America, 2009), 3–8; Jessie Ann Bourjaily and Phil Bourjaily, "5 Gun Safety Basics to Practice and Pass on," *Field & Stream*, October 30, 2019, https://www.fieldandstream.com/5-gun-safety-basics/.

92. https://www.cdc.gov/nchs/fastats/injury.htm

93. Jennifer Mascia, "26 States Will Let You Carry a Concealed Gun Without Making Sure You Know How to Shoot One," *The Trace*, February 2, 2016, https://www.thetrace.org/2016/02/live-fire-training-not-mandatory-concealed-carry-permits/.

94. Spitzer, *The Politics of Gun Control*, 85–90. The instrumentality effect has been studied from both criminological and medical perspectives. It also explains why the American murder rate is far higher than that of other Western nations, even though our crime rates are otherwise about the same. Unlike other developed nations, guns are far more prolific in the U.S. and account for over half of all U.S. murders, central to understanding the far greater likelihood of death.

95. For example, Yasser S. Selman, "Medico-legal Study of Shockwave Damage by High Velocity Missiles in Firearm Injuries," *Journal of the Faculty of Medicine,*

Baghdad 53 (October 2011): 401–405; Leana Wen, "What Bullets Do to Bodies," *New York Times*, June 15, 2017, https://www.nytimes.com/2017/06/15/opinion/virginia-baseball-shooting-gun-shot-wounds.html?_r=0; Ryan Hodnick, "Penetrating Trauma Wounds Challenge EMS Providers," *Journal of Emergency Medical Services* March 30, 2012, http://www.jems.com/artic les/print/volume-37/issue-4/patient-care/penetrating-trauma-wounds-challe nge-ems.html; Sarah Zhang, "What an AR-15 Can Do to the Human Body," *Wired*, June 17, 2016, https://www.wired.com/2016/06/ar-15-can-human-body/.

96. Quoted in Timothy Williams, "N.R.A. Backs Away from Article Criticizing Advocates of Carrying Guns in Public," *New York Times*, June 4, 2014, https://www.nytimes.com/2014/06/05/us/nra-backs-away-from-criticism-of-open-carry-advocates.html.

97. Jennifer Mascia, "'This Isn't Normal': Governing with Guns in the State House," *The Trace*, October 31, 2020, https://www.thetrace.org/2020/10/michigan-misso uri-washington-no-guns-inside-statehouse/.

98. "Armed Assembly: Guns, Demonstrations, and Political Violence in America," ACLED and Everytown for Gun Safety, August 2021, https://acleddata.com/2021/08/23/armed-assembly-guns-demonstrations-and-political-violence-in-america/?utm_source=The+Trace+mailing+list&utm_campaign=46681b2 doa-EMAIL_CAMPAIGN_2019_09_24_04_06_COPY_01&utm_medium=email&utm_term=0_f76c3ff31c-46681b2doa-69360165. The analysis defined armed demonstrations as "demonstrations in which individuals and groups—including militias, militant social movements, and unaffiliated individuals and groups—are present and identified as equipped with firearms in print, photographs, and/or video."

99. "Updated Armed Demonstration Data Released a Year After the 6 January Insurrection Show New Trends," The Armed Conflict Location & Event Data Project," https://acleddata.com/2022/01/05/updated-armed-demonstration-data-released-a-year-after-the-6-january-insurrection-show-new-trends/?utm _source=The+Trace+mailing+list&utm_campaign=589479c541-EMAIL_ CAMPAIGN_2019_09_24_04_06_COPY_01&utm_medium=email&utm_ term=0_f76c3ff31c-589479c541-69360165.

100. Robert J. Spitzer, "Why Are People Bringing Guns to Anti-quarantine Protests? To Be Intimidating." *Washington Post*, August 27, 2020, https://www.washing tonpost.com/outlook/2020/04/27/why-are-people-bringing-guns-anti-quarant ine-protests-be-intimidating/.

101. John Passantino et al., "Suspect in Fatal Portland Shooting of Right-Wing Activist Killed During Attempted Arrest, US Marshals Say," *CNN.com*, September 4, 2020, https://www.cnn.com/2020/09/04/us/portland-protest-suspected-killer/index.html; Chris Woodyard and Kevin McCoy, "'Arms race': How the Portland Shooting Shows Protesters on the Right and the Left Are Bringing Guns," *USA

Today, September 4, 2020, https://www.usatoday.com/story/news/2020/09/
04/portland-shooting-how-protesters-right-and-left-may-arm-themselves-rall
ies/5723571002/?utm_source=The+Trace+mailing+list&utm_campaign=cc6
afe0a3e-EMAIL_CAMPAIGN_2019_09_24_04_06_COPY_01&utm_med
ium=email&utm_term=0_f76c3ff31c-cc6afe0a3e-69360165.

102. Woodyard and McCoy, " 'Arms race.' "
103. Jonathan Obert, Andrew Poe, and Austin Sarat, eds., *The Lives of Guns*
(New York: Oxford University Press, 2019), 1.
104. Kathy McCormack, "Governor Cancels Inaugural, Citing Mask Protests at His
Home," *Associated Press,* December 30, 2020, https://apnews.com/article/arrests-
concord-coronavirus-pandemic-new-hampshire-74c5be34db1e55a287b4b1da4
bf89958.

CHAPTER 5

1. Judith McDaniel, "The Sanctuary Movement, Then and Now," *Religion & Politics,*
February 21, 2017, https://religionandpolitics.org/2017/02/21/the-sanctuary-
movement-then-and-now/.
2. McDaniel, "The Sanctuary Movement, Then and Now."
3. *Printz v. United States,* 521 U.S. 898 (1997).
4. Rick Su, "The Rise of Second Amendment Sanctuaries," *American Constitution
Society,* March 2021, 17, https://www.acslaw.org/wp-content/uploads/2021/03/
The-Rise-of-Second-Amendment-Sanctuaries.pdf; Shawn E. Fields, "Second
Amendment Sanctuaries," *Northwestern University Law Review* 115 (2020): 441–443.
5. Su, "The Rise of Second Amendment Sanctuaries," 1.
6. Tracy Garnar, Sione Lynn Pili Lister, and Jennifer Carlson, "Whiteness and
Impunity: Examining Virginia's Second Amendment Sanctuary Movement,"
Sociological Inquiry, 22 (2021): 1–26.
7. Jennifer Mascia, "Second Amendment Sanctuaries, Explained," *The Trace,* January
14, 2020, https://www.thetrace.org/2020/01/second-amendment-sanctuary-
movement/; Owen Daugherty, "Dozens of Virginia Counties Declare Themselves
'Second Amendment Sanctuaries' after Democrats Win State Legislature," *The
Hill,* December 7, 2019, https://thehill.com/homenews/state-watch/473503-
dozens-of-virginia-counties-declare-themselves-second-amendment; "What Are
So-Called "Second Amendment Sanctuaries?" n.d., https://www.bradyunited.
org/act/second-amendment-sanctuaries; Stephen Gruber-Miller, "These Iowa
Counties Voted to Become 'Second Amendment Sanctuaries.' Here's What That
Means," *Des Moines Register,* July 19, 2021, https://www.desmoinesregister.com/
story/news/politics/2021/07/19/iowa-jasper-hardin-counties-second-amendm
ent-sanctuaries-oppose-unconstitutional-gun-firearm-laws/7971733002/;
https://en.wikipedia.org/wiki/Second_Amendment_sanctuary; Sarah Okeson,
"Feds Sue Missouri Over Effort to Nullify Gun Laws," *DCReport,* February 25,

2022, https://www.dcreport.org/2022/02/25/feds-sue-missouri-over-effort-to-nullify-gun-laws/. From 2010 to 2014, four states enacted measures that claimed immunity from some federal gun laws, although they did not use the phrase Second Amendment sanctuary. Fields, "Second Amendment Sanctuaries," 446.

8. Thomas R. Dye and Susan A. McManus, *Politics in States and Communities*, 15th ed. (Boston: Pearson, 2015), 56–65.

9. J.W. Peltason and Sue Davis, *Corwin & Peltason's Understanding the Constitution*, 15th ed. (New York: Harcourt, 2000), 204–205.

10. Douglas Bradburn, "A Clamor in the Public Mind: Opposition to the Alien and Sedition Acts," *William and Mary Quarterly* 65(July 2008): 565–600.

11. James H. Read and Neal Allen, "Living, Dead, and Undead: Nullification Past and Present," *American Political Thought* 1(Fall 2012): 274.

12. William W. Freehling, ed., *The Nullification Era* (New York: Harper & Row, 1967), ix–xvii.

13. John C. Calhoun, "Fort Hill Address," in William W. Freehling, ed., *The Nullification Era*, 146; Merrill D. Peterson, *The Great Triumvirate: Webster, Clay, and Calhoun* (New York: Oxford University Press, 1987), 177–178, 186–192, 213–214.

14. William W. Freehling, *Prelude to Civil War* (New York: Harper & Row, 1966), 165; William H. Freehling, *The Road to Disunion, Vol. 1, Secessionists at Bay, 1776-1854* (New York: Oxford University Press, 1990), 257–260. The term "interposition" is sometimes used as a synonym for nullification, but also sometimes defined in contrary ways. Read and Allen, "Living, Dead, and Undead," 278.

15. Freehling, *Prelude to Civil War*, 171.

16. Read and Allen, "Living, Dead, and Undead," 268.

17. Read and Allen, "Living, Dead, and Undead," 283–285.

18. Read and Allen, "Living, Dead, and Undead," 268–269, 277.

19. Read and Allen, "Living, Dead, and Undead," 263–265. The states that enacted these measures were conservative midwestern and southern states.

20. Read and Allen, "Living, Dead, and Undead," 265–266. The Supreme Court ruled in 1942 that even purely intrastate commerce implicated interstate commerce and therefore could be subject to congressional regulation through its commerce power in *Wickard v. Filburn* (317 U.S. 111).

21. Benjamin Ginsberg et al., *We the People: Essentials 13th Edition* (New York: W.W. Norton, 2021), 67.

22. Erin Adele Scharff, "Hyper Preemption: A Reordering of the State–Local Relationship?" *Georgetown Law Journal* 106 (June 2018): 1475–1476.

23. Joseph Blocher, "Firearm Localism," *Yale Law Journal* 123 (January 2013): 130.

24. Scharff, "Hyper Preemption," 1476.

25. Rachel Simon, "State Preemption of Local Gun Regulations: Taking Aim at Barriers to Change in Firearm Policy," March 15, 2020, http://dx.doi.org/10.2139/ssrn.3623529.

26. Dave Fagundes and Darrell A. H. Miller argue that the *Hunter* doctrine "does not reflect the sociological reality of the modern municipal corporation," and is therefore outmoded. While that may be true as a matter of sociology, this intriguing normative argument does not sweep aside the existing state of the law of state-local relations. "The City's Second Amendment," *Cornell Law Review* 106 (March 2021): 682.

27. Fields, "Second Amendment Sanctuaries," 466–474.

28. Robert J. Spitzer, *Gun across America: Reconciling Gun Rules and Rights* (New York: Oxford University Press, 2015), ch. 2.

29. Jennifer Mascia, "In Much of the Country, Cities Can't Enact Their Own Gun Laws," *The Trace*, December 8, 2018, https://www.thetrace.org/2018/12/preempt ion-nra-local-gun-laws/.

30. "Preemption of Local Laws," Giffords Law Center, n.d., https://giffords.org/lawcen ter/gun-laws/policy-areas/other-laws-policies/preemption-of-local-laws/. The five states without gun preemption laws are Connecticut, Hawaii, Massachusetts, New Jersey, and New York.

31. "Tucson to Ignore Arizona's 'Second Amendment Sanctuary' Law," *AP*, July 6, 2021, https://apnews.com/article/joe-biden-az-state-wire-arizona-tucson-gun-politics-f1521fa4e6c05a10f140abcdd8cf394a?utm_source=The+Trace+mailing+list&utm_campaign=c4a7c7eb37-EMAIL_CAMPAIGN_2019_09_24_04_06_COPY_01&utm_medium=email&utm_term=0_f76c3ff31c-c4a7c7eb37-112434573&utm_source=The+Trace+mailing+list&utm_campaign=9cba8dc65d-EMAIL_CAMPAIGN_2019_08_29_06_04_COPY_01&utm_medium=email&utm_term=0_f76c3ff31c-9cba8dc65d-69360165.

32. Jon Skolnik, "Do Pro-gun 'Second Amendment Sanctuaries' Threaten a Constitutional Crisis?" *Salon*, April 20, 2021, https://www.salon.com/2021/04/20/do-pro-gun-second-amendment-sanctuaries-threaten-a-constitutional-crisis/.

33. Katherine Rosenberg-Douglas, "Second Amendment 'Sanctuary County' Movement Expands as Organizers Take Aim at New Gun Laws," *Chicago Tribune*, April 17, 2019, https://www.chicagotribune.com/news/breaking/ct-met-second-amendment-sanctuary-county-movement-illinois-20190416-story.html.

34. Fields, "Second Amendment Sanctuaries," 440–441.

35. Eric Lutz, "The Right's Latest Tactic on Gun Laws? Just Don't Enforce Them," *Rolling Stone*, May 28, 2019, https://www.rollingstone.com/politics/politics-featu res/second-amendment-sanctuaries-nra-839552/.

36. "What Are So-Called 'Second Amendment Sanctuaries?'" Brady Campaign to Prevent Gun Violence, n.d., https://www.bradyunited.org/act/second-amendm ent-sanctuaries.

37. Jennifer Mascia, "Missouri's 'Second Amendment Sanctuary' Law Could Complicate Police Efforts to Solve Gun Crimes," *The Trace*, August 17, 2021, https://www.thetrace.org/2021/08/missouri-second-amendment-sanctuary-law-gun-crime/?utm_source=The+Trace+mailing+list&utm_campaign=3429358

951-EMAIL_CAMPAIGN_2019_09_24_04_06_COPY_01&utm_medium= email&utm_term=0_f76c3ff31c-3429358951-69360165. This article reports that at least seventeen states have enacted sanctuary-type provisions, including eleven in 2021, but that includes the broadest possible definition of sanctuary resolutions, and incorporates state measures dating back more than a decade. See also Lindsay Whitehurst and Andrew Selsky, "Second Amendment Sanctuaries Facing 1st Court Test in Oregon," *AP*, May 16, 2021, https://apnews.com/article/us-news-ore gon-gun-politics-government-and-politics-1dec173dc5d6d7d5f343b933bb883368.

38. https://sanctuarycounties.com/, visited August 17, 2021. Another, similar website is https://constitutionalsanctuaries.com/.

39. Daniel Trotta, "Defiant U.S. Sheriffs Push Gun Sanctuaries, Imitating Liberals on Immigration," *Reuters*, March 4, 2019, https://www.reuters.com/article/us-usa-guns-sanctuary/defiant-u-s-sheriffs-push-gun-sanctuaries-imitating-liberals-on-immigration-idUSKCN1QL0ZC. The law, Initiative 1639, was later supplemented by state legislative action. The measures withstood legal challenge.

40. David Gutman, "Sheriffs Who Don't Enforce Washington's New Gun Law Could Be Liable, AG Bob Ferguson Says," *Seattle Times*, February 12, 2019, https://www. seattletimes.com/seattle-news/politics/sheriffs-who-dont-enforce-washingtons-new-gun-law-could-be-liable-ag-bob-ferguson-says/.

41. https://cdn5.creativecirclemedia.com/lafromboise/original/20210723-134204-60f8970d9d061.hires.jpg.

42. https://legistarweb-production.s3.amazonaws.com/uploads/attachment/pdf/384 821/2019_Sheriffs_Letter_Regarding_Firearms.pdf.

43. Bethany Blankley, "Nevada Sheriffs Express 'Second Amendment Sanctuary' Sentiment, Non-Compliance With Gun Registration Law," *The Center Square*, March 18, 2019, https://www.thecentersquare.com/nevada/nevada-sheriffs-expr ess-second-amendment-sanctuary-sentiment-non-compliance-with-gun-registrat ion-law/article_b6c50eee-49ac-11e9-abfd-d39cec23c07b.html; "Nevada Sheriffs Unanimously Reject Unconstitutional Gun Laws," *Gun Rights Watch*, June 15, 2019, https://gunrightswatch.com/news/2019/06/15/nevada/nevada-sheriffs-unanimously-reject-unconstitutional-gun-laws/.

44. Sarah Tabin, "Utah Sheriffs Say They Will Protect Second Amendment Rights," *The Salt Lake Tribune*, June 11, 2021, https://www.sltrib.com/news/2021/06/11/ utah-sheriffs-say-they/.

45. National Law Enforcement Officers Memorial Fund, n.d., https://nleomf.org/ facts-figures/law-enforcement-facts. A surge of retirements and resignations owing to a variety of factors converged in 2020 and 2021, including the COVID-19 pandemic, calls for police reform in the wake of concerns raised by the Black Lives Matter movement, an upsurge in crime, and plunging morale likely reduced the total number. Eric Westervelt, "Cops Say Low Morale And Department Scrutiny Are Driving Them Away From The Job," *NPR*, June 24, 2021, https://www.npr.

org/2021/06/24/1009578809/cops-say-low-morale-and-department-scrutiny-are-driving-them-away-from-the-job.

46. Kathy Morris, "Democratic Vs. Republican Jobs: Is Your Job Red Or Blue?," *Zippia*, November 2, 2020, https://www.zippia.com/advice/democratic-vs-republican-jobs/; see also "Democratic vs. Republican Occupations," n.d., http://verdantlabs.com/politics_of_professions/.

47. https://www.sheriffs.org/sites/default/files/uploads/documents/GovAffairs/State-by-State%20Election%20Chart%20updated%2008.13.15.pdf. The four states without elected sheriffs are Alaska, Connecticut, Hawaii, and Rhode Island.

48. "I Elected the Sheriff," *BallotReady*, January 23, 2018, https://medium.com/ball otready/i-elected-the-sheriff-2c70b95ef6cc. The two states that do not elect county sheriffs are Alaska and Connecticut.

49. David N. Falcone and L. Edward Wells, "The County Sheriff as a Distinctive Policing Modality," *American Journal of Police* 14 (1995): 127.

50. Falcone and Wells, "The County Sheriff as a Distinctive Policing Modality," 134–135.

51. Falcone and Wells, "The County Sheriff as a Distinctive Policing Modality," 136.

52. "Line in the Sand," *Southern Poverty Law Center*, June 13, 2016, https://www.splcen ter.org/fighting-hate/intelligence-report/2016/line-sand. The SPLC reported that a number of the sheriffs they spoke with found their names on the organization's list, even though they did not join and had no affiliation.

53. Ashley Powers, "The Renegade Sheriffs," *The New Yorker*, April 23, 2018, https://www.newyorker.com/magazine/2018/04/30/the-renegade-sheriffs.

54. James Tomberlin, "'Don't Elect Me': Sheriffs And The Need For Reform In County Law Enforcement," *Virginia Law Review* 104 (2018): 127.

55. Quoted in Martin Kaste, "When Sheriffs Won't Enforce The Law," *NPR*, February 21, 2019, https://www.npr.org/2019/02/21/696400737/when-sheriffs-wont-enfo rce-the-law.

56. Jonathan Thompson, "The Rise of the Sagebrush Sheriffs," *High Country News*, February 2, 2016, https://www.hcn.org/issues/48.2/the-rise-of-the-sagebrush-sheriffs; "Line in the Sand."

57. Christy E. Lopez, "Opinion: Beware the Extremist, Dangerous and Unconstitutional 'Constitutional Sheriffs,'" *Washington Post*, December 17, 2021, https://www.washingtonpost.com/opinions/2021/12/17/constitutional-sheriffs-extremist-dangerous-unconstitutional/.

58. Powers, "The Renegade Sheriffs"; Daniel Levitas, *The Terrorist Next Door* (New York: St. Martin's Press, 2004).

59. Matt Surtel, "Wyoming County Supervisors Take Second Amendment Stand," *Batavia News*, January 11, 2019, https://www.thedailynewsonline.com/news/wyoming-county-supervisors-take-second-amendment-stand/article_dca37410-3e5e-5439-ae22-09bca7039698.html.

60. Stephen T. Watson, "Grand Island Goes On Record Supporting 2nd Amendment, Opposing Gun Control Measures," *Buffalo News*, January 23, 2019, https://buff alonews.com/news/local/grand-island-goes-on-record-supporting-2nd-amendm ent-opposing-gun-control-measures/article_770e1b65-9745-5335-9c9a-0f06b8fea 70f.html.

61. Jason Subik, "Montgomery and Fulton County Sheriffs Reject 2nd Amendment Sanctuary Declaration," *The (Schenectady) Daily Gazette*, February 2, 2020, https://dailygazette.com/2020/02/02/montgomery-and-fulton-county-sheriffs-reject-2nd-amendment-sanctuary-declaration/.

62. Travis Dunn, "Solon Votes to Defy Future Gun Laws," *Cortland Standard*, March 6, 2020.

63. Travis Dunn, "'The Next Step,'" *Cortland Standard*, June 13, 2020, https://cortl andstandard.net/2020/06/13/2nd-amendment-sanctuary-push-spreads-across-us/. The townships of Truxton, Cuyler, and Cincinnatus all have populations of about one thousand each.

64. Louis M. Vanaria and Seymour B. Dunn, eds., *Industry and Leaders in 19th Century Cortland* (Cortland, NY: Cortland County Historical Society, 1988), 1–22.

65. *Cortland County New York* (New York: Windsor Publications, 1971), 15. When I went off to college I took with me a portable Smith-Corona typewriter. It has been many, many years since any of my students recognized the brand name.

66. Ashley Biviano, "Some Area Counties Want to Become 'Second Amendment Sanctuaries,'" *Binghamton Press & Sun-Bulletin*, February 11, 2020. Upstate counties where sanctuary movements have emerged include Broome, Chemung, Chenango, Delaware, Otsego, and Steuben.

67. Chris Potter, "Steuben County Gun Advocates Backed 2nd Amendment Sanctuary: Why County Denied Proposal," *Hornell Evening Tribune*, March 11, 2021, https://www.eveningtribune.com/story/news/local/2021/03/11/ny-gun-sanctuary-second-amendment-steuben-county-safe-act/4625000001/.

68. Nick Reisman, "Lawmakers Give Final Approval To Gun Control Bills," *Spectrum News1*, June 9, 2021, https://spectrumlocalnews.com/nys/central-ny/ny-state-of-politics/2021/06/09/lawmakers-give-final-approval-to-gun-control-bills.

69. Robert J. Spitzer, "New York State and the New York SAFE Act: A Case Study in Strict Gun Laws," *Albany Law Review* 78 (2014/2015): 749–787.

70. https://gunowners.org/second-amendment-sanctuaries-rhetoric-vs-reality/; GOASecAmSanc.pdf. See also The Tenth Amendment Center, https://tenthamen dmentcenter.com/legislation/2nd-amendment-preservation-act/.

71. Dunn, " 'The Next Step.'"

72. Dunn, "'The Next Step.'"

73. Erin Douglas, "Texas Abortion Law a "Radical Expansion" of Who Can Sue Whom, and an About-Face For Republicans on Civil Lawsuits," *Texas Tribune*, September 3, 2021, https://www.texastribune.org/2021/09/03/texas-republican-abortion-civil-lawsuits/.

74. Michael S. Schmidt, "Behind the Texas Abortion Law, a Persevering Conservative Lawyer," *New York Times*, September 12, 2021, https://www.nytimes.com/2021/09/12/us/politics/texas-abortion-lawyer-jonathan-mitchell.html; Jonathan F. Mitchell, "The Writ-of-Erasure Fallacy," *Virginia Law Review* 104 (2018): 933–1019. Mitchell, deeply religious, was a law clerk for Justice Antonin Scalia, and spent seven years formulating this strategy to make it more difficult for the courts to intervene.

75. Jennifer Mascia, "Could Gun Restrictions Modeled on Texas's Anti-Abortion Law Work?" *The Trace*, January 19, 2022, https://www.thetrace.org/2022/01/texas-abortion-law-applied-to-guns-california-new-york/

76. All quotes from Furlin and Wehbe are from a transcript of "Forum on Second Amendment Preservation Laws," Institute for Civic Engagement, SUNY Cortland, September 15, 2020, https://sunycortland.webex.com/webappng/sites/sunyc ortland/recording/26e4973d68f942f68b34a69240d247d1/playback. Cortland County Legislator Ann Homer also participated in the forum. My thanks to Institute Director John Suarez for his thoughtful assistance.

77. https://www.churchofjesuschrist.org/study/ensign/1992/02/the-divinely-inspi red-constitution?lang=eng.

78. Erica Turret, Chelsea Parsons, and Adam Skaggs, "Second Amendment Sanctuaries: A Legally Dubious Protest Movement," *The Journal of Law, Medicine & Ethics*, 48(Winter 2020): 105–111.

79. Spitzer, *Guns across America*, Ch. 2.

80. Robert J. Spitzer, *The Politics of Gun Control*, 8th ed. (New York: Routledge, 2021), 216.

81. Scharff, "Hyper Preemption," 1477. The relevant home rule provision is found in Article IX of the state Constitution.

82. Scharff, "Hyper Preemption," 1478.

83. Garnar, Lister, and Carlson, "Whiteness and Impunity," 5. Their study is based on an analysis of over two hundred fifty documents from Virginia Second Amendment sanctuary resolutions from 2019 to 2020.

84. Read and Allen, "Living, Dead, and Undead," 290.

85. Lutz, "The Right's Latest Tactic on Gun Laws? Just Don't Enforce Them."

86. Dunn, "'The Next Step.'"

87. Jennifer Mascia, "Missouri's 'Second Amendment Sanctuary' Law Could Complicate Police Efforts to Solve Gun Crimes," *The Trace*, August 17, 2021, https://www.thetrace.org/2021/08/missouri-second-amendment-sanctuary-law-gun-crime/?utm_source=The+Trace+mailing+list&utm_campaign=552860d 166-EMAIL_CAMPAIGN_2019_09_24_04_06_COPY_01&utm_medium= email&utm_term=0_f76c3ff31c-552860d166-69360165; Glenn Thrush, "Justice Dept. Says Missouri's Gun Law Hobbles Drug and Weapons Inquiries," *New York Times*, August 18, 2021, https://www.nytimes.com/2021/08/18/us/politics/misso uri-gun-law.html; Glenn Thrush, "Inside Missouri's '2nd Amendment Sanctuary'

Fight," *New York Times*, September 9, 2021, https://www.nytimes.com/2021/09/09/us/politics/missouri-gun-law.html.

88. Thrush, "Inside Missouri's '2nd Amendment Sanctuary' Fight"; Brian Freskos and Alain Stephens, "The Brothers Behind an Extreme Gun-Rights Network That Republicans Call a Big Scam," *The Trace*, June 23, 2020, https://www.thetrace.org/2020/06/dorr-brothers-gun-rights-activism/.

89. "Gov. Parson Says There Are 'Things We Can Correct' About Second Amendment Preservation Act," *KCTV*, September 28, 2021, https://www.kctv5.com/news/local_news/gov-parson-says-there-are-things-we-can-correct-about-second-amendment-preservation-act/video_9735d304-6abd-5b43-aea7-319b376a9efo.html?utm_source=The+Trace+mailing+list&utm_campaign=e3bfe35674-EMAIL_CAMPAIGN_2019_08_29_06_04_COPY_01&utm_medium=email&utm_term=0_f76c3ff31c-e3bfe35674-69360165.

90. Southern Poverty Law Center, "The Year in Hate and Extremism 2020," https://www.splcenter.org/news/2021/02/05/year-hate-and-extremism-far-right-extremists-coalescing-broad-based-loosely-affiliated.

91. Kirk Siegler, "Federal Appeals Court Upholds Dismissal Of Cliven Bundy Case," *NPR*, August 6, 2020, https://www.npr.org/2020/08/06/899886777/federal-appeals-court-upholds-dismissal-of-cliven-bundy-case.

92. Jonathan Allen, "Trump Pardons Oregon Ranchers Who Inspired Refuge Standoff," *Reuters*, July 10, 2018, https://www.reuters.com/article/us-oregon-standoff-trump/trump-pardons-oregon-ranchers-who-inspired-refuge-standoff-idUSKBN1KO21Q.

93. *Olmstead v. United States*, 277 U.S. 438, 485 (1928).

CHAPTER 6

1. "James J. Gallagher, Because He Lost His Job, Shoots Mayor W. J. Gaynor," *The Buffalo Times*, August 9, 1910.

2. Todd Errington, "Robert Todd Lincoln and Presidential Assassinations," National Park Service, n.d., https://www.nps.gov/articles/000/robert-todd-lincoln-and-presidential-assassiations-not-formal-title.htm.

3. Lee Kennett and James LaVerne Anderson, *The Gun in America* (Westport, CT: Greenwood Press, 1975), 171–179; Alexander DeConde, *Gun Violence in America* (Boston: Northeastern University Press, 2001), 107–109.

4. Kennett and Anderson, *The Gun in America*, 174.

5. Kennett and Anderson, *The Gun in America*, 174.

6. "Revolver Killings Fast Increasing," *New York Times*, January 30, 1911.

7. One criticism seeking to undercut the legitimacy and intent of the Sullivan law argued that Tammany Hall in the person of Sullivan was looking for a way to give the appearance of cracking down on notorious city gangs that also worked for Tammany without actually cracking down on them: "Enter Big Tim [Sullivan] with the

perfect solution: Ostensibly disarm the gangs—and ordinary citizens, too—while still keeping them on the streets." Michael A. Walsh, "The Strange Birth of NY's Gun Laws," *New York Post*, January 16, 2012, https://nypost.com/2012/01/16/the-strange-birth-of-nys-gun-laws/. Sullivan biographer Richard F. Welsh confronted this criticism but came to a different conclusion: "Cynics suggested that Big Tim pushed through his law so Tammany could keep their gangster allies under control. Hoodlums who forgot who really ran things in the city could be easily arrested if found with a gun—or if one was slipped into their pocket. The Big Feller surely heard the charges and likely shrugged them off. If there were political benefits from doing the right thing, what was the problem? But all the available evidence indicates that Tim's fight to bring firearms under control sprang from heartfelt conviction." *King of the Bowery: Big Tim Sullivan, Tammany Hall, and New York City from the Gilded Age to the Progressive Era* (Albany, NY: SUNY Press, 2009), 146.

8. Peter Duffy, "100 Years Ago, the Shot That Spurred New York's Gun-Control Law," *New York Times*, January 23, 2011, https://cityroom.blogs.nytimes.com/2011/01/23/100-years-ago-the-shot-that-spurred-new-yorks-gun-control-law/; Kennett and Anderson, *The Gun in America*, 178–182.

9. Ch. 608, § 1, 1913 N.Y. Laws 1627, 1627–1630; David D. Jensen, "The Sullivan Law at 100," *Government, Law and Policy Journal* 14 (Summer 2012): 6.

10. For example, "the Sullivan Law was prompted by xenophobic fears within the mainstream white Anglo-Saxon leadership of New York, and specifically targeted at Italian immigrants." James A. Beckman, "Sullivan Law," *Guns in American Society*, 2nd ed., Gregg Lee Carter, ed. (Santa Barbara, CA: ABC-CLIO, 2012), 799.

11. *Laws of the State of New York, Vol. 1* (Albany, NY: J.B. Lyon Co. 1905), Ch. 92, 130.

12. https://law.onecle.com/new-york/penal/PEN0400.00_400.00.html.

13. "Concealed Carry," Giffords Law Center, n.d., https://giffords.org/lawcenter/gun-laws/policy-areas/guns-in-public/concealed-carry/.

14. As the owner of a state concealed carry pistol permit, which I received in 2013, I can report that I found the process reasonable, useful, and beneficial as a matter of public policy. An account of my experience is found in Robert J. Spitzer, *Guns across America: Reconciling Gun Rules and Rights* (New York: Oxford University Press, 2015), 171–179.

15. *Kachalsky v. County of Westchester*, 701 F.3d 81 (2nd Cir. 2012); *cert. denied Kachalsky v. Cacace*, 569 U.S. 918 (2013).

16. Robert J. Spitzer, "Gun Law History in the United States and Second Amendment Rights," *Law and Contemporary Problems* 80, 2 (2017): 63–67.

17. Jennifer Mascia, "The Supreme Court's Next Big Gun Case, Explained," *The Trace*, May 18, 2021, https://www.thetrace.org/2021/05/supreme-court-gun-rights-concealed-carry-new-york-corlett/.

18. Robert J. Spitzer, "New York State and the New York SAFE Act," *Albany Law Review* 78 (2014/2015): 749–787.

19. Michael Siegel et al., "Easiness of Legal Access to Concealed Firearm Permits and Homicide Rates in the United States," *American Journal of Public Health* 107(December 1, 2017): 1923–1929. This study finds that homicide rates are eleven percent higher in weak permit states.

20. John J. Donohue, Abhay Aneja, and Kyle D. Weber, "Right-to-Carry Laws and Violent Crime: A Comprehensive Assessment Using Panel Data and a State-Level Synthetic Control Analysis," *Journal of Empirical Legal Studies* 16 (June 2019): 198–247.

21. Michael Siegel, et al., "The Impact of State Firearm Laws on Homicide Rates in Suburban and Rural Areas Compared to Large Cities in the United States, 1991–2016," *Journal of Rural Health* 36 (March 2020): 255–265, https://pubmed.ncbi.nlm.nih.gov/31361355/

22. David I. Swedler, et al., "Firearm Prevalence and Homicides of Law Enforcement Officers in the United States," *American Journal of Public Health* 105 (October 2015): 2042–2048, https://pubmed.ncbi.nlm.nih.gov/26270316/

23. David Hemenway, Deborah Azrael, and Matthew Miller, "Whose Guns Are Stolen? The Epidemiology of Gun Theft Victims," *Injury Epidemiology* 4 (2017); Jeffrey DeSimone, Sara Markowitz, and Jing Xu, "Child Access Prevention Laws and Nonfatal Gun Injuries," *Southern Economic Journal* 80 (2013): 5–25. In addition, actual cases of successful gun defense are rare and increase the risk that the victim will be harmed. David Hemenway and Sara J. Solnick, "The Epidemiology of Self-Defense Gun Use: Evidence from the National Crime Victimization Surveys 2007–2011," *Preventive Medicine* 79 (April 21, 2015): 22–27; Charles C. Branas et al., "Investigating the Link Between Gun Possession and Gun Assault," *American Journal of Public Health* 99 (November 2009): 2034–2040.

24. "Gun Violence in Illinois," Everytown for Gun Safety, April 2020, https://maps.everytownresearch.org/wp-content/uploads/2020/04/Every-State-Fact-Sheet-2.0-042720-Illinois.pdf. An earlier study of Missouri's homicide rate before and after it repealed its 2007 permit-to-purchase handgun law found that, controlling for other factors, the firearm homicide rate increased twenty-three percent in the three years after repeal, and sixteen percent five years after repeal. The non-firearm homicide rate was unaffected by the law change. Daniel Webster, Cassandra Kercher Crifasi, and Jon S. Vernick, "Effects of the Repeal of Missouri's Handgun Purchaser Licensing Law on Homicides," *Journal of Urban Health* 91 (April 2014): 293–302.

25. Abundant writing addresses these and other areas. A good summary of these efforts from the political right is found in Ian Millhiser, *The Agenda: How a Republican Supreme Court Is Reshaping America* (New York: Columbia Global Reports, 2021). Millhiser does not include an examination of gun rights in his book.

26. Alan Feuer, "The Texas Abortion Law Creates a Kind of Bounty Hunter. Here's How It Works," *New York Times*, September 10, 2021, https://www.nytimes.com/2021/09/10/us/politics/texas-abortion-law-facts.html.

27. Robert J. Spitzer, "Gun Law History in the United States and Second Amendment Rights.".

28. Gordon E. Dean, "Organized Crime and Our Changing Criminal Law," *Commercial Law Journal* (August 1932): 380.

29. Jeffrey M. Jones, "Approval of U.S. Supreme Court Down to 40%, a New Low," *Gallup*, September 23, 2021, https://news.gallup.com/poll/354908/approval-supr eme-court-down-new-low.aspx.

30. "Marquette Law School Supreme Court Poll September 7–16, 2021," https://law. marquette.edu/poll/wp-content/uploads/2021/09/MLSPSC04Toplines_Cou rtItems.html.

31. Jack M. Balkin, "*Bush v. Gore* and the Boundary Between Law and Politics," *Yale Law Journal* 110 (June 2001): 1407–1458.

32. Robert Barnes and Seung Min Kim, "Supreme Court Observers See Trouble Ahead as Public Approval of Justices Erodes," *Washington Post*, September 26, 2021, https://www.washingtonpost.com/politics/courts_law/supreme-court-pub lic-opinion/2021/09/25/379b51ec-1c6c-11ec-bcb8-0cb135811007_story.html; Ruth Marcus, "The Supreme Court's Crisis of Legitimacy," *Washington Post*, October 1, 2021, https://www.washingtonpost.com/opinions/2021/10/01/supreme-court-cri sis-of-legitimacy/.

33. William J. Riordan, *Plunkitt of Tammany Hall* (New York: E.P. Dutton, 1963), 3.

Index

For the benefit of digital users, indexed terms that span two pages (e.g., 52–53) may, on occasion, appear on only one of those pages.

Tables are indicated by *t* following the page number

Afghanistan War (2001-21), 1–2
African Americans, 10–13, 81
AK-47 Kalashnikov rifle, 27, 29
Alabama, 79*t*
Alaska, 98
Alien and Sedition Acts, 95
Alito, Samuel, 7, 13–14, 135n.79
Allen, Neal, 96–97, 112
Altschuler, Glenn C., 81–82
American Bar Association, 2
American Revolution, 11
American Suppressor Association (ASA), 64, 69–70
ammunition regulations, 2–3, 26, 33–36, 34*t*, 50, 108–9, 121–22, 123. *See also* large capacity magazines (LCMs)
Antifa, 90
AR-15 rifle
   extremist organizations and, 40–41
   first production (late 1950s) of, 27
   lethality and destructiveness of, 42–43
   M16 as military version of, 27
   noise level associated with, 64
   self-defense and, 46–47

semi-automatic firing design of, 27
silencers and, 52
Arizona, 57*t*, 79*t*, 82*t*, 93, 98–100
Arkansas, 79*t*
ArmaLite Company, 27
Arpaio, Joe, 105–6
Articles of Confederation, 95, 97
Article VI (US Constitution), 95, 97
assault weapons. *See also* fully automatic firearms; semi-automatic firearms
   crimes committed with, 37, 39–40
   defining qualities of, 28–29
   estimated number in United States of, 36–37
   extremist organizations and, 40–41
   federal ban (1994-2004) on, 28, 29–30, 37, 39, 45, 50
   gangs' use of, 39–40
   Heller II case and, 14
   lethality and destructiveness of, 41–43, 47–48
   marketing of, 27–29
   mass shootings and, 1–2, 29–30, 37–38

assault weapons (*cont.*)
military origins and applications of, 23, 27, 29, 30–31, 36
Miller v. Bonta and, 46–47
National Rifle Association and, 28–29
noise level associated with, 64
police killed by shooters with, 38–39, 45–46
profit for manufacturers of, 46
self-defense and, 46–48
states' regulations regarding, 14–15, 23, 29–30, 39, 50, 94–95, 108–9, 112, 123
Auerbach, Herman, 59
Aurora (Colorado) movie theater shooting (2012), 37–38, 44–45
automatic weapons. *See* fully automatic firearms; semi-automatic firearms

background checks for gun purchases
Brady Handgun Violence Prevention Act of 1993 and, 8, 104, 111–12
public opinion regarding, 3
sanctuary movement's opposition to, 8, 100, 101–2, 104, 106
silencers and, 52–53, 55, 65, 67–68, 70
state laws regarding, 108–9
Barber, Oliver, 77
Barrett, Amy Coney, 7, 13–15
Baum, Dan, 87–88
Benitez, Roger, 25–26, 46–50
Bensel, Richard Franklin, 81
Berra, Yogi, 1
Biden, Joe, 1–2, 6–7
Bill of Rights, 15–16, 115, 123. *See also specific amendments*
Black Codes, 11–12
Black Hand, 117
Black Lives Matter (BLM), 41, 72, 74, 89–90
Black Militias, 11–12
Black Panthers, 11, 84
Blackstone, William, 76–77

Blocher, Joseph, 84
Blumin, Stuart M., 81–82
Boogaloo Bois, 41, 74–75, 89–90
Brady Handgun Violence Prevention Act of 1993, 8, 104, 111–12
Brandeis, Louis, 115
brandishing. *See also* carrying of firearms
extremist groups and, 74–75, 89–90, 124
intent and, 78–80
of knives and swords, 77–78, 80
McCloskey case (2020) and, 72–73
at polling places, 83
at public protests, 24, 41, 74–76, 83–84, 86–87, 89–91, 122–23
state laws restricting, 73–74, 77–81, 79*t*, 122–23
Browning Automatic Rifle (BAR), 1–2
Brown v. Board of Education, 97
bump stocks, 1–2, 94–95
Bundy, Cliven, 114–15
Bureau of Alcohol, Tobacco, Firearms, and Explosives (ATF), 67–68
Bush, George H.W., 4–5
Bush, George W., 5
Busse, Ryan, 40–41

Calhoun, John C., 96
California
ammunition restrictions in, 33–35, 34*t*
assault weapons ban in, 14–15, 29–30, 46
Black Panther protests in, 84
brandishing laws in, 79*t*
concealed gun carry restrictions in, 9
extremist organizations in, 40
large capacity magazine ban in, 25, 30–31, 48
sanctuary cities in, 93
silencer ban in, 53
waiting period for gun purchases in, 10
Campbell, David, 100

Capone, Al ("Scarface"), 61
Carroll County (Maryland), 100
carrying of firearms. *See also* brandishing
  absence of training requirements
    for, 87–88
  concealed gun carrying and, 9–10, 17–
    18, 32, 50, 121
  extremist organizations and, 74–75,
    89–90, 124
  First Amendment and, 83
  gun owners' perception of
    empowerment and, 86
  "hoplophobia" and, 87–90
  National Rifle Association and,
    80, 88–89
  open carry and, 73–76, 83, 88–89, 121
  at polling places, 81–83, 82*t*
  public opinion regarding, 24, 86–87
  at public protests, 24, 41, 74–76, 83–
    84, 86–87, 89–91, 122–23
  Second Amendment and, 24, 83–84,
    118, 122–23
  security dilemma principle and, 85–86
  at state capitols, 84, 89
  Sullivan Law (1911) and, 117–18
  time and place restrictions for, 81
  weapons effect and, 84
  weapons instrumentality effect and, 88
Castle doctrine, 73–74
Cato Institute, 8–9
Christian Patriot movement, 105
Cincinnatus (New York), 107
Civil War, 31, 97
Clark, Champ, 61–62
Clark, Paul, 62
Colfax (Louisiana) massacre (1873), 12–
    13, 133n.54
Colorado, 30
Colt Company, 27, 30–31, 121
Columbia (Missouri), 113–14
Columbine High School shooting
    (1999), 37–38

concealed gun carry
  Heller case and, 17–18
  Peruta v. California and, 9
  Rogers v. Grewal and, 10
  Second Amendment and, 10,
    17–18
  states' regulations regarding, 9–10,
    17–18, 32, 50, 121
Connecticut, 30
Constitutional Sheriffs movement, 104–
    6, 114–15
Cooper, Jeff, 87–88
Cooper v. Aaron, 97
Cornell, Saul, 11–12, 50, 76–77
Cortland County (New York), 107–9
Country Justice (Dalton), 76–77
COVID-19, protests against public
    health measures regarding, 24, 41,
    74–75, 84, 89–90, 91, 100–1
Cummings, Homer S., 63
Czolgosz, Leon, 116–17

Davis, J.A.G., 77
Dayton (Ohio) mass shooting
    (2019), 44–45
D.C. v. Heller. See Heller case (*D.C. v.
    Heller*, 2008)
Delaware, 53, 57*t*, 79*t*, 82–83, 82*t*
Diaz, Tom, 28
District of Columbia. See also *Heller*
    case; *Heller II* case
  ammunition magazine restrictions in,
    33–35, 34*t*
  assault weapons ban in, 14, 30
  automatic weapons restrictions (1932)
    in, 32–33
  gun registration regulations in, 14
  January 6 riots (2021) in, 40–
    41, 104–5
  silencer ban in, 53
  US Court of Appeals in, 5–6, 14
Donohue, John J., 38–39

Dorr, Aaron, 114
Duncan v. Becerra, 25–31, 48–49

Effingham County (Illinois), 100
El Salvador, 93
Epps, Garrett, 84
extremist organizations
  assault weapons and, 40–41
  carrying of firearms by, 74–75, 89–
    90, 124
  takeover of federal lands by, 114–15

Federalist Society, 4–7, 20
Feinstein, Dianne, 38
felons' gun rights, 15, 17
Fifteenth Amendment, 5, 97
Filindra, Alexandra, 86–87
Firearms Freedoms laws, 98
First Amendment, 16, 83
Fleischer, Ari, 66
Floyd, George, 72
Fort Lauderdale airport mass shooting
  (2017), 66
Fourteenth Amendment, 9, 97, 98, 110–11
Fourth Amendment, 10, 110–11
Fugitive Slave Act, 93
Fuller, Claude, 62
fully automatic firearms. *See also* assault
  weapons
  crimes committed with, 70
  federal registration system for, 14–15
  National Firearms Act of 1934 and
    restrictions on, 13, 32, 35, 70, 121
  states' regulations regarding, 2, 26–27,
    32–33, 50, 121
Furlin, Stephen A., 110–12

Gale, William Potter, 105
Gallagher, James J., 116
gangs, 39–40, 59–61, 121
Gardner, Kim, 73
Garfield, James A., 116–17

Gaynor, William J., 116–17
Georgia, 79*t*, 80, 82*t*
ghost guns, 108
Gienapp, Jonathan, 20
Giffords, Gabrielle, 43, 45
Ginsberg, "Doggy" Henry, 60
Girandoni air rifle, 30–31, 140–41n.38
Goldsborough, Fitzhugh Coyle, 117
Gonzalez, Susan and Mike, 48–49
Gorsuch, Neil, 7, 9, 13–14
Grand Island (New York), 106
Great Britain, 11, 76–78, 122–23
Green, Christina Taylor, 45
Guatemala, 93
Guiteau, Charles, 116–17
Gun Owners of America organization, 54
gun silencers. *See* silencers
gun trafficking, 39–40, 113–14
Gura, Alan, 8–9

Halbrook, Stephen, 62–63, 76
handguns
  crimes committed with, 37
  estimated number in United
    States of, 36
  lethality and destructiveness of, 42–43
  mass shootings and, 38
  self-defense and, 47–48
  states' licensing regulations
    regarding, 2
  theft of, 48–49
Harding, Warren G., 1–2
Hawaii, 30, 33–35, 34*t*, 53, 57*t*
Hearing Protection Act, 52–53, 64
Heller case (*D.C. v. Heller*, 2008)
  concealed gun carrying and, 17–18
  historical gun law provenance
    standard and, 17, 35
  individual Second Amendment right
    to own handguns for self-protection
    at home established by, 3–4, 8–9,
    16–17, 26

Originalism and, 20–21
as precedent for other gun rights cases,
13–14, 19
restrictions on guns permitted
under, 17–18
Heller II case (*Heller v. D.C.*, 2011), 14
Helms, Mark, 107
HK-91semiautomatic military assault
rifle, 28, 40
home rule authority, 98–99, 112
"hoplophobia," 87–90
Hornaday, William T., 56
Hunter v. City of Pittsburgh, 99–100

Idaho, 79*t*, 98
Illinois
ammunition magazine restrictions in,
33–35, 34*t*
automatic weapons restrictions in, 33
crimes committed using silencers in, 60
sanctuary movement in, 94–95, 100
silencer ban in, 53
Indiana, 79*t*, 80
Ingram Mac 10 submachine gun, 40
International Association of Chiefs of
Police, 39–41
Iowa, 79*t*
Iraq War (2003-2012), 1–2, 42

Jackson, Andrew, 96
January 6 riots (Washington DC, 2021),
40–41, 104–5
Jefferson, Thomas, 110–11
Justice Department, 4, 67–68, 109

Kansas, 53–54, 79*t*
Kanter v. Barr, 15
Kavanaugh, Brett, 7, 10, 13–15
Keene, David, 46
Kelly, Mark, 45
Kenosha (Wisconsin) demonstrations
(2020), 75–76

Kentucky, 95
Kopel, David, 62–63
Ku Klux Klan, 11–12

Lacombe, Matthew J., 13
large capacity magazines (LCMs)
crimes committed using, 37, 45–
46, 50–51
definition of, 1–2, 23, 43
Duncan v. Becerra and, 25–26,
31, 48–49
federal restrictions (1994-2004) on, 37
mass shootings and, 37–38, 43–46
police officers killed by assault
weapons fire and, 39–41, 45–46
profit for manufacturers of, 46
Second Amendment and, 25–26,
49, 124–25
self-defense and, 48–50
states' regulations regarding, 1–2,
14–15, 23, 25–26, 30–31, 33–35, 39,
43–45, 48, 94–95, 112
Las Vegas (Nevada) mass shooting
(2017), 37–38
Lee, Mike, 53
Lewis County (New York), 101
Liebell, Susan P., 21–22
Lincoln, Robert Todd, 116–17
Living Constitution, 19–22
Long Island Railroad shooting (1993), 43
Louisiana, 33–35, 34*t*, 57*t*, 82*t*
Lowi, Theodore J., 21–22

M16 rifle, 17–18, 27, 29
machine guns, 2, 32, 35, 121. *See also* fully
automatic firearms; semi-automatic
firearms
Mack, Richard, 104–5
Madison, James, 19–20
Mailing of Firearms Act of 1927, 2
Maine, 56, 57*t*, 78, 79*t*
Maisch, Patricia, 45

Malheur National Wildlife Refuge
    takeover (2016), 114–15
Maryland, 30, 81–82, 82*t*, 100
Massachusetts, 30, 32–35, 34*t*, 53, 57*t*,
    77–78, 79*t*
mass shootings. *See also specific shootings*
    assault weapons and, 1–2, 29–
    30, 37–38
    definition of, 37–38, 143n.83
    firearms restrictions passed
        following, 29–30
    handguns and, 38
    large capacity magazines and, 37–
        38, 43–46
    semi-automatic weapons and, 38, 44
    silencers and, 68
Maxim, Hiram, 55–56, 59–60, 63
Maxim silencers, 56–62, 57*t*, 122
McCloskey, Mark T. and Patricia
    N., 72–73
McConnell, Mitch, 5–6
McCord, Mary, 91
McDonald v. Chicago, 9, 13–15
McKinley, William, 116–17
Mearsheimer, John J., 85–86
Meese, Edwin, 4
mentally ill persons, 17
Merry, Melissa K., 40
Michigan, 26, 32–35, 34*t*, 57*t*, 75,
    79*t*, 89–90
Michigan Liberty Militia, 89–90
Miller, Darrell A.H., 83–84
Miller v. Bonta, 46–47
Minnesota, 30, 32–35, 34*t*, 57*t*, 69
Miranda v. Arizona, 85
Mississippi, 78–80, 79*t*
Missouri
    ammunition magazine restrictions in,
        33–35, 34*t*
    ban on weapons at polling places and
        government buildings in, 82*t*
    brandishing laws in, 79*t*

crimes committed using
    silencers in, 60
domestic violence homicides
    in, 113–14
open carry law in, 73–74
sanctuary movement in, 94–95, 113–15
Second Amendment Preservation Act
    in, 113–14
sheriffs in, 114
Mitchell, Jonathan F., 109
Montana, 79*t*, 98
Moran, George Clarence "Bugs," 61
Murphy, Bruce Allen, 20–21
Murphy, Paul L., 21

National Conference of Commissioners
    on Uniform State Laws, 2
National Firearms Act of 1934 (NFA)
    fully automatic weapons regulated
        under, 13, 32, 35, 70, 121
    silencers regulated under, 23–24, 32,
        52–54, 62–63, 68–69, 70, 122
National Hearing Conservation
    Association (NHCA), 64–65
National Rifle Association (NRA)
    "armed citizen stories"
        promoted by, 48
    assault weapons and, 28–29
    carrying of firearms and, 80, 88–89
    Heller case (2008) and, 8–9
    model laws proposed by, 2
    sanctuary movement and, 100, 114
    self-defense and, 48
    silencers and, 63
    state preemption laws and, 99–100
    Supreme Court nominations
        supported by, 13
National Shooting Sports Foundation
    (NSSF), 28–29, 36, 63–64
Nevada, 79*t*, 102
New Black Panther Party, 89–90
New Hampshire, 78, 79*t*, 91

New Jersey
ammunition magazine restrictions in,
33–35, 34*t*
assault weapons ban in, 30
brandishing laws in, 78, 79*t*
concealed carry regulations in, 10
crimes committed using silencers
in, 59–60
large capacity magazine ban in, 30
silencer ban in, 53, 56, 57*t*
New Mexico, 79*t*, 80, 82*t*
New York City, 13–14, 59–60, 110–11, 117
New York State
assault weapons ban in, 30
ban on weapons at polling places and
government buildings in, 82–83, 82*t*
brandishing laws in, 77–78, 79*t*
constitution of, 110–11
large capacity magazine ban in, 30
New York SAFE Act of 2013 and, 39,
106, 108–9
red flag law in, 108
sanctuary movement in, 101, 106–9
silencer ban in, 53, 57*t*
Sullivan Law, 117–19, 173–74n.7
*New York State Rifle & Pistol Association
(NYSRPA) v. Bruen*, 118–19
Ninth Amendment, 16
Ninth Circuit Court of Appeals, 9–
10, 26
North Carolina, 33–35, 34*t*, 57*t*, 78, 79*t*
nullification doctrine, 24, 92–93, 95–98,
112, 123
*N.Y. State Rifle & Pistol Association v.
City of New York*, 13–14

Oath Keepers, 41, 89–90
Obama, Barack, 5–6
Ohio, 26, 33, 34*t*
Oklahoma, 79*t*, 82*t*
open carry, 73–76, 83, 88–89, 121. *See also*
brandishing

Oregon, 33–35, 34*t*, 79*t*, 110–11
Originalism
definition of, 19
Federalist Society and, 4–7, 20
gun rights and, 15, 18–20
Heller case and, 20–21
historians' criticisms of, 20–21
organized campaigns to appoint
judges who subscribe to, 4
"Originalism 1.0" *versus* "Originalism
2.0" and, 20
Scalia and, 19–21
Orlando (Florida) mass shooting (2016),
37–38, 44–45

Parkland (Florida) school shooting
(2018), 37–38, 43
Parson, Mike, 113–14
Patriot Prayer organization, 89–90
Pennsylvania, 33–35, 34*t*, 57*t*, 79*t*
pepperbox firearm, 30–31
Peruta v. California, 9
Peterson, Phillip, 29
Phillips, David Graham, 117
Pittsburgh (Pennsylvania), 56
Plunkitt, George Washington, 125
Portland (Oregon) protests
(2020), 90–91
Posner, Richard, 21
Posse Comitatus movement, 105
preferred freedoms doctrine, 16
Printz v. U.S., 8–9, 104
Proud Boys, 89–90
Puckle Gun, 30–31
Pulse nightclub mass shooting (Orlando,
Florida, 2016), 37–38, 44–45

Rakove, Jack, 20–21
Rasenberger, Jim, 31
Read, James H., 96–97, 112
Reagan, Ronald, 4, 6
Reckord, Milton, 62

Reconstruction Era, 11–12, 50
red flag laws, 2–3, 100, 108, 112
Refugee Act (1980), 93
registration of firearms
    crime rate reduction and, 70
    federal register for fully automatic
        firearms and, 14–15
    Heller II case and, 14
    states' regulations regarding, 14–15
Reid, Harry, 5–6
Republican Party, 4–5, 11–12, 73
Rhee, Peter, 42–43
Rhode Island, 26, 32–35, 34*t*, 53, 57*t*
Rittenhouse, Kyle, 75–76
Roberts, John, 7
Robin, Corey, 10–11
Rogers v. Grewal, 10
Roosevelt, Theodore, 61–62
Ruger 10/22 .22 LR Rifle, 64
Russell, William, 77

sanctuary movement
    assault weapons laws and, 94–95
    background checks for gun purchases
        opposed by, 8, 100, 101–2, 104, 106
    claims of gun laws' unconstitutionality
        cited in, 94–95, 106
    federalism and, 92–93, 95, 98, 111–
        12, 115
    Firearms Freedoms laws and, 98
    home rule authority and, 98–99, 112
    immigrant sanctuary movement
        and, 93–94
    large-capacity magazine laws and, 94–95
    local governments as primary locus
        of, 98–100
    nullification doctrine and, 24, 92–93,
        95–98, 112, 123
    private citizen lawsuits against
        government officials and, 120
    sheriffs and, 101–7, 114
    state preemption laws and, 99–100

Sandy Hook elementary school shooting
    (2012), 37–38, 44–45, 108–9
sawed-off shotguns, 1–2, 17, 32, 62
Scalia, Antonin, 15, 19–21
Second Amendment. *See also* sanctuary
        movement
    African Americans' gun rights
        and, 10–12
    carrying of firearms and, 24, 83–84,
        118, 122–23
    concealed gun carry and, 10, 17–18
    First Congress debates (1789)
        on, 16–17
    Fourteenth Amendment and, 9
    Heller case (2008) and, 3–4, 8–9,
        16–17, 26
    individual gun rights and, 3–4, 8–
        9, 16–17
    intermediate scrutiny standard and, 18
    Kanter v. Barr and, 15
    large capacity magazines and, 25–26,
        49, 124–25
    milita-based gun rights and, 8–
        9, 16–17
    *N.Y. State Rifle & Pistol Association v.
        City of New York* and, 14
    Printz v. U.S. and, 8–9, 104
    self-defense rights and, 3–4, 8–9, 13,
        16–17, 26
    silencers and, 26, 53–54, 124–25
Second Amendment Protection Act
    (Kansas), 53–54
security dilemma principle, 85–86
segregation in the United States, 11–13,
        97–98, 123
self-defense
    African Americans and, 13
    assault weapons and, 46–48
    Castle doctrine and, 73–74
    common law tradition and, 13
    handguns and, 47–48
    Heller case and, 3–4, 8–9, 16–17, 26

large capacity magazines and, 48–50
number of annual self-protection
   actions involving firearms in United
   States and, 65–66
Second Amendment and, 3–4, 8–9, 13,
   16–17, 26
stand your ground laws and, 73–74
semi-automatic firearms. *See also* assault
   weapons
bump stocks and, 1–2
lethality and destructiveness of, 41–43
mass shootings and, 38, 44
states' regulations regarding, 2, 23, 26–
   27, 30, 32–33, 50, 101–2, 121
Senate of the United States, 5–6, 38, 53
Seventh Amendment, 16
sheriffs
   Constitutional Sheriffs movement
      and, 104–6, 114–15
   elections for, 103
   January 6 rioters and, 104–5
   police chiefs compared to, 103
   political beliefs among, 103–4
   rural orientation of, 104
   sanctuary movement and, 101–7, 114
ShotSpotter technology, 69
silencers
   campaign to deregulate use of, 23–24,
      52–53, 63–66, 70–71, 122
   commercial interests of manufacturers
      of, 69–70, 71
   crimes committed using, 55–63, 67–
      69, 70, 122
   defining qualities of, 54–55
   estimated number in United
      States of, 55
   federal background check required for
      purchasing, 52–53, 55, 65, 67–68, 70
   hearing protection and, 52–53, 63–66,
      70–71, 122
   hunting and, 56, 61–63, 64, 67, 69
   invention of, 55–56

mass shootings and, 68
Maxim silencers and, 56–62, 57*t*, 122
National Firearms Act of 1934 and
   federal restrictions on, 23–24, 32,
   52–54, 62–63, 68–69, 70, 122
public opinion regarding, 55–56, 60
recoil reduction and, 63–64
safety value of firearm noise
   and, 66–67
sale to private foreign sources
   of, 69–70
Second Amendment and, 26, 53–
   54, 124–25
Silencers Helping Us Save Hearing
   (SHUSH Act) and, 53
states' regulations regarding, 1–2, 53,
   56, 57*t*, 69, 70, 122
U.S. v. Cox and, 53–54
Silvester v. Becerra, 10
Skousen, W. Cleon, 105
Solon (New York), 107–8
South Carolina, 33, 34*t*, 79*t*, 96
South Dakota, 33, 34*t*, 98
Sportsmen's Heritage and Recreational
   Enhancement Act (SHARE
   Act), 52–53
stand your ground laws, 73–74
Statute of Northampton (England,
   1328), 77–78
Steuben County (New York), 108
Stewart, James, 77
STG 44 ("Sturmgewehr"), 27
Stockton (California) mass shooting
   (1989), 37–38
St. Valentine's Day massacre (1929), 61
Su, Rick, 94
Sullivan, Jim, 27
Sullivan Law (New York State, 1911),
   117–19, 173–74n.7
Sununu, Chris, 91
suppressors. *See* silencers
Sutton, Lloyd, 113

Tennessee, 78, 79t, 82–83, 82t, 98
Tenth Amendment, 98
Tenth Circuit Court of Appeals, 53–54
Texas, 33–35, 34t, 79t, 82t, 109, 120
Third Amendment, 16
Thirteenth Amendment, 97
Thomas, Clarence
    African Americans' gun rights
        and, 10–11
    Federalist Society and, 7
    Heller case and, 8
    McDonald v. Chicago and, 9
    *N.Y. State Rifle & Pistol Association v.
        City of New York* and, 13–14
    Peruta v. California and, 9
    Printz v. U.S., 8–9
    Second Amendment jurisprudence of,
        8–13, 15–16, 18, 123
    Silvester v. Becerra and, 10
Three Percenters, 41, 89–90
Tommy guns, 1–2, 32, 44–45
Trump, Donald
    armed public supporters of, 40–
        41, 89–90
    Federalist Society and, 5, 6–7
    federal judicial appointments made
        by, 5–7
    January 6 riots (2021) and, 40–41
    pardons issued by, 105–6, 114–15
    sale of silencers to private foreign
        sources allowed under, 69–70
    Supreme Court appointments made
        by, 5, 13–14
Trump, Donald Jr., 69–70
Truxton (New York), 107, 113
Tucson (Arizona), 99–100
Tulsa (Oklahoma) race massacre (1923),
    12–13, 133n.54

Uniform Firearms Act, 2
Union Leagues, 11–12

U.S. Revolver Association (USRA), 2
U.S. v. Cox, 53–54
U.S. v. Peters, 97–98
Utah, 98, 102

Vaseghi, Bardia, 84
Vermont, 30, 33–35, 34t, 57t
Vietnam War, 27, 93
Virginia
    ammunition magazine restrictions in,
        33–35, 34t
    automatic weapons restrictions
        in, 30, 33
    Black Militias during Reconstruction
        Era in, 11–12
    brandishing laws in, 78, 79t
    nullification resolutions (1798) in, 95
    protests against COVID
        restrictions in, 84
    sanctuary movement in, 94–95
Virginia Beach mass shooting (2019), 68
Volokh, Eugene, 83–84

waiting periods for gun purchases, 3,
    10, 101–2
Waldron, Josh, 69–70
Washington DC. *See* District of
    Columbia
Washington State, 30, 33–35, 34t, 79t,
    101–2, 110–11
Wehbe, Gus, 110–12
West Virginia, 79t
Wharton, Francis, 77
Williams, Knox, 64
Williams, Michael B., 69–70
Winkler, Adam, 76
Wisconsin, 33–35, 34t, 75–76
World War I, 1–2
World War II, 27, 29
Wyoming, 57t, 79t, 80, 98, 106
Wyoming County (New York), 101, 106